R. L. STOREY

The End of
the House of Lancaster

ALAN SUTTON
1986

ALAN SUTTON PUBLISHING
BRUNSWICK ROAD · GLOUCESTER

Copyright © R.L. Storey, 1966, 1986

First published by Barrie & Rockliff, 1966
This new edition first published, 1986

British Library Cataloguing in Publication Data

Storey, Robin
The end of the house of Lancaster.
1. Great Britain—History—Wars of the roses.
I. Title
942.04   DA250

ISBN 0-86299-290-7

Printed and bound in Great Britain
by the Guernsey Press Company Limited
Guernsey, Channel Islands

Contents

Genealogical Tables

Maps

PREFACE

The fifth centenary of Edward IV's assumption of the English crown was scarcely an occasion for national celebration. At the Public Record Office, the event was marked by the production of an exhibition of records illustrating the Wars of the Roses. As the Assistant Keeper responsible for their selection, I was agreeably impressed by the public interest taken in this exhibition. Some of my then colleagues were kind enough to suggest that I should write a book on the same subject, and for this encouragement and their assistance I remain most grateful, and in particular to Mr H. N. Blakiston and Mr H. C. Johnson.

This is not, however, a book about the Wars of the Roses, but an attempt to explain how and why they began, since, as will be shown, the traditional view that they originated in conflicting hereditary claims to the throne is not justified by the facts. A key to this problem seemed to emerge as I browsed through judicial records of Henry VI's reign. In a period when literary sources are meagre and the rolls of the great departments impassively formal, the indictments of King's Bench provide fascinating details about the social scene. Of course criminal records do not reflect more than a fraction of human activity, nor can those of this time always be accepted at their face value, but they form an invaluable supplement to the little we know about the people of mid-fifteenth-century England, while a number considerably expand our knowledge of the public crises of Henry's last years.

Since these judicial records concern individuals and events in many parts of the country, it is difficult to present their evidence in a coherent pattern. Personal quarrels and disorders in various counties

all contributed to the outbreak of civil war. In order to establish some
continuity, however, the central theme of this book will be the king's
government and its relations with Richard, duke of York. The narrative is broken to study developments in certain districts which, at
particular points in the main chronology, came to affect politics at a
national level. These provincial diversions permit us to examine
sections of Lancastrian society.

I have incurred many debts of gratitude in the preparation of this
book. In its early stages, I profited from discussions with Mr A. F.
Bottomley and Dr R. M. Jeffs. Mr T. B. Pugh most kindly read the
whole work in typescript and corrected errors in detail. My colleagues
in the History Department of Nottingham University have given me
the benefit of their criticism; Professor J. C. Holt and Dr G. W. O.
Woodward have been particularly generous in this respect. I am
grateful also to all who have been responsible for the publication of
this book; my task has been lightened by their courtesy and efficiency.
Finally I would like to record my deep obligation to my wife for
her unfailing interest and help.

R. L. STOREY

Nottingham
17 July 1966

FOREWORD

Twenty years have passed since this book was published. In the meanwhile, the period in question has ceased to be one of the empty quarters of English history, as the appended list of publications amply testifies. Modern study of England's history in the later middle ages lost its founding genius with the death of K.B. McFarlane in 1966. More recently, the untimely death of his pupil, Charles Ross, removed the guiding hand of a productive group of younger scholars. A wider association of fifteenth-century specialists owes its inception to the late Stanley Chrimes, who convoked our first assembly at Cardiff in 1970. This informal colloquium now meets biennially and enjoys the boon of a sympathetic publisher. Some of the company at the last gathering persuaded him (and me) to reprint this volume.

The main purpose of *The End* was to report on my reconnaissance in the Public Record Office for information bearing on the outbreak of the Wars of the Roses. This operation was made possible by my freedom as an assistant keeper to investigate the whole range of the contents of the Office in Chancery Lane, including some then unsorted and not available to the public searcher (illustrated in Barnes, 1978), although not the unsorted files of King's Bench; they were in an outside repository, and their potential value still awaits full exploitation (Meekings, 1975; Powell, 1979, 1985). Sources hitherto unknown have been found in the libraries of Trinity College, Dublin, and Harvard University. The latter discovery is of transcripts of important council meetings during Henry VI's insanity (Griffiths, 1984). Dr Harriss announced the discovery of John Benet's chronicle in 1965, so causing me to make some additions in proof to notes. Now published, it reveals first-hand knowledge of events in London from 1447 to 1462 and gives more particulars about incidents for which my principal source were the records of King's Bench. Benet shows, for instance, that Lord Saye was indicted and condemned before a properly constituted commission of oyer and terminer which Cade's rebels hijacked during their occupation of London. The chronicle is mainly factual, but it betrays an increasingly 'Yorkist' bias, with Henry VI being deposed 'because he ruled *tirannice* as his grandfather and father had done'; in this context, *tirannice* obviously means 'unlawfully', reflecting the Yorkist view that the Lancastrian kings were all usurpers (Harriss, 1972; Gransden, 1982, 256–7). The superb new edition of the Paston letters and papers must also be welcomed, although with some qualification by the chronologically-minded (Davis, 1971–6).

Professor Griffiths' magisterial volume has thoroughly traversed the ground sketched in *The End*. He accepts that Henry took an active part in government, at least until 1453, in contrast to the view of Mr McFarlane which I heavily endorsed (McFarlane, 1936, 399–400; below, esp. 38–42), although he is critical of the king's natural aptitude to exercise personal monarchy. He also suggests, however, that Henry was incapable of developing any talent for statecraft, more than once referring to him as inexperienced; indeed, he quotes a Prussian agent reporting Henry as 'very young and inexperienced' in 1450 – after fourteen years of personal rule and as old as his father was in the year of Agincourt! (Griffiths, 1981, esp. 251–4). This foreign observer seems to confirm alleged opinions of humble subjects about the king's immature face and deportment (below, 34–5). Sir John Fortescue's determination to secure Thomas Carver's conviction for treason suggests that the king's council regarded such chatter as dangerous (Meekings, 1975). Certainly Henry himself cannot be held responsible for the 'execution' of the Kentish woman who berated him in 1443: she died by *peine forte et dure* because she had refused to plead (Griffiths, 1981, 253). While Professor Griffiths sees such royal conduct as an aberration, to Dr Wolffe it is of a piece with the unforgiving and vindictive facets of Henry's character (Wolffe, 1981, esp. 125–32). This malign view of the king's personality is hard to credit in the light of Dr Lovatt's more recent reappraisal of John Blacman's memoir, although its exhortatory purpose calls for caution; it is a new kind of hagiography, portraying Henry as a model of lay piety (Lovatt, 1981, 1984; Richmond, 1983). The 'schizophrenic quality of English diplomacy' in the 1440s (Ferguson, 1972, 9) may have owed something to royal intervention in the cause of peace. Given Henry's piety, however, it is curious that his influence had little weight in Rome when bishops were appointed (Betcherman, 1966). John Benet's comment, under the year 1449, seems nearer the mark: 'under the most noble and Christian King Henry, the wicked duke of Suffolk ruled in England'. New studies of the king's council have confirmed its contraction during Suffolk's heyday, and his calamitous personal direction of political and military operations in France (Brown, 1969; Virgoe, 1970; Allmand, 1983; Keen, 1974; Pollard, 1983; Vale, 1970).

The duke's malignant influence in East Anglia has been further illustrated from Sir John Fastolf's difficulties (Smith, 1984). His local rival, the duke of Norfolk, was equally ready to champion unscrupulous retainers (Virgoe, 1980). That neither ducal house completely dominated county society was shown in parliamentary elections (Virgoe, 1966), while Dr Richmond's engaging study of John Hopton suggests that attachment to a 'good lord' was not a prerequisite for a peaceful life (Richmond, 1981). Without a collection of Hopton letters, however, there is room for scepticism. The uniquely fortuitous survival of the Paston collection must arouse the envy of all scholars with interests in other parts of England. One may, for instance, hazard the opinion that the correspondence of a Westmorland family like the Crackenthorpes would tell of experiences more harrowing than any endured by the Pastons; they would, no doubt, have alleged oppressions by Richard Neville, earl of Salisbury, and his equivalents to Tuddenham and Heydon. Studies of Salisbury's retainers, and of his influence in parliamentary elections, indicate that his standing in northern England closely paralleled that of William de la Pole in East Anglia (Jalland, 1972, 1976; Pollard, 1976, 1979). In both cases, an essential ingredient of their regional supremacy was their intimate place in the circle ruling the

Lancastrian court. Exclusion from its favour undermined local consequence, as the Courtenay earls of Devon painfully understood (Cherry, 1979, 1981).

With a typically judicious summary of the final rebellion against Henry's government, Dr Thomson points to a divergence between the explanation of Mr McFarlane and my own. Despite my large reliance on 'new' sources, however, I do not dispute that the 'inanity' of Henry VI was the basic cause of the opening rounds of the Wars of the Roses: disorder had escalated because his personal authority was non-existent. He had not followed the example of his forebears in building up a political affinity directly attached to his person and capable of overawing any other retinue in the kingdom (Pugh, 1972, 108). If my original views on bastard feudalism are less than convincing, I hope that amends are found elsewhere (Storey, 1983). A feature of Henry's government which I had not appreciated earlier was that very few of his servants in administrative office were ordained clergy. For over two centuries, until the time of Henry V, there were at least 200 'king's clerks' serving in departments of state, the royal household and other offices, who could be rewarded with ecclesiastical preferment and thus at no cost to the king. Before the end of the minority, most of Henry's officials were laymen, and consequently had to be provided with secular benefits. In addition to this new charge on royal patronage, the quality of administration may have been adversely affected by this process of secularization. Unlike their clerical predecessors, these lay bureaucrats had families to support and, ideally, endow as landed gentry (Storey, 1982, 1984). Another additional consideration is the role of the episcopate at the end of Henry's reign. There were long-standing clerical grievances which his regime had failed to remedy. It is arguable that some prelates favoured Richard of York in order to protect the Church (Storey, 1972, 1984). York's own propaganda against the Lancastrian court may (Keen, 1973, 453–7; McCulloch, 1983) or may not (Barron, 1981; Ross, 1981) have won popular support, but it must be remembered that the Church had the best-organized means to spread opinions throughout the country.

On the other hand, it is highly conjectural what reception was given to statements about national issues, whether they were disseminated inside churches by calls for prayers and processions, or as broadsheets fastened to their doors (e.g. Virgoe, 1973). Reactions will have varied from place to place, and even local unanimity was unlikely. It is therefore an important development in historical scholarship that increased attention is being given to the structure of society in the shires. The aristocracy has been firmly identified as a class (McFarlane, 1973). Its stature has been illuminated by its part in resolving disagreements between gentry (Rowney, 1982; Powell, 1983). No lord, however, could be assured of the unswerving loyalty of the gentry forming his affinity (McFarlane, 1981, 17–19). The structure of those affinities was complex, and the interests and expectations of individual members far from uniform or, indeed, always compatible. Networks of gentry-alliances, moreover, had a vitality of their own (e.g. Carpenter, 1980; Wright, 1983; see also Rawcliffe, 1979, 1986). Further studies may disclose regional variants. Meanwhile, the associated problem of defining the gentry class in this period is at last receiving the attention it deserves (Harriss, 1981; Jones, 1986). We will be in a better position to understand why Henry VI was deposed when we are more fully informed about the nation which for so long tolerated, but finally disowned him. The second objective is infinitely more important.

WORKS CITED

with other recent publications about his period (abbreviations as below, 242–3).

ALLMAND, C.T., *Lancastrian Normandy, 1415–1450* (Oxford 1983).

ARMSTRONG, C.A.J., *England, France and Burgundy in the Fifteenth Century* (collected papers; 1983).

ARNOLD, C., 'The Commission of the Peace for the West Riding of Yorkshire, 1437–1509', POLLARD, 1984, 116–38.

ARCHER, R.E., 'Rich Old Ladies: The Problem of Late Medieval Dowagers', ibid., 15–35.

BARNES, P.M., ed., 'The chancery corpus cum causa file, 10–11 Edward IV', *Medieval Legal Records*, ed R.F. Hunnisett and J.B. Post (1978), 430–76.

BARRON, C.M., 'London and the Crown 1451–61', HIGHFIELD, 1981, 88–109.

BELLAMY, J.G., *The Law of Treason in England in the Later Middle Ages* (Cambridge, 1970).

——, *Crime and Public Order in England in the Later Middle Ages* (1973).

BETCHERMAN, L.R., 'The making of bishops in the Lancastrian period', *Speculum*, 41 (1966), 397–419.

BLATCHER, M., *The Court of King's Bench 1450–1550* (1978).

BROWN, A.L., 'The King's Councillors in Fifteenth-Century England', *THRS*, 5th ser. 19 (1969), 95–118.

——, *The early history of the clerkship of the Council* (Glasgow, 1969).

CARPENTER, M.C., 'The Beauchamp affinity: a study of bastard feudalism at work', *EHR*, 95 (1980), 515–32.

CHERRY, M., 'The Courtenay Earls of Devon: the Formation and Disintegration of a Late-Medieval Aristocratic Affinity', *Southern History*, 1 (1979), 71–97.

——, 'The Struggle for Power in Mid-fifteenth-century Devonshire', GRIFFITHS, *Patronage*, 1981, 123–44.

CHRIMES, S.B., C.D. ROSS and R.A. GRIFFITHS, eds., *Fifteenth-century England 1399–1509* (Manchester, 1972).

CLOUGH, C.H., ed., *Profession, Vocation and Culture in Later Medieval England* (Liverpool, 1982).

CRAWFORD, A., 'The King's Burden?: the Consequences of Royal Marriage in Fifteenth-century England', GRIFFITHS, *Patronage*, 1981, 33–56.

CURRY, A., 'The First English Standing Army? Military Organization in Lancastrian Normandy, 1420–1450', ROSS, 1979, 193–208.

DAVIES, R.G., and J.H. DENTON, *The English Parliament in the Middle Ages* (Manchester, 1981).

DAVIS, N., ed., *Paston Letters and Papers of the Fifteenth Century*, 2 parts (Oxford, 1971–6).

DOBSON, R.B., *Durham Priory 1400–1450* (Cambridge, 1973).

——, 'Urban Decline in late Medieval England', *TRHS*, 5th ser. 27 (1977), 1–22.

——, ed., *The Church, Politics and Patronage in the Fifteenth Century* (Gloucester, 1984).

DU BOULAY, F.R.H., *The Lordship of Canterbury: an essay on medieval society* (1966).

——, *An Age of Ambition: English society in the late Middle Ages* (1970).

DUNNING, R.W., 'Thomas, Lord Dacre, and the West March towards Scotland, ?1435', *BIHR*, 41 (1968), 95–9

DYER, C., 'A Redistribution of Incomes in Fifteenth-Century England', *Past and Present*, 39 (1968), 11–33.

——, *Lords and Peasants in a Changing Society: The Estates of the Bishopric of Worcester, 680–1540* (Cambridge, 1980).

EDWARDS, J.G., 'The Huntingdonshire parliamentary election of 1450', *Essays in medieval history presented to Bertie Wilkinson*, ed. T.A. Sandquist and M.R. Powicke (Toronto, 1969), 383–95.

FERGUSON, J., *English Diplomacy 1422–1461* (Oxford, 1972).

GILLINGHAM, J.B., *The Wars of the Roses: Peace and Conflict in Fifteenth-Century England* (1981).

GOODMAN, A.E., *The Wars of the Roses: Military Activity and English Society 1452–97* (1981).

GRANSDEN, A., *Historical Writing in England*, ii, *c.1307 to the Early Sixteenth Century* (1982).

GRIFFITHS, R.A., 'Local Rivalries and National Politics: the Percies, the Nevilles, and the Duke of Exeter, 1452–1455', *Speculum*, 43 (1968), 589–632.

——, 'The Trial of Eleanor Cobham: an episode in the fall of Duke Humphrey of Gloucester', *BJRL*, 51 (1968–9), 381–99.

——, 'Wales and the Marches', CHRIMES, 1972, 145–72.

——, 'Duke Richard of York's intentions in 1450 and the origin of the Wars of the Roses', *Journal of Medieval History*, 1 (1975), 187–209.

——, 'The Winchester Session of the 1449 Parliament: A Further Comment', *Huntington Library Quarterly*, 42 (1978–9), 181–91.

——, 'The Sense of Dynasty in the Reign of Henry VI', ROSS, 1979, 13–31.

GRIFFITHS, R.A., *The Reign of King Henry the Sixth: The exercise of royal authority, 1422–1461* (1981).

——, ed., *Patronage, The Crown and the Provinces in Later Medieval England* (Gloucester, 1981).

——, 'The hazards of civil war: the Mountford family and the "Wars of the Roses"', *Midland History*, 5 (1981), 1–19.

——, 'The King's Council and the first Protectorate of the Duke of York, 1453–1454', *EHR*, 99 (1984), 67–81.

HARDING, A., *The law courts of medieval England* (1973).

HARE, J.N., 'The Wiltshire Risings of 1450: political and economic discontent in mid-fifteenth century England', *Southern History*, 4 (1982), 13–31.

HARRIS, M., ed., 'The Account of the Great Household of Humphrey, First Duke of Buckingham, for the year 1452–3', *Camden Miscellany XXVIII*, Camden Soc., 4th ser. 29 (1984), 1–57.

HARRISS, G.L., 'Cardinal Beaufort – Patriot or Usurer?', *TRHS*, 5th ser. 20 (1970), 129–48.

——, and M.A. HARRISS, eds., 'John Benet's Chronicle for the years 1400 to 1462', *Camden Miscellany XXIV*, Camden Soc., 4th ser. 9 (1972), 151–252.

——, Introduction to McFARLANE, 1981, ix–xxvii.

HARVEY, J.H., ed., *William Worcestre, Itineraries* (Oxford, 1969).

HATCHER, J., *Plague, Population and the English Economy, 1348–1530* (1977).

HERBERT, A., 'Herefordshire, 1431–61: some Aspects of Society and Public Order', GRIFFITHS, *Patronage*, 1981, 103–22.

HIGHFIELD, J.R.L., and R.A. JEFFS., eds., *The Crown and Local Communities in England and France in the Fifteenth Century* (Gloucester, 1981).

HORROX, R., 'Urban Patronage and Patrons in the Fifteenth Century', GRIFFITHS, *Patronage*, 1981, 145–66.

IVES, E.W., 'The common lawyers', CLOUGH, 1982, 181–217.

JALLAND, P., 'The Influence of the Aristocracy on Shire Elections in the North of England, 1450–70', *Speculum*, 47 (1972), 483–507.

——, 'The "Revolution" in Northern Borough Representation in

Mid-Fifteenth-Century England', *Northern History*, 11 (1976), 27–51.

JONES, M.K., 'John Beaufort, Duke of Somerset, and the French Expedition of 1443', GRIFFITHS, *Patronage*, 1981, 79–102.

JONES, Michael, ed., *Gentry and Lesser Nobility in Late Medieval Europe* (Gloucester, 1986).

KEEN, M.H., *England in the Later Middle Ages* (1973).

——, and M.J. DANIEL, 'English Diplomacy and the Sack of Fougères in 1449', *History*, 59 (1974), 375–91.

LANDER, J.R., *Crown and Nobility 1450–1509* (collected papers; 1976).

LOVATT, R.W., 'John Blacman: biographer of Henry VI', *The Writing of History in the Middle Ages*, ed. R.H.C. Davis and J.M. Wallace-Hadrill (Oxford, 1981), 415–44.

——, 'A Collector of Apocryphal Anecdotes: John Blacman Revisited', POLLARD, 1984, 172–97.

McCULLOCH, D., and E.D. JONES, 'Lancastrian Politics, the French War, and the Rise of the Popular Element', *Speculum*, 58 (1983), 95–138.

McFARLANE, K.B., 'England: The Lancastrian Kings, 1399–1461', *Cambridge Medieval History*, 8 (1936, reprinted 1959), 363–417.

——, *The Nobility of Later Medieval England* (Oxford, 1973).

——, *England in the Fifteenth Century: Collected Essays* (1981).

MEEKINGS, C.A.F., 'Thomas Kerver's Case, 1444', *EHR*, 90 (1975), 331–46.

MYERS, A.E., ed., *English Historical Documents 1327–1485* (1969).

NEVILLE, C.J., 'Gaol Delivery in the Border Counties, 1439–1459; some preliminary observations', *Northern History*, 19 (1983), 45–60.

PHYTHIAN-ADAMS, C., *Desolation of a city: Coventry and the urban crisis of the late middle ages* (Cambridge, 1979).

POLLARD, A.J., 'The northern retainers of Richard Nevill, earl of Salisbury', *Northern History*, 11 (1976), 52–69.

——, 'The Richmondshire Community of Gentry during the Wars of the Roses', ROSS, 1979, 37–59.

——, *John Talbot and the War in France 1427–1453* (1983).

POLLARD, A.J., ed., *Property and Politics: Essays in Later Medieval English History* (Gloucester, 1984).

POWELL, E., 'Public Order and Law Enforcement in Shropshire and Staffordshire in the Early Fifteenth Century' (Oxford University D.Phil. thesis, 1979).

——, 'Arbitration and the Law in England in the Late Middle Ages', *TRHS*, 5th ser. 33 (1983), 49–68.

——, 'The Restoration of Law and Order', *Henry V: the Practice of Kingship*, ed. G.L. HARRISS (Oxford, 1985), 53–74.

POWELL, J.E., and K. WALLIS, *The House of Lords in the Middle Ages* (1968).

PUGH, T.B., 'The magnates, knights and gentry', CHRIMES, 1972, 86–128.

——, ed., *Glamorgan County History*, III, *The middle ages* (Cardiff, 1971).

RAWCLIFFE, C., *The Staffords, Earls of Stafford and Dukes of Buckingham, 1394–1521* (Cambridge, 1978).

——, 'Baronial Councils in the Later Middle Ages', ROSS, 1979, 87–108.

——, and S. Flower, 'English Noblemen and Their Advisers: Consultation and Collaboration in the Later Middle Ages', *Journal of British Studies*, 25 (1986), 157–77.

RICHMOND, C.F., 'The Nobility and the Wars of the Roses 1459–61', *Nottingham Mediaeval Studies*, 21 (1977), 71–86.

——, *John Hopton: A Fifteenth-Century Suffolk Gentleman* (Cambridge, 1981).

——, 'After McFarlane' (review article), *History*, 68 (1983), 46–60.

ROBERTSON, C.A., 'Local Government and the King's "Affinity" in fifteenth-century Leicestershire and Warwickshire', *Transactions of the Leicestershire Archaeological and Historical Society*, 52 (1976–7), 37–45.

ROSENTHAL, J.T., 'The Estates and Finances of Richard, Duke of York (1411–60)', *Studies in Medieval and Renaissance History*, 2 (1965), 117–204.

——, 'Feuds and Private Peace-Making: a Fifteenth-Century Example'. *Nottingham Mediaeval Studies*, 14 (1970), 84–90.

ROSKELL, J.S., *Parliaments and Politics in Late Medieval England* (collected papers, 3 vols.; 1982–4).

ROSS, C.D., *Edward IV* (1975).

——, ed., *Patronage, Pedigree and Power in Later Medieval England* (Gloucester, 1979).

——, 'Rumour, Propaganda and Public Opinion during the Wars of the Roses', GRIFFITHS, *Patronage*, 1981, 15–32.

ROWNEY, I., 'Arbitration in Gentry Disputes of the Later Middle Ages', *History*, 67 (1982), 367–76.

SMITH, A., 'Litigation and Politics: Sir John Fastolf's defence of his English property', POLLARD, 1984, 59–75.

STOREY, R.L., 'Lincolnshire and the Wars of the Roses', *Nottingham Mediaeval Studies*, 14 (1970), 64–83.

——, *Diocesan Administration in Fifteenth-Century England*, Borthwick Papers, 16 (York, 2nd edition, 1972; reprint, 1981).

——, 'The north of England', CHRIMES, 1972, 129–44.

——, 'Gentleman-bureaucrats', CLOUGH, 1982, 90–129.

——, Bastard Feudalism Revisited', *Bulletin of the Manorial Society of Great Britain*, 3 (1983), 7–15.

——, 'Episcopal King-Makers in the Fifteenth Century', DOBSON, 1984, 82–98.

——, 'England: Amsterhandel im 15. und 16. Jahrhundert', *Amsterhandel im Spätmittelalter und im 16. Jahrhundert*, ed. Ilja Mieck (Berlin, 1984), 196–204.

——, 'The Universities during the Wars of the Roses', *England in the Fifteenth Century: Proceedings of the 1986 Harlaxton Symposium*, ed. D.T. Williams (1987).

SUMMERSON, H., 'Crime and Society in Medieval Cumberland', *Transactions of the Cumberland and Westmorland Antiquarian and Archaeological Society*, 82 (1982), 111–24.

THOMSON, J.A.F., 'John de la Pole, Duke of Suffolk', *Speculum*, 54 (1979), 528–42.

——, *The Transformation of Medieval England 1370–1529* (1983).

VALE, M.G.A., 'The last years of English Gascony, 1451–1453', *TRHS*, 5th ser. 19 (1969), 119–38.

——, *English Gascony, 1399–1453* (Oxford, 1970).

VIRGOE, R., 'Three Suffolk Parliamentary Elections of the Mid-fifteenth Century', *BIHR*, 39 (1966), 185—96.

——, 'The Composition of the King's Council, 1437–61', *BIHR*, 43 (1970), 134–60.

VIRGOE, R., 'William Tailboys and Lord Cromwell: crime and politics in Lancastrian England', *BJRL*, 55 (1972–3), 459–82.

——, 'The Cambridgeshire Election of 1439', *BIHR*, 46 (1973), 95–101.

——, 'The Murder of James Andrew: Suffolk Faction in the 1430s', *Proceedings of the Suffolk Institute of Archaeology and History*, 34 (1980), 263–8.

——, 'The Crown, Magnates and Local Government in Fifteenth-Century East Anglia', HIGHFIELD, 1981, 72–87.

——, 'The Parliamentary Subsidy of 1450', *BIHR*, 55 (1982), 125–38.

WILSON, E., 'A Poem Presented to William Waynflete as Bishop of Winchester', *Middle English Studies*, ed. D. Gray and E.G. Stanley (Oxford, 1983), 127–51.

WOLFFE, B.P., *Henry VI* (1981).

WRIGHT, S.M., *The Derbyshire Gentry in the Fifteenth Century* (Derbyshire Record Society, 8, 1983).

Some corrigenda

p.7, 1.6. *For* Châtillon *read* Castillon (also p.129, 1.15).

p.61, 1.6. *For* Stafford *read* Strafford.

p.130, 1.9. *For* Tattersall *read* Tattershall.

Finally, I wish to record, yet again, my gratitude to my valuable colleague, Dr Michael Jones, for his constructive criticism of this additional material.

R.L. STOREY

Nottingham
17 July 1986

INTRODUCTION

"The Wars of the Roses"

The royal line of Lancaster ended, as it had begun, with the deposition of a king. On 4 March 1461, Edward, earl of March, took possession of the throne of England with the agreement of a handful of lords, the acclaim of the citizens of London and the blessing of his uncle, the archbishop of Canterbury. This assumption of the crown had yet to be made good by the issue of war. A dangerous concentration of hostile magnates held northern England. It had already twice defeated the forces of York, at Wakefield (30 December 1460), where Edward's father, Duke Richard, had been slain, and at the second battle of St. Albans (17 February 1461). This army had retired to the north when it failed to take London, taking with it Henry VI, its chief prize on the field of St. Albans. Edward soon gave chase. On 29 March, at Towton in central Yorkshire, there was fought the greatest battle, in point of numbers, in the entire course of "the Wars of the Roses"; both parties were at full strength, although even the lowest contemporary estimate of 20,000 men a side is probably an exaggeration. The determined onslaught of Edward's forces shattered the enemies' line and pressed them back into a swollen stream. Following recent precedents, the defeated leaders were shown no mercy; prisoners were executed without delay. Henry VI, Queen Margaret and the remnant of their followers made for Scotland, leaving garrisons in a few Northumbrian castles. After a visit to Newcastle-upon-Tyne, Edward returned southward by way of Lancashire and the west midlands to quell possible malcontents there. King now in fact as well as name, he issued writs calling a parliament to meet in July. This had to be postponed on account of danger from Scotland and the general confusion which made men afraid to travel. By the end of September, however, after a progress by Edward through southern and western England, only on the Scottish border and at Harlech did Henry VI's supporters continue to offer resistance.

When Edward IV's first parliament was eventually held in November, the faithful commons presented him with "a declaration of the royal title". That the victorious head of the house of York was the legitimate king of England was certainly not a proposition which this parliament would care to dispute. This declaration, however, has more significance than as a constitutional endorsement of military success. In it there appears the earliest expression of an historical myth which has coloured our interpretation of fifteenth-century England until modern times. Henry, earl of Derby, son of John of Gaunt, duke of Lancaster, it stated, had (in 1399) "temerously, against righteousness and justice, by force of arms, against his faith and allegiance"* raised war against Richard II, the true and anointed king; and not content with usurping the crown, he was moved by unnatural wickedness to murder the deposed king. This outrageous crime "against God's law, man's allegiance and oath of fidelity" doomed its perpetrators to the uttermost torments of Hell. All Christian people had been appalled, and "their heavy exclamation . . . soundeth into God's hearing in Heaven". In consequence, the realm of England "has suffered the charge of intolerable persecution, punishment and tribulation" and had "in the time of the said usurpation fallen from renown into misery, wretchedness, desolation, shameful and sorrowful decline". Instead of enjoying its wonted peace and plenty, good government and justice, the country had been afflicted with "unrest, inward war and trouble, unrighteousness, shedding and effusion of innocent blood, abuse of the laws" and all manner of crimes.[1]

This picture of a country torn by intestinal strife from the close of the fourteenth century recurs in the history of Edward Hall, a masterpiece of Tudor propaganda published in the first year of Edward VI's reign (1547). Hall's title page announced his theme. It is

---

* Extracts from fifteenth- and sixteenth-century English texts have been rendered in modern spelling.

[1] References to sources, signalled in the text by small raised numbers, are listed at the end of the book. Footnotes are signalled by asterisks etc.

"The union of the two noble and illustrious families of Lancaster and York, being long in continual dissension for the crown of this noble realm . . . beginning at the time of King Henry the Fourth, the first author of this division", and continuing to the reign of Henry VIII, "the indubitable flower and very heir of both the said lineages". Hall had adopted for his own purposes the same argument as Edward IV had put forward.* Shakespeare received Hall's interpretation of fifteenth-century history through the plagiaristic *Chronicles* of Raphael Holinshed, and his history plays have immortalised the dynastic conflict of Lancaster and York. Like Hall, he traces its origin from the deposition of Richard II.

> The blood of England shall manure the ground,
> And future ages groan for this foul act;
>
> .   .   .   .   .   .
>
> It will the woefullest division prove,
> That ever fell upon this cursed earth.[3]

For the subjects of the Tudors, of course, the end of this division came with the victory of Henry Tudor at Bosworth and his marriage to Elizabeth of York. But they had common ground with the supporters of Edward IV in regarding the tragic events of 1399 as the beginning of England's winter of discontent.

Sixty years later, when armies joined battle to decide claims to the crown of England, the circumstances of Richard II's deposition did undoubtedly become an issue of importance. The enemies of Lancaster could then assert that Henry IV had not been Richard's lawful heir. Edmund Mortimer, earl of March, had the best hereditary title as the great-grandson of Lionel, duke of Clarence, the second son of Edward III. John of Gaunt, Henry's father, was Edward's third son. In 1399, however, the claims of Edmund Mortimer were apparently ignored, or if mentioned, set aside on the grounds of his youth or because his descent from Edward III came through a female. There was, after all, no accepted legal doctrine governing the descent of the English crown. The only rule observed since 1216 had been that the eldest son succeeded his father as king, but neither precedent nor convention provided for failure of direct heirs of the king's body.

* This was no coincidence, for Hall undoubtedly knew the Yorkist manifesto; he made use of it in preparing an oration which he put into the mouth of Richard, duke of York.[2]

Indeed, at the beginning of the sixteenth century a Venetian ambassador could state, as if reporting a quaint native custom, that if the succession to their crown were ever in doubt, the English would settle the question by force of arms, on the understanding that "he who lost the day, lost the kingdom also".[4]

Henry IV was accepted as king in an assembly comprising the majority, and certainly the most powerful, of the nobility, and the knights and burgesses elected for a parliament. His position was by no means assured, and in the first six years of the reign he was threatened by a series of rebellions and conspiracies, but he defeated all attempts against his life and throne; if the nation was not solidly behind Henry of Lancaster, at the least he had more support than Richard had enjoyed in his last year. Henry's government was not popular, it was strongly opposed by the commons in a number of parliaments, but their protests were against its incompetence and financial weakness; they did not question its legitimacy. Again, Henry surmounted these crises, and he died in full possession of the crown's prerogative authority. His son and grandson succeeded to the throne without challenge. The Mortimer claim failed to command a following. It was espoused by the Percies in their revolt in 1403, and in 1415 by a trio of noble malcontents whose plot to assassinate Henry V was betrayed by the earl of March himself. More than forty years were to pass before another claimant came forward to dispute the Lancastrian title to the crown. There is, therefore, no foundation for the myth that from 1399 onward English society was irreparably split into two hostile parties, the adherents of the usurping house of Lancaster, and the advocates of the legitimate Mortimer line.

The emergence of factions grouped under the representatives of these two royal lines in the second half of the century was an entirely new development. That these parties came to fight for possession of the throne is a matter of history. Towton had secured the crown for Edward IV and, after his flight abroad in 1470, he regained it by his victories at Barnet and Tewkesbury (1471); while Henry VII replaced Richard III at Bosworth (1485) and secured his position at Stoke-by-Newark (1487). It is then natural that we should think of this conflict as a dynastic struggle. Yet the earliest victories of York at St. Albans (1455) and Northampton (1460) did not bring about the deposition of Henry VI; he became a prisoner but he remained king. Initially, therefore, the friends of York did not take up arms to put their leader on the throne. Not until 1461 did the logic of their situation persuade them to crown him and so take advantage of his claim to be the legitimate heir of Richard II.

The original cause of the "Wars of the Roses" was thus not a dispute over the hereditary rights of Lancaster and York to possession of the crown of England. This has, of course, already been realised by some modern historians. Indeed, it was the opinion of a contemporary writer that the personal quarrel of the dukes of York and Somerset was the initial reason for the civil wars.* More recently, scholars have been viewing the conflict as no more than a sordid scramble by various great lords for control of the king's government.⁵ Modern research in economic history, moreover, has disclosed the financial difficulties of fifteenth-century peers and has thus suggested a further motive for their political manoeuvres.† These explanations are the more credible when considered against the picture provided by fifteenth-century writers of a kingdom in a state of disintegration, in their accounts of the poverty and incompetence of the government of Henry VI, its unpopularity as a result of the English defeat in France and the weakness of its authority in a country dominated by great landed magnates.

Here we are on firmer ground. But no explanation for the outbreak of the wars can be considered satisfactory unless it can also account for the ability of the protagonists to raise armies. Historians discussing the formation of the parties have tended to look at this problem from the wrong end; having already determined what the causes of the conflict were, they have gone on to draw up roll-calls of "Lancastrians" and "Yorkists" from the lists of casualties and victory honours, and then assume that these men had for some time past upheld the causes of their leaders. If instead we attempt to trace the formation of parties from before the outbreak of fighting a far less simple pattern emerges. By examining the careers of individuals, we can seek to establish why they gave active support to either York or Lancaster, and their reasons for so doing, it may be claimed, were the real causes of the wars. The Nevilles, for instance, are usually counted as "Yorkists", and the fact of their kinship with Richard of York has been taken as proof that they could never have been anything else. Yet, in fact, they were by no means eager to identify themselves with York and only came to do so as a result of their own difficulties.‡ Like other

---

* See p. 74 below.   † See pp. 19-20 below.   ‡ See Chapter IX.

well-known champions of Lancaster and York, they upheld their leader's cause because they needed his friendship. And a cause adopted out of necessity is unlikely to retain devotion. When a man's reasons for joining one party became less urgent and the rival faction seemed to offer greater advantages, he suffered no agonies of conscience in accepting his new leader as his rightful king. When Edward IV's triumph seemed complete, former adherents of Lancaster were ready to enter his service; the celebrated efficiency of Henry VII's administration was due to his employment of experienced "Yorkist" officials. Throughout the period of conflict, personal loyalties were continually shifting. In such circumstances it is unrealistic to label individuals as "Lancastrian" or "Yorkist".

The name "Wars of the Roses" is equally misleading. That it is a modern invention★ is not a serious objection, for convenience appears to demand that historians should remedy the failure of contemporaries to provide acceptable names for their wars and battles. A more cogent criticism is that the title is misconceived. It was presumably inspired by Shakespeare, whose imagery owed nothing to Hall's history. The roses plucked in that famous scene in the Temple Garden, the white by York, the red by Somerset, become the emblems which distinguish the champions of York's royal title from the defenders of Henry VI, until in the last act of the cycle, the ultimate victor, Henry of Richmond, announces his intention "to unite the white rose and the red".[7] In fact, the red rose is not known as a badge of Henry VI, although his forbears had it as one of several devices. Richard of York did have a badge of the white rose, but it was only one of several family emblems. "Wars of the Roses" calls to mind a picture of two armies with every member wearing a rose of the appropriate colour, as a kind of uniform. Actually only the personal retainers of a leader would have carried his device; the followers of his noble allies would have worn the liveries of their own lords. Properly speaking, these were not armies at all, but confederations of private forces. Neither principal had sufficient private resources to raise a large host; the king was as dependent on baronial retinues as was his rival to muster a strong following.

These baronial contingents were not standing private armies. It has often been said that they were, that they comprised the retinues which the lords had formed for service in France and had brought home

★ It first appeared in Scott's *Anne of Geierstein* (1829).[6]

after the end of the Hundred Years War. In fact, few of the leaders in either camp had ever served in France. The last occasion when the nobility crossed the Channel in strength was in 1429, and since then the French wars had lost their attraction and few peers cared to serve. Of the exceptions, the first earl of Shrewsbury was killed and his retinue largely destroyed at the battle of Châtillon; the duke of York did hold the loyalty of a number of his officers, but the duke of Somerset's soldiers mutinied on their return to England and almost succeeded in killing him.* It is unlikely that there were more than two or three thousand able-bodied, front-line veterans of the French wars in England at the end of Henry VI's reign. No doubt a good number of them took part in the civil war, but they could not have amounted to a high proportion of the combatants.

The baronial forces were also confederations. Household servants, admittedly numerous, still formed only the core of a magnate's retinue, for it included companies brought by country gentry who had accepted his lordship, and even these subordinate retinues might include parties raised by their captain's clients among the lesser squirearchy of their neighbourhoods. The country gentleman who followed his noble patron into battle was no more devoted to the merits of Lancastrian or Yorkist legitimacy, and when circumstances changed he was no less ready to transfer his loyalty to another champion.

The title "Wars of the Roses" has a still more serious defect. It directs attention to the dynastic issue, to the battles and their political results. These mêlées are sometimes looked upon as the death throes of a war-minded aristocracy, of a degenerate chivalry which had outlived its usefulness; they are interesting as spectacles, but their significance is superficial. The country as a whole, it is often said, was barely affected by this blue-blooded bickering. Of a population of between two and two and a half millions, it is unlikely that more than fifty thousand ever took part in the battles. For most, life went on as before. The people of several entire counties never saw even the passage of armies, and, on the whole, non-combatants rarely suffered military outrage: the ravages of the "northern men" in their march on London in the winter of 1460-1 were an exception. Armies sought each other to do battle, they did not attempt lengthy campaigns to subjugate territories; no town had to stand a siege.

* See pp. 75, 80.

Yet the wars came about because of the general state of English society. The Yorkist manifesto of 1461 was not exaggerating when it said that riot, murder, robbery and the like had flourished in the time of Henry VI. And offenders were to be found in all ranks of society, even among those responsible for upholding the law in their own countryside. The feuds of the nobility in the more outlying parts of the kingdom attained the proportions of private wars. The quarrels of gentry led to the movements of large companies of armed men, with seizure of property or manslaughter and sack as their ostensible objectives. Nor were these disturbances confined to the counties north of Trent or west of Severn and Exe: southern Lincolnshire was alarmed by the exploits of Sir William Tailbois;[8] in Bedfordshire, the commission of the peace was unable to hold its sessions because of the feud of Lords Grey and Fanhope;[9] the troubled state of Norfolk and Suffolk is already well known through the testimony of the *Paston Letters*; the quarrel of the Stafford and Harcourt families led to a miniature campaign in Oxfordshire.* Nor, again, as the cases of York, Norwich and Hereford reveal,† did towns remain immune from the dangers of disorder.

> In every shire with jacks and sallets‡ clean,
> Misrule doth rise and maketh neighbours war.[10]

The semi-military operations of nobility and gentry were undertaken without any fear of intervention by the crown, for it had no standing army available for police duties, and its orders to keep the peace were contemptuously ignored. Known offenders were sooner or later subjected to the formal procedures of the judicial system, but there was apparently little danger of conviction and punishment. Juries of country gentry would not convict their own kind.§ Instead of keeping order and protecting the weak, the law was more commonly misapplied to the advantage of those able to control it. The corruption and oppression of local government was the main burden of the Kentish rebels of 1450. "The complaint of the commons of Kent" shows us why English society was falling apart, why the crown, its officers, and with them the whole legal system, were losing

---

* See pp. 57-8 below.
† See pp. 127-8, 142-6, and Appendices III and VI.
‡ *I.e.* protective jackets and helmets.
§ The *Rex* sections of the King's Bench plea rolls suggest that only habitual criminals like highway robbers were ever convicted.

the respect and essential co-operation of the king's subjects.* It is easy to regard the Kentish rising as an isolated incident, unconnected with the baronial wars which began five years later; but it has a very definite place in the same pattern of social collapse.

The anti-clericalism of the period must be seen in the same context. Criticism of the Church, or, more particularly, of individual clergy or certain of their orders, had been common in late medieval England. What distinguishes the anti-clericalism of the mid-fifteenth century is its unusually vicious character. Prelates had been killed from time to time in the past, but for two bishops to be murdered by mobs in one year, as in 1450, was without parallel, and two others were threatened with violence. No doubt the political connections of these bishops accounted for their unpopularity, but their fate indicates how little the populace respected their episcopal status. Parish clergy were also the victims of violence.[11] In 1456, a group of Kentish rebels demanded that all priests having more than one benefice should be put to death and the remainder castrated.[12] The clergy were more commonly subjected to persecution by abuse of the law. In 1444, the convocation of Canterbury complained of the perjuries and false accusations being made against churchmen;[13] certainly there are many cases still on record of priests being accused of rape or the theft of church goods.[14] It need not be supposed that all these charges were false, and in other ways the English clergy were not wholly undeserving of the low esteem in which they were held. But the Church was an integral part of medieval life, and in an age when the secular bonds of English society were in a state of disintegration, it was hardly remarkable that its ecclesiastical institutions should also be under attack.

The civil wars were the outcome of this collapse of law and order, because it was in these conditions of insecurity that the baronial retinues were built up to the proportions of small armies. The greater peers had long made a practice of engaging considerable numbers of men. Those with extensive possessions required men to manage their property, stewards, councillors and a host of minor officials; for these positions, in which an able layman could make a profitable career, professional competence was the most important qualification. Professional retainers of this type might serve more than one lord in the course of their careers. Many other knights and esquires were engaged

* See Chapter III.

for a different purpose. A magnate's reputation and political influence was to a large extent dependent upon the size and social quality of the company which, wearing his livery, would ride with him, both locally and when he went to attend parliaments and councils. The man who sealed an indenture★ binding him to perform these services received his patron's undertaking to pay a regular pension and reimburse the costs of attendance and also a promise of "good lordship". These retainers were not necessarily recruited from the gentry who held their lands from their "good lord", but might be the tenants of the king or another lord. Although they undertook to serve their lord for life, this undertaking was not always kept and some retainers are known to have transferred their allegiance to other lords.

This system of personal service has been called "bastard feudalism",[15] a name which implies that it was a debased imitation of the original type of feudalism and, albeit wrongly, that it was illegal and inimical to social order. In fact, parliament had attempted to regulate rather than abolish it. What was forbidden, by statutes dating from 1275, was maintenance in litigation, that is, the support of litigants in their suits by improper manipulation of the processes of law or by more overt forms of interference like the intimidation of juries. "Bastard feudalism" is often equated with "livery and maintenance", but the two were not necessarily coterminous. Maintenance of litigation was illegal, but the granting of liveries by lords to their pensioners was not. It had, indeed, the sanction of a statute of 1390; this act forbad men below the rank of banneret to give liveries, but retainers of lords were licensed to wear their patrons' liveries provided that they were at the time engaged on his service. Claims have been made recently that "bastard feudalism" could prove to be beneficial as a means of giving stability to local society; the lord could keep the peace among his followers, settling their disputes by his arbitration. Provided that the king was able to control the lords, "bastard feudalism" had a valuable place in the organisation of national life.[16]

The fact remains that the emergence of this system was a retrograde step. The original feudalism, itself the product of the need for protection in the Europe of the Dark Ages, had been introduced to England

---

★ The indented deed was the normal form of document for a contract in medieval England, for business transactions of all kinds as well as for engagement of services. It cannot therefore be argued that the king's practice of raising armies by indenture inspired the baronial method of building retinues on the grounds that the same kind of document was employed.

by William the Conqueror as a means of holding the country and providing himself with an army, and at the same time rewarding those who had come with him from the continent. Gradually his successors had undermined the feudal order, and, instead of ruling the country through the agency of a small number of great tenants-in-chief, developed a new pattern of government based on the co-operation of all the free landed classes. The most potent weapon in the royal task of centralisation had been the law. The king showed that his justice was better than that of any baronial court, and litigants came to prefer the royal court; its procedure was more impartial and speedy, and its decisions were enforced by the king's local officers.

The central institutions of the English judicial system had been established by the end of the thirteenth century. The court of Common Pleas at Westminster tried the private suits of subjects from all parts of England save those few privileged territories, like the Bishopric of Durham, where tenants were still obliged to sue in their lord's court. Plaintiffs came to Common Pleas to make their claims to lands, services, revenues, goods, debts and damages. Similar pleas were also entertained in the chief royal court of King's Bench, usually at Westminster, although it occasionally went on circuit until the reign of Henry V. King's Bench exercised an immediate criminal jurisdiction as well in the county where it happened to be, and it also tried cases of serious crimes which had originally been opened by indictments in local courts. To supplement their work at Westminster, and carry the authority of the royal courts into the country as a whole, the justices of both benches were commissioned at least once a year to visit every county town. Here they presided over the assizes in which litigants sought possession of lands and they also tried all the inmates of the county gaol, men arrested on charges of felony by the sheriff, coroners and other officers responsible for the local preservation of the king's peace.

The development of the royal judicial system led to the establishment of a new relationship between the king and the landed gentry; whether they were his immediate tenants or those of great feudatories, these knights and squires found themselves increasingly called upon to act as jurors in the king's courts, as royal commissioners and officers in his administration of the shires, and they were frequently summoned to the capital to give verdicts or to report on the performance of their duties. Eventually members of this class, elected by the county freeholders, were summoned to take their places as knights of the shires in parliament. Thus, at the close of the thirteenth century, the class which bore the unpaid burden of local government and legal administration was recognised as a partner, albeit a junior one, in the king's government of the realm.

As parliament became one of the regular institutions of government in the fourteenth century, the country gentry eligible for election came to value the status and opportunities of the shire knight. These early parliaments were short but frequent, depending on the king's needs to call them. Far from shunning the interruption to their rural lives, many ex-members were ready to seek re-election, some serving as often as a dozen times. This continuity of personnel enabled the commons in parliament to develop their organisation and procedure and to establish traditions and privileges. Although they were not, like the lords, admitted to the king's confidence and asked to consider affairs of state, the crown at times thought it advisable to make declarations of policy for their enlightenment. The commons took, and were allowed, a closer interest in economic affairs, in the preservation of public order and the correction of injustices. They won the king's recognition that he could not tax the realm without their consent, and this weapon they occasionally exploited to secure remedies of grievances, even to the point of forcing the king to dismiss incompetent or corrupt ministers and to accept regulations for the conduct of his council. The king also conceded that permanent amendments or additions to the law of the land could only be effected by statutes enacted in parliament, and these likewise required the assent of the commons. From this recognition of their part in legislation, they went on to attain almost a monopoly in the initiation of statutes. Petitions from the commons praying for relief in particular cases had frequently formed the basis of enactments of general remedies, but in the second quarter of the fifteenth century almost every addition to the statute book originated in the commons.

The limitations imposed on royal authority in the spheres of legislation and taxation led Sir John Fortescue, in his celebrated analysis of the governance of fifteenth-century England, to describe the country's polity as a lordship both political and royal; he contrasted England with France, a lordship only royal, in which the king held arbitrary authority and could make laws and impose taxes at his pleasure. Fortescue professed to believe that England's laws had been given to her by that legendary first king of Britain, the Trojan Brutus, but he also attributed the difference between her legal system and that of France to contrasts in the distribution of wealth in the two countries. Whereas the average French peasant was miserably poor, and so a wretched fellow without the spirit to revolt or take to crime, there were in England many men enjoying comfortable livelihoods.[17]

This claim for England is well supported by the returns made in 1436 when incomes from land were assessed for taxation; from these it has been calculated that there were approximately 7,000 commoners in the country holding lands with an annual value exceeding £5,* and there were probably at least twice as many who were qualified to vote in parliamentary elections after the franchise had been restricted in 1429 to those with freehold land worth no less than forty shillings a year. Of the 7,000, an estimated 183 had an average annual income of £208, some 750 an average of £60 and 1,200 had £24.[19] These admitted figures may err on the low side because of the purpose for which they were required, and they do not relate to all possible sources of income. But they uphold Fortescue's statement that there were in every county considerable numbers of men free from the cares of poverty and thus, he claimed, able to make judgments when called upon to act as jurors. Among the wealthier commoners there were at least 2,000 qualified for appointment as county justices of the peace when, in 1439, parliament ordained that the minimum income from land of such justices should not be less than £20.

In Fortescue's opinion, the English were particularly fortunate to enjoy the safeguards of the method of trial by jury. How much more happy were they than subjects of the king of France who could be condemned on the testimony of two witnesses. Fortescue's comparison, however, did not go far enough. The relative wealth of the two populations did not provide the full explanation of their different systems of law. The contrast between the revenues of the two kings *vis-à-vis* their subjects was even more significant. The revenues of the

---

* It is not possible to express medieval money in modern values: the same multiplier could not be applied to every price. The figures given on this page will permit some comparison. In addition, the following average wages and prices in 1450 might be noted:

Daily wages: farm labourers, 4d.; masons, 6¼d. or 5¼d.; carpenters, 5¼d.; thatchers and tilers, 5d.

Prices: wheat, 5s. 10d. per quarter; oatmeal, 5s. 0d. per quarter; beef, 4s. 1d. per cwt.; mutton, 4s. 6d. per cwt.; butter, ½d. per pound; eggs, 5¼d. for 120.[18]

French king permitted him to engage a large, professional corps of administrators and judges, whereas the king of England, with far less resources, was dependent on the unpaid services of country gentry for the administration of justice in the shires.

By the early fourteenth century, it had become obvious that the king's professional judges were unable to cope with a mounting crime-wave, and the eventual solution was the creation of commissions of the peace to exercise criminal jurisdiction in the shires. In arriving at this solution in the statute of 1361, Edward III had in fact given way to the wishes of the commons; they had exploited their control over taxation to gain a concession both for the cause of public order and for the enhancement of their own local importance, for justices of the peace were selected from the same class of men who provided the counties with representatives in parliament. In the same reign, the commons also extracted the king's undertaking that the senior officer responsible for each shire's good order and judicial administration, the sheriff, should be changed every year in order to prevent the perpetuation of corrupt practices. Again, it was the same class of gentry who were called upon to provide recruits to the shrievalty. Thus the descendants of those lesser tenants who had been drawn into the crown's local administration by royal command won statutory recognition of their indispensability for the preservation of the king's peace.

By this time the *raison d'être* of feudalism had also disappeared. Already by the twelfth century, kings found the feudal levy an impractical means of raising an army for employment on the continent, and towards the end of the thirteenth century there was a growing tendency to engage and pay men for a longer term than the forty days prescribed by feudal custom. The armies raised by Edward III for the French wars were all paid, the greatest tenants-in-chief as well as other men being retained by contract to serve the king for wages for the whole period of their service. The wages of these indentured armies were provided by parliamentary subsidies levied throughout the country and customs duties imposed on certain imports and exports, of which wool was the most important. The burden of war thus ceased to be almost exclusively the unpaid responsibility of those who held land and was now spread over a larger section of the population as taxpayers and consumers of dutiable imports.

Feudalism, however, did remain as the basis of English land-law. In theory, land was not owned but "held"; the earl with fifty or more manors scattered throughout a score of counties and the petty squire with a fraction of a knight's fee were equally tenants-in-chief of the king if they held directly from the crown, that is, without any intermediate lord. In practice, however, a tenant-in-chief had nearly as absolute a title to his estates as any landowner in the modern sense. He could sell his lands, grant them to trustees, mortgage or lease them, create an entail by a number of conveyances or divide them among his children. It is true that the crown had by statute made it obligatory for tenants-in-chief to obtain royal licences before making such dispositions, but this was a formality only, obtainable at a price, or acquired after the event by the purchase of a pardon. The tenant's right to make these arrangements was not disputed. He could defend his title to his lands in a court of law, even against the crown. The crown's feudal authority remained, but most estates only felt it when a tenant died, when the king's officers took possession. If the heir, generally the eldest son, was over twenty-one years of age, he did homage to the king and paid a relief before entering his inheritance; but if he were a minor, the property was held by the king or his grantees until the heir came of age. The marriage of wards and widows was another feudal perquisite of the crown; the former could be sold to aspiring parents-in-law, while widows required the king's licence to re-marry. Yet several of these incidents could be avoided by the creation of trusts which preserved estates from royal occupation.

"Bastard feudalism" threatened to destroy the constitutional and legal progress achieved since the twelfth century. Baronial courts had gone out of business because of the greater attractions of the common law, by the same law under-tenants could feel secure in the possession of their property. With the growing influence of central government in the local administration of the law, and their own participation in its work, members of the middle landed class tended to think of themselves as subjects of the king rather than as the men of their territorial lords; they served in his local government, while they were no longer likely to be called upon to give their lords the military service which was the condition of their tenure. But now the baronage was again making these landed gentry its immediate dependents. There might be a clause saving a retainer's loyalty to the king in his indenture with a lord, but for all practical purposes he was that lord's man and followed his lead in national as well as local affairs. The institutions of the king's local administration and of the common law continued to function, but their impartiality and effectiveness were being destroyed. Officials and juries were subjected to pressure from magnates fulfilling their promises of "good lordship" by maintaining their retainers in their suits.

As the parasitic hold of "bastard feudalism" on royal justice grew stronger,[20] it became a matter of crucial importance for every man of property to have his own "good lord". A man injured or threatened by a powerful enemy could put no trust in the king's courts to give him justice or protection; his adversary might have influential friends in the central or local administration, he might be the retainer of a peer able to pack a jury or strong enough to intimidate it. The remedy was to find a patron whose influence and material resources would at least match those of the enemy. Aggressive country gentry likewise found it advisable to have a "good lord" who would defend them from the legal or other consequences of their misdeeds. Some men may have engaged themselves to lords for the sake of the fees or pensions paid as part of the terms of their indentures, but it is improbable that this consideration was the chief attraction to most retainers. The pension rarely exceeded £10 a year, and, even if useful, an emolument on this scale was not likely to induce a squire or knight of much substance to put himself at the disposal of a peer, with all that this might entail.

Since his lord's protection was vital to a retainer's safety, he would not dare to refuse to perform his side of the bargain. No doubt some retainers kept an eye open for a more effectual champion, and deserted for service under a new "good lord" when the first was losing the influence on which the retainer depended for his own security. Yet such fickleness is immaterial. The relevant fact was that even the most time-serving retainer was always at the command of some lord, and thus ready to take his place in some baronial retinue. On the other hand, many examples are provided by the northern counties of retainers who adhered to their lords through years of crisis. But steadfast or not, if the lord for the time being became actively engaged in the conflict of Lancaster and York, his retainers had no choice but to follow him into battle.

Few could have foreseen this extreme development when they

sealed their indentures, but there always was a strong possibility of having to take part in semi-military operations locally. "Bastard feudalism" did not bring stability to those districts where more than one lord had recruited retainers if the relations of those lords were hostile.* When groups of country gentry were already coming to blows, they inevitably attached themselves to different patrons. The feuds were continued under the banners of their leaders, but not necessarily with their approval, and finally transferred, as if to a supreme court, to the battlefields of the civil war.

In the reign of Henry VI, "bastard feudalism" developed without restraint and made its own momentum, creating the conditions which encouraged the recruitment of baronial retinues and thus still further strengthening its hold on English society. The fact that the collapse of law and order which led to the upsurge of "bastard feudalism" was general suggests a cause common to the whole country. Earlier generations of historians used to find an explanation in the end of the Hundred Years War in 1453; with the first battle of the Wars of the Roses coming so soon afterwards in 1455, it seemed to them that bellicose Englishmen, deprived of their continental battle-grounds, could not be expected to settle at home and naturally soon took to fighting among themselves. We have already dismissed the notion that the civil wars were fought by ready-made contingents of veterans from the French wars. Moreover, the breakdown of public order in England long preceded the final defeat in France. It is doubtful if other effects of the war caused serious dislocation to English life. Only a minute proportion of the country's manpower, less than one per cent, was engaged in France for long periods. Much of the cost was carried by European purchasers of English wool, and while money was taken from the land in the form of direct taxation, wealth came back to the country in the hands of soldiers who had won ransoms and other prizes of war.[21]

The fifteenth century as a whole can certainly not be characterised as a period of poverty and desolation, as the Yorkist manifesto of 1461 alleged. We have still too much visible evidence of its architectural achievements to believe this, above all in the parish churches of East Anglia and the Cotswolds. Yet it is very questionable if much of

---

* It is hard to understand why modern apologists for "bastard feudalism" can at the one time proclaim its stabilising properties and also bring forward cases to show the transient nature of the bonds between lord and man.

this building can be attributed to the middle years of the century. Its third quarter was a period of depression in both trade and agriculture. There had been a decline in the country's export trade at the opening of the century, followed by a recovery in the 1420's, but from about the opening of the last stage of the Hundred Years War in 1449 a second depression had begun. At the same time as French and Burgundian markets were closed to English trade, there was a serious breach with the Hanseatic League which interrupted trade with the Netherlands and the Baltic. The value of wool exported fell by a quarter of the pre-1450 average, and this commodity had accounted for ninety-five per cent of the country's exports. Then the conquest of Gascony by the French crippled the wine trade: the amount of red wine imported by English merchants fell to one-third of its previous total.[22] Apart from the damage caused by these disasters to native trading interests, the repercussions on wool growers and the woollen cloth industry must have been severe, for the home market was unable to absorb the unexported products. Underemployment may therefore partially explain the restiveness of some urban populations.* Finally, the revenues of the crown also suffered through the fall of its receipts from customs charges on wool and wine, which had been the largest single item in its income.

Nine-tenths of the population lived by agriculture. Here the depression had a longer history, dating from the second decade of the fourteenth century. The catastrophic harvests of that time had at least arrested the previous danger of over-population, and later the Black Death of 1348-9 and its subsequent visitations had caused an appalling loss of life. This spelt the final demise of the traditional manorial economy supported by the unpaid labour of unfree tenants tied to their native soil. To fill the gaps in their working force, lords of manors tried to attract labourers from elsewhere by offering wages, and the conditions of the surviving tenants were improved so that they should not be tempted to leave. More commonly, the proprietors gave up the attempt to farm their own land and leased it in portions to tenants free of all charges except rents. Such tenants were not always readily found, and records of decreasing rents and entry fines,

---

* The disturbance at Norwich, however, took place before the depression of the 1450's, although this explanation may hold good in the case of the city of York.

of empty holdings and even of deserted villages bear witness to an acute scarcity of agricultural manpower.

The evidence of wages and prices in the fifteenth century suggests that the population continued to diminish. The prices of cereals and other primary crops remained steady, but wages of labourers went on rising so that by mid-century their value, at least in regard to basic foodstuffs, was more than double what it had been in 1300. This was equally the case with the wages of masons, carpenters and other artisans, indicating that there was no serious drift of labour from the land to the towns;[23] it also suggests that men put out of work by the dislocation of overseas trade would have been able to find other employment. This was, as a great authority has said, "the golden age of the English labourer, if we are to interpret the wages he earned by the cost of the necessaries of life. At no time were wages, relatively speaking, so high, and at no time was food so cheap."[24] So far as the average member of the working class was concerned, therefore, the fifteenth century was a period of prosperity, and he had no compelling economic motive to leave his place of work to make a living by more hazardous and possibly less lawful means.

The well-being of the peasantry, however, was the result of the difficulties of the landowner. There had been a redistribution of rural wealth. The low rents and relatively high wages enjoyed by yeomen and labourers naturally ensued in declining revenues for the landed classes. Despite this, the late medieval magnate kept a large domestic establishment and incurred heavy expenses for wages, food, wine and clothing; his rank demanded both splendour and lavish generosity in entertainment and largesse. Yet even the greatest magnates were unable to meet the cost of this extravagant way of life. The earl of Warwick's expenditure in 1420-1 included £787 spent on clothing alone from an income of £2,918, and in addition £103 for a piece of velvet worked with gold.[25] In 1450, the duke of Buckingham's income was apparently insufficient for the costs of his household.[26] At the same time, the lords were lengthening their wages-bills by recruiting larger numbers of gentry as retainers. Before we ask whether and how the baronage attempted to find additional sources of profit to compensate for the fall in its revenue from land, it might be legitimate to question whether some, at least, were really aware of their critical financial position or sufficiently alarmed to search for compensation; there is little reason to believe that the fifteenth-century nobility tried to curtail its expenditure, and the signs are that, like its counterpart in the following century, it lived on a grand scale and obliviously headed for bankruptcy.

The simplest way for a landed family to offset falling revenue was through marriages to heiresses or well-dowered widows; both expedients augmented the income of the earls of Northumberland.[27] This remedy was not freely available, and the competition for ladies of property tempted some importunate suitors to employ forcible methods in their courtship.[28] The French wars had offered prospects of enrichment, but after about 1430 the opportunities here had begun to dwindle. The recession in trade and ensuing industrial stagnation lessened the prospects of profit by direct participation or indirectly by obtaining perquisites from municipal bodies ready to pay for baronial goodwill. There remained royal patronage: offices of profit, pensions, wardships and marriages of feudal heirs and widows and other incidents were at the king's disposal. But the king's revenue had declined more steeply than any other, and his means were insufficient to satisfy all claimants to his bounty.

Competition for royal favours could then account for baronial rivalries. The political gangsterdom of the times could have been the consequence of the nobility's shrinking revenues.[29] In the case of the earls of Northumberland, however, the family's financial difficulties were the result, not the cause, of the struggle for influence on both national and local levels; between a third and a half of its gross landed revenues was consumed by fees to its officers and retainers, and its indebtedness was less than the arrears of wages due for services to the crown.[30] An awareness of impending economic disaster may possibly have added to the tenacity of some contestants for political influence and sharpened the zeal of litigants pursuing claims to lands and other revenues. What it will not explain is how the parties grouped themselves as they did in the civil wars, why particular peers chose to associate themselves with one leader in preference to another, why the English monarchy became the plaything of faction, or why there should have been this collapse in so long-established a system of law and order.

The threat of public disorder was never far distant in medieval England: hardly a generation passed without some major disturbance. This was as present a danger in years of economic progress as in times of recess: the great boom in seigneurial prosperity had not yet burst when Edward II was forced to submit to the Lords Ordainers in 1310. Despite the establishment of a centralised judicial system and a network of local officers and magistrates responsible to the crown, the internal peace of the kingdom was poised on a razor's edge. It rested, above all, on the natural hazards of a hereditary monarchy. The preservation of public peace was the constant burden of the crown. In his coronation oath the king swore to uphold the laws of the land and give justice to his people; he was vested, under the law, with unlimited executive authority so that he could fulfil this charge; but it was dependent upon the quality of his personal stature whether he could unfailingly command his subjects' obedience. It was a vital necessity for the country's domestic well-being that every king should possess the strength of character and mental calibre necessary to inspire effective government and ensure the respect of his subjects to himself and thus to the country's legal and administrative institutions. But hereditary succession is a lottery. If a king's heir lacked the qualities requisite to his office, the framework of government and judicature would not perish, but they would no longer serve the purposes for which they had been designed.

What made the personal qualities of each king a matter of such crucial importance was his relationship with the peerage. This was the most sensitive point in the constitution of medieval England. Whatever Sir John Fortescue might say about the restraints of law and custom on the authority of the crown, the brutal fact was that the chief limitation on the power of the sovereign was the straitness of his means. After these had provided for the costs of his household, the support of his family, the upkeep of his buildings, and the wages and expenses of his ministers and numerous servants in the departments of government and of the officers and garrisons of the regular defence establishments, there was little if any balance remaining for emergencies. The king's revenues did not permit him to keep more than the skeleton of a standing army. In normal circumstances this was enough. His household provided a nucleus for a national host when the country was threatened by external enemies or factious revolt; if the former, his summonses to service would be obeyed without question, but if a rebellion broke out, a king would be in critical danger if the lords refused to mobilise their followers in his support. In more settled times, even, the co-operation of his most influential subjects was essential for the smooth operation of his government.

Harmony between the crown and the lords was the keystone of public order.

The English nobility had been transformed since the reigns of the Norman kings.[31] Time alone had removed many great names of the early feudal period; some titles had disappeared entirely, others survived because they had been resuscitated by the crown. Before parliaments were held, the only tenants-in-chief distinguished by having titles were the earls. There were thirteen earldoms in 1422. Warwick alone dated from the eleventh century, Arundel, Devon and Oxford from the twelfth, but only Oxford was held by a direct heir male of the first to hold the title. The remaining earldoms had been created by Edward III and Richard II. The four dukedoms in 1422 were more recent: Richard was the third duke of York since 1385, but Bedford, Gloucester and Exeter were creations of Henry V, all fated to die with their holders.* In addition, there were some two score men who can be termed lords because they were summoned in person to parliament. By this time it was an established convention that the son of a man called to parliament should enjoy the same distinction when he inherited his father's lands, or the right to a summons could be transferred to the husband or son of an heiress. Additions were continually being made to this category of lesser peers, but for a variety of mainly natural causes their total number did not rise significantly.

Titled and untitled peerages owed their creation to the crown. They were conferred only as acts of the royal prerogative, as marks of the king's favour, to distinguish members of his own family circle and to reward notable services in war or government. The majority of peerages in the fifteenth century were neither ancient or feudal; their existence was a consequence of the emergence of a non-feudal institution, parliament. The lords, however, were also tenants-in-chief. Peerages were only given to men who had the landed resources thought necessary to support their dignity. The returns of 1436 show that the lords, some fifty all told, declared a total income from land of £40,000. Individual incomes varied greatly. Only thirteen peers admitted to having estates yielding more than £1,000 a year, and half of the remainder had less than £400. There was little to distinguish this last group from the wealthier commoners apart from their

---

* Exeter was revived in 1444 when the earl of Huntingdon was promoted to ducal rank.

writs of summons, and, like the gentry, they tended to attach themselves to the greater peers. These dozen magnates accounted for more
than half the reported baronial revenues; three peers – the duke of
York and the earls of Stafford* and Warwick – together with their
widowed mothers held between them a quarter of the entire baronial
wealth. The dukes of Gloucester and Norfolk† and the earl of Suffolk
each had about £2,000 a year, and were followed by the earls of
Huntingdon, Salisbury, Somerset and Northumberland, and Lords
Cromwell, Lovel, Talbot‡ and Tiptoft with incomes of between
£1,300 and £1,000.[32]

These outstandingly well-endowed peers owed their wealth,
largely, to the fortune of marriage alliances with other noble houses
which had failed to continue in the male line. The value of landed
property may have been declining, but heiresses augmented the
fortunes of houses which were able to produce male heirs. In any
case, the incomes of the magnates remained on a level surpassing
those of other landed families, and they inevitably held a dominant
place in English society. The overmighty subject, as Fortescue called
him, was however not an irresponsible tyrant, a feudal reactionary.
Social manners and living conditions had naturally changed a great
deal since the twelfth century. The expansion of international com-
merce and the greater internal order achieved by the Angevin kings
permitted new standards of domestic comfort and private ease; space
and light became more important desiderata than military security in
the planning of baronial mansions. A high standard of living required
adequate financial provision; it depended upon an administrative
organisation to bring to its master all the revenues to which he was
entitled. With his estates dispersed through half the counties of
England, the great lord had a strong vested interest in the preservation
of public order. His dearest ambition was doubtless the continuity and
prosperity of his house, which he or his recent forbears had tried to
safeguard by the creation of entails; he would not lightly hazard his
family's fortunes by the reckless abuse of power.

The landed resources of the lords gave them a major stake in the
well-being of the country, and by popular sentiment they were
accorded an undefined part in the governance of the realm; they were,

---

* Created duke of Buckingham in 1444.
† The dukedom of Norfolk was restored in 1425.
‡ Created earl of Shrewsbury in 1442.

it was said, "the king's natural councillors". With important pre-
occupations in their own estates and a disinclination, if not inaptitude,
to routine administrative work, they had no wish to be tied to regular
attendance in official positions in the central government. It was
sufficient that the king should consult them on major issues of policy
at periodic assemblies, in parliaments and great councils.* Provided
that the king showed proper regard to their ambitions and prejudices,
they were content to leave the conduct of government to him and
the ministers and councillors of his choice. There were always a few
individual peers attendant on the king or ready to accept military or
civil office under him, but if the king could be said to have ruled under
the shadow of the baronage, its supervision was generally remote.

In maintaining harmonious relations with the lords, there were
many assets in the king's favour. Firstly was a natural predisposition
to accept his leadership, which was grounded in tradition, sentiment
and notions of honour; his authority was sanctified by the solemnities
of the coronation and recognised by the lords' oaths of fealty. The
crown was the fount of honour and rewarded notable services with
favours flattering to a lord's self-esteem. The king was not obliged to
buy the favour of the lords with expensive grants of lands, offices and
privileges. He might make concessions to their dynastic ambitions,
giving the licences necessary for their entails and the like, and he
might uphold their repute by showing favour to their protégés, but
there was no need to be lavish. Nothing made a greater contribution
to harmony than an identity of tastes and pursuits. The lords were
most likely to respect a king with a desire for military glory and the
martial qualities to realise it, a lover of chivalrous pageantry and
courtly pomp, an ardent follower of the chase and yet also a faithful
son of the Church. Further, if the king's government earned the
goodwill of the gentry and commons, the lords' ability to threaten
him would be considerably reduced; thus the earlier plots against
Henry IV ended in disaster because humble subjects turned violently
against the noble rebels.

It is misleading, moreover, to refer to the peerage *en bloc* as if it
formed a normally coherent body. Its members had individual as
well as common interests, they were connected by marriage alliances
but they did not have a corporate organisation. The king had to deal
with them as single persons. His resources were no match for those

* Meetings usually of lords spiritual and temporal only.

of the entire baronage, but he could cope with isolated miscreant peers. In so doing, if the offender's misdeeds were manifestly inimical to good government, the king could count on the rest of the lords to uphold him. Hereditary peerages were subject to the same accidents of birth as the monarchy; there was no guarantee that every lord would have a full sense of responsibility for his actions and could keep his violent passions under control. But lords were as likely to quarrel with each other over precedence or local consequence or property as to oppose the royal authority. The abatement of noble quarrels was the most important single task of the king's council. This was the highest tribunal in the land, exercising the inalienable judicial powers of the crown, and it showed particular concern for feuds which could result in serious disorder.

The emergence of the overmighty subject, the magnate whose estates embraced several inheritances, both simplified the king's task of wooing the lords and also brought new dangers. He now had fewer individuals to deal with; if he could satisfy them, the rest of the baronage would follow suit. On the other hand, these magnates were conscious of their strength and more difficult to restrain. As long as their private interests divided them, however, the king was not endangered by their potential strength. It was only when his policies threatened the interests of the whole class that he encountered serious difficulties. Richard II had fallen because, preferring the arts to war, he had estranged the sympathies of the peers, and his despotic pretensions had united them against him. The reign had ended with such unlikely comrades-in-arms as the Nevilles and Percies putting Henry of Lancaster on the throne, while the country in general remained indifferent to Richard's appeals for aid.

The prestige of the monarchy may have been impaired by Henry IV's usurpation, but its inherent strength was realised in full under his son Henry V. He did more than wage a victorious war of conquest in France. John Harding, writing for the eye of Edward IV, could say of the second Lancastrian king:

> His shadow so obumbered all England,
> That peace and law [were] kept continuant.[33]

Henry's subjects were not all as law-abiding as Harding would have us believe, but forty years later his reign could reasonably be thought of as a golden age of order and justice.

The subsequent decline began in the long minority of Henry VI. The constitutional issues raised by this minority, particularly the proposal to set up a regency and its defeat by the exponents of conciliar government, have received more scholarly attention than the general domestic consequences. It may be suspected that, in the absence of the personal influence of a king, the more considerable tenants-in-chief felt freer to develop their local interests. However conscientiously the lords of the council applied themselves to the problems of central government, to diplomacy and the French war, it is doubtful whether they attempted to restrain those of their colleagues who used high-handed methods to extend their personal authority in the districts where their estates lay. Certainly, the council took action when baronial disputes threatened serious breaches of the peace, but its members, following the precept "dog does not eat dog", were likely to adopt a policy of non-interference in each other's local operations. Factional tension in the council, moreover, prompted its secular peers to increase their retinues: in 1432, seven baronial councillors were ordered not to bring more than their customary trains of domestic retainers when they attended parliament; and the earls of Northumberland and Warwick are known to have made appreciable additions to their lists of pensioners in the years about 1430.[34]

A parallel upsurge in the worse aspects of "bastard feudalism" is revealed by the growing number of parliamentary petitions concerning disorder and illegal maintenance. Complaints of abuses of the law had undeniably been a staple ingredient of parliamentary bills since their inception, but from 1427 the volume of petitions on this subject and the gravity of their allegations indicate that members were becoming seriously alarmed. In 1427 it was said that knights and others below baronial rank had been granting liveries beyond the statutory limitations but they were escaping prosecution because juries were prevented from making indictments by "great maintenance". One of a number of petitions regarding disorder presented by the commons in 1429 asked for an elaboration of a statute of 1391 which empowered justices of the peace to restore a man to land from which he had been forcibly expelled; these violent entries were now being made "daily", and some of the wrongful occupants were gifting the property so seized to lords and others in order to have their maintenance.

In the same parliament, the members of the king's council were required to take an oath that they would not harbour murderers, robbers, "oppressors of the people" and other "open misdoers" and not to uphold their causes in courts of law. As maintenance of this kind had long been forbidden by statutes, this measure indicates how ineffective they were, and it also suggests parliament's suspicions about the behaviour of the lords of the council. In the parliament of 1433, at the request of the commons, all the prelates and lords took the same oath, and it was later administered to scores of knights, esquires and municipal officers in every county.[35]

Had Henry VI, when he came of age, been a king of the same calibre as his father, the drift to anarchy would have been checked. It was a national disaster that for forty years the throne was occupied by a king without the capacity to rule. Henry's failings were entirely negative. Because of his personal deficiencies, the monarchy virtually fell into abeyance. Not only did he lack the force of character necessary to earn the respect of the lords and so persuade them, as need arose, to submit their private disputes to the judgment of his council; he let the council itself fall into the grasp of a small baronial faction and thus, probably without his knowledge, the crown itself became a party in these quarrels. And for want of justice, or rather through fear that the justice of the king's council would not be impartial, magnates with enemies in the council attached themselves to the natural leader of the opposition to the royal court, the duke of York. These compacts with York were the most extreme kind of maintenance, and they gave him the armed strength he required to force a conclusion in his dispute with the faction enjoying the king's favour.

The Wars of the Roses were thus the outcome of an escalation of private feuds. Gentry, with understandable lack of confidence in the processes of law, attached themselves to lords who could give them protection against their personal enemies and in return supported their patrons in private wars with their peers. These baronial hostilities similarly resulted in the contestants aligning themselves with the major political rivals, and thus drawing their retainers into the conflict of Lancaster and York. These private wars which preceded the Wars of the Roses admittedly involved only a small if powerful section of the peerage, but neither did all members of the nobility take an active part in the civil war. Those lords who had already taken the field against their private enemies were the most militant protagonists of the rival princes.

At the levels of both gentry and baronage, there was the same basic cause for these associations, the failure of the crown to administer justice with vigour and obvious impartiality. Because it was dominated by a faction, the king's council lost its stature as the tribunal for pacifying hostile lords. The same faction corrupted the administration of justice in the shires for the benefit of its clients. Henry did not directly antagonise the peers against himself. As late as 1460, even those who had recently fought against his standard refused to renounce their oaths of fealty. Unlike civil wars in contemporary Europe, in the France of Louis XI or the Naples of Ferrante I, those in England did not originate in hostility to the king. Baronial revolts abroad were provoked by the increasingly despotic nature of royal government, but here civil war came for the very opposite reason, for what contemporaries called "the lack of politic rule and governance".

I

Henry VI

Henry of Windsor was born on 6 December 1421, the son of Henry V and Catharine of France. Nine months later, his father, "the flower of Christian chivalry", victor of Agincourt, conqueror of Normandy and, since the treaty of Troyes, "heir and regent of the kingdom of France", died in the royal castle in the Bois de Vincennes, outside the walls of Paris. From 1 September 1422, the government of England was carried on in the name of Henry VI. It was solemnly recorded on the close roll of Chancery that on 28 September his father's chancellor, the bishop of Durham, came before Henry at Windsor and in the presence of the lords of the council delivered the great seal into the hands of the king, who thereupon committed this major instrument of authority to a temporary keeper. There is no suggestion in the record that circumstances were other than normal, that the king was not a fully responsible, adult monarch in complete charge of his administration. The fiction was preserved in all subsequent formal acts of government. Parliaments were summoned to his presence, and when Henry himself did not preside, the parliamentary records make it clear that it was he who appointed a deputy to sit in his place. Official letters all issued in the name of *Henricus Dei gracia rex Anglie et Francie et dominus Hibernie*. Chancellor, treasurer and all other officers of the central government as well as of local administrations drew their authority from his letters of commission. In their turn, subjects addressed letters and petitions "to the king our sovereign lord" with suitable expressions of reverence for his majesty and dread of the royal indignation.

The official records, as they often do, conceal the reality. It was of course not the king who ruled but his council. Royal letters do reveal this body's activity: Henry's grants were said to have been made "with the assent of our council". In fact, it was the council alone which authorised all acts of government until the king came of age. In the first years of his reign, these councillors were all men who had been similarly employed by Henry V – the senior ministers of state and members of his council in England, and some of the officers previously engaged in the administration of Normandy. Apart from a short visit to England in 1421, Henry V had been directing his armies in France from 1417 until his death, but despite this long absence he kept a very firm control over the administration in England: there was a royal lieutenant, with a council to advise him, but they rarely presumed to initiate any action without the king's prior consent. Under Henry V, the power and prestige of the monarchy reached a peak it had not known for many decades; many more were to pass before the crown again enjoyed an authority as uncontested as it had been on the day of his death. Henry V had not ignored the claim of the baronage to be his natural counsellors, but the strength of his personality, and the reputation which military victory had brought him, enabled him to dominate the lords and to restrain any aspirations to a position of effective influence.

The succession to this formidable monarch of an infant of nine months offered the lords a golden opportunity to attain real control over the royal administration. The most recent precedent, the minority of Richard II, pointed to the establishment of a council of bishops and temporal peers as the chief agent of government. The duke of Gloucester, Henry V's youngest brother, opposed this arrangement, claiming instead that he should be regent, and it appears that Henry in his last will had decreed Gloucester's appointment. Had Gloucester been successful, the authority, prerogatives and patronage of the crown would have been wielded by his hands alone, and so kept intact until Henry VI could take full charge. Instead, the crown was virtually put into commission. Bishop Beaufort and other members of the council may well have been inspired by distrust of Gloucester, as well as by a desire to share in the profits of government; for certainly some councillors can be shown to have furthered their private interests, by obtaining grants from the crown and by promoting the petitions of their dependents. Yet there was nothing abnormal in this: a king of full age was always being solicited for favours, and as he desired the goodwill of the peers he would not have rejected all their requests.

The council of Henry VI's minority gave English government a stable core. Its members are not to be written off as self-seeking magnates, unsuited to bearing the responsibilities of supreme authority. Most of the bishops and junior peers, Ralph Cromwell for instance, had served under Henry V, and his ability to choose servants of real worth was not denied. These experienced clerical and secular administrators and diplomats formed a majority in the score of councillors, and were the most regular in their attendance. The leading temporal peers were also members, but whatever their qualifications as statesmen it was of great advantage to the peace of the realm that the most mighty subjects should be brought together at the royal council: personal differences could be thrashed out there, with the other members mediating. Apart from the recurrent quarrel of Gloucester and Beaufort, the period of the royal minority was comparatively free from the serious kind of disorder engendered by the disputes of magnates, and the efforts of the other councillors to keep the peace between these and other contestants testifies to a collective sense of responsibility for the stability of the kingdom.

The date when the king was held to have come of age is not disclosed by any formal record. It has been presumed that the departure for France of the king's tutor, the earl of Warwick, in the autumn of 1437, marked the end of Henry's minority. In fact, Warwick had been relieved of his responsibility for Henry's upbringing on 19 May 1436,[1] and it is likely that the personal rule dates from this year. The telling phrase, "with the assent of our council", is not to be found in an increasing proportion of royal warrants from August 1436 onwards; from the following November a growing volume of petitions was granted with the only authorisation being the royal sign-manual, "R. H."; and by January 1437 the office of king's secretary was fully established, a clear indication of personal activity by the monarch himself. The prelates and temporal lords had met in a great council in October 1436, and it is most probable that they had agreed that the time had come when Henry should conduct his government in fact as well as in name.[2] It was not then remarkable that a boy of fifteen should be entrusted with so great a charge of responsibility: Henry's father had been no older when he was put in charge of military operations against the Welsh rebels, and the commons in the parliament of 1380 had thought that, at thirteen, Richard II was old enough to govern without a council. Henry VI, indeed, had already shown a precocious desire to enjoy his prerogatives which brought upon him a rebuke from the council in November 1434; but his advisers rejoiced that he then possessed "as great understanding and feeling as ever they saw or knew in any prince or other person of his age".[3]

Henry's education from the age of six had been entrusted by the council to Richard Beauchamp, earl of Warwick, a comrade in arms of Henry V from the time of Glendower's revolt and reputedly a flower of chivalry. Warwick was instructed that before all things he was to teach the king to worship and fear God, and generally to encourage him to seek to do good and shun evil by telling of instances in times passed of the grace and prosperity befalling virtuous kings and their subjects and of the calamities which overtook the unrighteous. The earl was also charged to have the king taught his letters, languages, good manners and other things "it fitteth so great a prince to be learned of". Warwick was licensed to chastise his charge when he misbehaved or refused to do his lessons.[4] In 1432, Warwick was becoming apprehensive of the great responsibility laid upon him and sought an amplification of his authority. He reported that Henry had grown in stature and in "conceit and knowledge of his high and royal authority and estate", and so he was coming to resent the earl's "chastising of him for his faults"; he had made some companions who distracted him from his lessons and had conversed with them on unsuitable topics. The council promised to support Warwick when he punished the boy and confirmed his authority to dismiss unworthy associates and to remove the king to such places as he thought desirable for his health and safety.[5] The council's rebuke of the king two years later shows that Warwick had been unable to enforce discipline and to keep Henry immune from companions who urged him to assert himself for their advantage. Warwick was doubtless a stern tutor, but as one of the richest landowners in England and Wales he was presumably at times distracted from giving his full attention to the king. Henry's later life shows that he was free from private vice, but his fatal weakness had already been foreshadowed, the ease with which he fell under the influence of his immediate associates.

The indications that the young king was impatient to take up the reins of government proved to be illusory: in fact, we may doubt if the seemingly precocious attempts of Henry to wield authority amounted to anything more than a desire to gratify suitors for his bounty. That members of his entourage were applying to him for favours is evident, and no doubt they urged him to assert a right to exercise the royal patronage. If Henry had gone so far as to issue orders for grants of crown office or property, the council would certainly have regarded this as interference in their administration. It would be unwise to put too much stress on the council's testimonial to Henry's "understanding and feeling" in 1434. There is no sound reason for doubting, at this time, that he possessed some intelligence, perhaps even the promise of more than average intellectual gifts; although no official record, destined for preservation, would refrain from the superlative where the king's qualities were concerned. If there were such promise, it was not to be realised: there is nothing exceptional in a "bright" boy disappointing the early hopes of his parents. No medieval Englishman, however, would have regarded intelligence as the most essential quality in his king, and certainly the behaviour of some of the leading secular peers in the last years of Henry's reign suggests that the mental calibre of the ruling class was far from distinguished.

The traditional portrait of Henry's character is largely derived from the notes compiled by his admiring chaplain, John Blacman,[6] and from the comments of Yorkist chroniclers written after his deposition. While Blacman extols the king's piety, humility and other Christian virtues, those writing in the time of Edward IV referred to Henry as an idiot, "by God's doom of small intelligence".[7] The accounts of both friend and foes, indeed, disclose Henry as a devout and kindly simpleton. There is also the undisputed fact of Henry's insanity in 1453 and 1454, of his complete mental and physical prostration following a violent shock. This breakdown, so apparently similar to the equally sudden collapse of his French grandfather, Charles VI, at approximately the same period of life, suggests that Henry's bad heredity can be held to account for his feebleness of mind. None of the literary evidence concerning Henry's mental condition now available dates from before 1453, and it is tempting to write off the testimony of Yorkist chronicles as hostile propaganda. There is, however, some material not previously cited in this connection which does, at least, raise some doubt about the state of Henry's mind before he became conspicuously insane.

The records of the court of King's Bench in this period include a number of charges of seditious speech. Sometimes these are no more than allegations and do not lead to a conviction. In some instances, the charge was made by an approver, that is, a felon turning "king's evidence" in a last attempt to avoid execution.* It cannot generally be accepted that the particular words ascribed to a person were really said by him. Yet the fact remains that somebody did think of making these particular observations about Henry, and it may well be that the accuser had heard them in conversation with other people. The geographical distribution of the alleged offences, and the presence of a common element in some of the supposed statements, does suggest that they reflect contemporary opinion of the king.

The earliest of the charges specifying words spoken against the king was made against a yeoman of Farningham, in Kent, for saying, in 1442, that "the king is a lunatic, as his father was". Guilty or not, the accused thought it worth his while to buy the king's pardon.[8] The case of Thomas Carver, "gentleman", of Reading, attracted a good deal of notice at the time. He had listened to the sermon delivered before the king and his court at Abingdon by John Curtis, a Dominican friar, on Palm Sunday (6 April), 1444, and on the following day he repeated the preacher's text with undue approval. This was "Woe to thee, O land, when thy king is a child".† Carver went on to say that if the king were as much a man as the Dauphin of France, who was the same age as Henry, he would be holding his French lands in peace. Carver was sentenced to die as a traitor, but the king commuted the penalty to imprisonment.‡ There are other references to this theme of the king's childishness, although he was now more than twenty-five years of age. In 1447, an approver claimed that a London draper had said that Henry was "not in his person as his noble progenitors have been, for his visage was not favoured, for he had not

* See Appendix I for a remarkable appeal.

† Ecclesiastes x, 16.

‡ The warrant for Carver's pardon instructed the chancellor to include a clause that the king would not show favour to any similar offenders, even to his closest kinsmen, but would cause them to be punished according to the "exigence of their trespass". The chancellor was also told to see that the pardon was "in no wise openly noised but kept as secret as you may". In fact, the pardon was known to a London chronicler. On being pardoned, Carver was kept in Wallingford Castle until August 1447.[9]

unto a child's face and is not steadfast of wit as other kings have been before".[10] At Ely, in 1449, a tailor accused a "Dutchman" of treason for saying that the king "looked more like a child than a man". A husbandman of Cley in Norfolk was said by another approver to have called the king a fool.[11] Then in 1450, a yeoman of Brightling, Sussex, was formally indicted of having declared in the market place there "that the king was a natural fool, and would ofttimes hold a staff in his hands with a bird on the end, playing therewith as a fool, and that another king must be ordained to rule the land, saying that the king was no person able to rule the land".[12] This is not weighty evidence, but it does suggest what the king's humbler subjects were saying about him in the common exchange of daily life; and it does provide a contemporary link with the Yorkist picture of the "simple" king.

The impersonal administrative records of Henry's government naturally offer no positive evidence to confirm these rumours, but they are equally incapable of being cited to reject them. We have already seen that the official acts of the time of Henry's minority were drawn up in a form implying that it was the king who directed his administration, and if, for instance, it could be solemnly recorded on the parliament roll that he presided over the assembly of 1425, it is impossible to deduce from notices of his presence in parliaments and councils in the 1440's that he was any more active a participant then than he had been at the age of three. Records of meetings of the king's council, indeed, do not indicate that Henry regularly attended its sessions. While it sat at Westminster, the king was frequently absent from the capital. It was hardly essential for a king to preside over all the meetings of his council; much of its business was of a routine, executive nature, but previous kings had preferred not to lose regular, direct contact with their ministers. It was also advisable for a king to show himself to his subjects in various parts of the realm, and to be accessible to them, but for ten years after 1436 Henry rarely left the Home Counties, residing in his palaces at Windsor, Sheen,* Kennington, Eltham and Berkhamsted.[13]

This restricted itinerary could be explained by delicate health alone, but he did survive long journeys in other periods of his life: he had been taken to Paris for his coronation as king of France in 1430; in 1448 he spent several months travelling through East Anglia and

* Now Richmond, Surrey.

eventually to Durham in the autumn; in 1451 and 1452 he made lengthy tours through southern and western England; and finally, in the twelve months before his capture in 1465, he wandered over the fell country of northern England, from one loyal refuge to another. It is hard to believe that Henry was not robust. His comparatively restricted movements in his earlier years require another explanation: lack of inclination would be the least disputable, since it was certainly not preoccupation with the business of the central government in Westminster.

Blacman tells how he was with the king in his chamber at Eltham reading works of devotion when they were disturbed by a duke knocking on the door, and Henry complained "They do so interrupt that by day or night I can scarcely snatch a moment to be refreshed by reading any holy teaching without disturbance". Apart from illustrating Blacman's text "His delight was in the law of the Lord by day and by night", and the obvious distaste of Henry for temporal business, this anecdote does not suggest that the king was entirely incapable: the fact that he was subjected to constant interruptions from his devotions shows that his council thought it necessary to refer to him. Had Henry been a complete simpleton, it would have ignored him and executed its decisions without troubling to ask for his consent. It is unlikely that he would often give his full attention to such business or do more than agree with the proposals laid before him, but as long as he was recognisably a sane person, his ministers, for their own immunity, observed the established forms of government by applying for his warrants for their actions. Seen through the eyes of Blacman, Henry appears as one whose thoughts were withdrawn from mundane things.

The only significant temporal achievement of the reign which can be attributed to Henry's active interest was the double foundation of the colleges of Eton and King's, Cambridge, and their purpose was to honour God and serve the Church by educating poor boys to be learned priests. Yet Henry's detachment was not complete. Thomas Carver would hardly have escaped the ferocious penalty for treason had the king not learned of his trial and intervened to spare his life.* Henry abhorred bloodshed, even of wild beasts, and he was sickened by the grisly remains of traitors. Blacman ascribed to the king's compassion the pardon granted to four "nobles" convicted of treason

* No petition for mercy from Carver has been traced.

who were already on the scaffold when his writ was delivered: this notice can only refer to the five members of the duke of Gloucester's household who were condemned for sedition and were reprieved at the last minute, in 1447, "out of reverence for the passion of Christ and the Virgin Mary".[14]

As early as 1438 the council had warned Henry against granting pardons without full consideration of their consequences. Although it was thinking about a pardon, or, more accurately, an acquittance, to a collector of customs which had lost the Exchequer two thousand marks,* a more general caution would not have been out of place, for Henry did do "to himself therein great disavail"[15] when he tempered justice with such frequent mercy that its power to deter men from crime was undermined. The patent rolls suggest that Henry was rarely unwilling to grant his pardon, even to those who were murderers by their own admission.† Henry's generosity was notorious. While Blacman extols the king's private charity, the records of his government give abundant proof of his lavish dispensation of crown patronage: grants of estates, wardships, offices of profit and pensions, of gifts of money and remissions of debt, flowed from his bounty without heed of the cost. Again, the council warned the king that he jeopardised his own revenues, and these were already inadequate. The most striking illustration of Henry's prodigality was the grant of the stewardship of the duchy of Cornwall when the office was already held by another man.‡

Crown patronage was rarely exercised on the king's own initiative: it was prompted by the application of aspiring beneficiaries. For many years past it had been customary for kings to be urged by petitions to grant specified favours to those presenting them, the constabulary of a castle, for instance, or a sum of money or an annual gift of wine. Petitions frequently gave some cause why the king should grant such requests; this might be pity for the suppliant's poverty or appreciation of his services. It is unlikely that the majority of petitions were delivered direct to the king, and most were probably given to an officer of the royal household to be forwarded to him or, at some periods, to his council, which might discuss whether the suppliant's case deserved consideration; but the final authorisation of a successful request was the king's warrant. From the time of Henry VI, this assent was generally signified by the king putting his sign-

* A mark was 13s. 4d. † See Appendix II. ‡ See p. 87 below.

manual to the bill. Numerous files of petitions thus approved by him survive, some also bearing his words "Nous avouns graunte".[16] The exercise of the royal prerogative of mercy and the dispensation of crown patronage were thus two aspects of a king's normal functions which Henry did perform. What is crucial here, however, is the question of through whose hands these petitions were presented. Who controlled access to the king? As he usually resided in a royal castle or palace outside London, he was not often easy to approach.

This point is really part of the larger problem of what control Henry had over his government after 1436, what kind of voice he had in "the great business of the king and the kingdom". Official minutes show the council discussing matters of war and peace, making contracts with military commanders and instructing embassies; it called before it great persons whose private quarrels disturbed the country; it tried to remedy the lamentable state of the crown's finances. Whether Henry was present or not when these major topics were under consideration, it is not possible to assess from this evidence alone how much he contributed to the formulation of policy. It might be supposed that an examination of the appointments of ministers would provide one way of assessing the king's influence. The great officers of state and of the royal household held office only for the duration of the king's pleasure. Sometimes such appointments were made under pressure but there is no reason to suppose that Henry was not free to choose his ministers in 1436 or in the following decade. Yet the lists of Henry's great officers of state offer only negative evidence on the question of his interest in their selection. The three chief ministers in 1436 had all been appointed by the council three or four years earlier: Bishop Stafford remained chancellor until 1450, and Lord Cromwell and William Lyndwood both continued for another seven years in their offices of treasurer and keeper of the privy seal. Nor was there any change in the senior household offices: the earl of Suffolk was steward from 1433 to 1446, and Sir William Philip, appointed chamberlain in 1432, carried on until a few months before his death in 1441.[17] The regime established in the last years of Henry's minority was not disturbed by his coming of age.

The same impression is given by the composition of the council, although some historians have discerned an assertion of the king's independence in the record of an act on 13 November 1437. This reports that the king appointed certain councillors to discuss and determine business relating to his governments of England and France, the improvement of his finances and the enforcement of justice "forasmuch as he shall not more attend to them in his own person as oft as he would"; but he reserved for himself the right to grant pardons and make appointments to church benefices and crown offices, and required the council to submit to his decision all matters of great weight and any others on which they were unable to agree. Now, this transaction took place in the great council,* and on the previous day it had decided that the former councillors should be reappointed, with four additions, and that its members were to have the same powers as were given to Henry IV's council in parliament.[18] Thus was the famous ordinance of 1406 resurrected. Henry IV had only accepted it as the price for a desperately needed financial grant, after his administration had been attacked in a parliament whose recalcitrance had kept it in being for the unprecedented length of nine months. Its articles mainly prescribed rules for the council's conduct of business in an attempt to gain for it the confidence of both the king and his subjects, but one provision appeared to threaten the king's authority by stipulating that all warrants should receive its assent, excepting only grants of pardons and the same kind of appointments as Henry VI reserved in 1437; this would have made the king unable to incur expenditure without the council's consent. Had this ordinance been effective, "a conciliar sieve would have been riveted over the flow of the king's personal initiative".[19] The reappointment of councillors in 1437 must be considered as a measure forced on the king. He had by then been exercising his powers of patronage for the past twelve months, and the manner in which he had done so had sufficiently perturbed the lords of the great council to make this attempt to curb his powers. There was no disputing his ultimate responsibility for the conduct of government but it was imperative that some check should be placed on his freedom to grant away his livelihood.

The administrative history of the next ten years discloses a conflict between the council established in 1437 and the executive authority of the crown. Eventually it was the council which succumbed; deprived of real power and without direct access to the king, its members gradually ceased to attend its unproductive sessions.[20] It was not, however, the personality of the king which emerged as the

* See footnote on p. 24.

most potent force in his government, but the earl of Suffolk and a group of associates headed by Bishops Ayscough of Salisbury and Moleyns of Chichester, with John Stafford,* the perennial chancellor, ready, at the least, to follow in their wake. The public denunciation of these men in 1450 leaves no doubt of the popular feeling that they were to blame for the country's disasters: they had made the king their puppet, they had given him evil counsel and enriched themselves from his bounty to the impoverishment of the realm. Earlier, in 1447, an approver claimed to have heard it said that Suffolk and Ayscough had such control over the king "that his rule is nought".†

According to Dr Thomas Gascoigne, Lord Say, who was chamberlain of the household from 1447 to 1450,[22] censored sermons delivered at court lest the king should hear any criticism of his "privy – or, more truly, depraved – council".[23] Henry's ignorance of the management of his government is also illustrated by Gascoigne when he tells how the king asked him why he was not a bishop.[24] Was he really not aware that the crown had almost absolute control over episcopal appointments? It might be supposed that with his strong religious feelings, Henry would have used this authority to ensure that the bishops elected in his time were men with high qualities for spiritual office. In fact, purely secular considerations continued to determine recruitment to the highest church offices; the only new tendency was a preference for clerks who held positions in the households of the king and queen, and an increase in the proportion of younger sons of the highest nobility.

The rise of Suffolk and his group to power was a gradual process, for the concentration of executive authority at the king's court was opposed by the old council. Moreover, Suffolk cannot be considered as the leader of a faction until after the retirement of Cardinal Beaufort. His subsequent political ascendancy, however, was founded on the personal relationship he had been establishing with the king over the course of a number of years. He had, after all, been steward of the household since Henry was thirteen. He had been selected for this office by his fellow councillors, and their choice had much in its favour. William de la Pole had many qualities to commend him for

---

* Bishop of Bath and Wells, 1424–43, archbishop of Canterbury 1443–52.

† Ayscough was blamed for the king having no heir: when Henry wished to have "his sport" with the queen, Ayscough counselled him not to "come nigh her".[21]

the most senior position in the royal court. At the time he was thirty-seven years of age, the fourth earl of his line and thus no *parvenu*.*
Beside possessing estates in his own right, he had married a considerable heiress, Alice Chaucer, who as the widow of Thomas Montagu, earl of Salisbury, also possessed dower lands; her kinship to the Beauforts added to her attractions. Suffolk's long record of service in the French wars was a further point in his favour; although not brilliantly successful, he had been entrusted with important commands and appears to have won a reputation for chivalrous conduct. Henry VI would hardly have been attracted by Suffolk had he been merely an experienced warrior. By the standards of the time, the earl was a highly civilised man, and a number of verses by him, in both French and English, suggest true feeling; while his foundation at Ewelme bears witness that he was at least as devout and generous as his peers.

The man most closely linked with him in popular abuse, William Ayscough, had also been about the court for several years. The earliest surviving warrant signed by the young king, on 27 October 1436, was his petition for a canonry in Lincoln Cathedral.[25] As the king's confessor, his influence over Henry would inevitably have been strong, and he continued to hold this position after his consecration as bishop of Salisbury in 1438.[26]

From 1438 royal warrants drafted at court by Adam Moleyns, the clerk of the council,† bear the names of those present. Rarely do more than four names appear: the chancellor, Suffolk, Ayscough, one or two household officials, occasionally the treasurer or keeper of the privy seal; sometimes it was only Suffolk and Moleyns, and a formal notice of the king's presence is often missing. Moleyn's endorsement of a petition was enough to convert it into an adequate authorisation for letters under the great seal or a payment at the Exchequer. Thus were the king's responsibilities for the direction of his government discharged: Henry allowed the executive powers of the crown to be exercised by a small group of men who had gained his trust.

In July 1445, a French embassy came to London to discuss a treaty of peace. On three days they were received by the king. He came

* His critics, however, did not forget that his great-grandfather had been a merchant at Hull in the time of Edward III. He was created marquess of Suffolk in 1444 and duke in 1448.

† He became keeper of the privy seal in 1444 and bishop of Chichester in 1445.

down from his seat to greet them, touching the hand of each French-
man and slightly raising his cap to their leaders. He seemingly
attended closely to what they had to say and "made a very good
appearance of being well pleased and very joyful"; when they spoke
of King Charles's affection for him, he uncovered and repeatedly
exclaimed "Saint Jehan, grant mercis", and he made similar inter-
jections when his own ministers referred to his regard for the French
king. Beyond this, Henry said nothing. He left it to his councillors,
Cardinal Kemp, Suffolk and the chancellor, to reply. This is not a
picture of an idiot. Henry was able to take his part in the formalities
with grace and urbanity, and he obviously followed the various
speeches with some understanding. Yet his simplicity is revealed: a
diplomatic confrontation is no place for enthusiastic expressions of
goodwill. The ambassadors believed that Henry remonstrated with
his ministers for their lack of cordiality,[27] but the latter were too
experienced in negotiations with the French enemy to commit
similar indiscretions. That Henry confined himself to a mainly cere-
monial part shows that he was well schooled; he was accustomed to
leaving the serious work of government to others. If in all his public
appearances he was generally content to take so purely formal a part,
save for an embarrassing habit of interrupting ministerial speeches
with unguarded remarks, it cannot be wondered that his subjects
came to speculate about the state of his mind. Nor can we reject the
Yorkists' portrait of Henry as merely hostile propaganda. One of
their chroniclers wrote:

> In this same time [1459-60], the realm of England was
> out of all good governance, as it had be[en] many days
> before, for the king was simple, and led by covetous
> counsel, and owed more than he was worth.[28]

This is not the whole truth – the responsibility of Henry's subjects is
ignored – but the author was justified in regarding the king's artless
nature as the primary cause of the breakdown of Lancastrian government.

II

Indictment of a Regime

"Now is the fox driven to hole; hoo to him, hoo! hoo!" So opens a contemporary ballad exulting in the arrest of the duke of Suffolk.[1] He was committed to the Tower of London on 28 January 1450, on the insistent demand of the house of commons. The members claimed that there were widespread rumours that the duke was in league with the king of France and preparing to betray England to him. Eight specific charges were presented on 7 February. One alleged a conspiracy between Suffolk and French ambassadors in 1447, when it was arranged that an invading army would depose Henry VI and place Suffolk's son on the throne as the husband of Margaret Beaufort, daughter of the late duke of Somerset. Other articles declared that Suffolk had regularly betrayed diplomatic and military secrets to the French; that he had procured the release of the duke of Orleans,* and for his own profit only had caused Le Mans and the county of Maine to be surrendered. According to the record, the king decreed that the proceedings should be stayed, giving rise to a belief that Suffolk had been pardoned, but the lords were also ready to see him brought to trial and ordered that he should answer the charges.

The commons brought in a second set of articles against him on 9 March which included a number relating to his influence on the domestic condition of the country and its government. Suffolk refused to plead, preferring to appeal direct to the king. He denied the first eight charges and showed how absurd some were. The new

* Captured at Agincourt, released in 1440.

43

chancellor*, speaking for the king on 17 March, said that Henry held that Suffolk was "neither declared nor charged" by the first set of articles, and that the second bill did not make any charges of a criminal nature. The king, therefore, not acting as a judge but because Suffolk had submitted to him, ordered his banishment from England for a period of five years.[2] On his release from prison, the duke narrowly escaped mob violence in London, but the ship taking him to Calais was intercepted by *The Nicholas of the Tower*, whose crew took it upon themselves to arraign, condemn and behead the fallen minister.[3] He had been the most hated man in the country. One popular poem on the death of "Jack Napes" concluded

> . . . all England joyfully may sing,
> The commendation with *Placebo* and *Dirige*.[4]

The parliament which impeached Suffolk had met on 6 November 1449. It was the second to be called that year. The first had been opened on 12 February and it was finally dismissed on 16 July. Taken in conjunction with the meagreness of its grant of taxation, the length of its session suggests that the commons were not very well disposed to the king's administration. The summons of the second parliament was prompted by the renewal of the French war, and the commons could anticipate a further application for financial assistance. That they should not have gathered in a mood of satisfaction with the ministry was inevitable, but the news from France made their hostility certain. From July, Normandy was being overrun by three French armies, and the English garrisons, undermined by the disaffection of the native population, surrendered one by one. On 19 October the citizens of Rouen drove the garrison into the castle, and on the 23rd it capitulated to the French king.

Before the truce of 1444 the tide of war had definitely been running against the English, but its movement had generally been slow, and their conquests seemed to be threatened with slow erosion rather than sudden inundation. Paris had been lost after the duke of Burgundy changed sides in 1435, but Pontoise, England's last foothold in the Île de France, was not finally lost until 1441. In 1442 the French began the conquest of Gascony, and after the failure of a relief force under the duke of Somerset, the English council was obliged to stave off defeat by negotiating a truce and the marriage of Henry to Margaret of Anjou, and subsequently to evacuate the remaining fortresses in

---

* Cardinal Kemp. Stafford resigned on 31st January 1450

Maine and Anjou as the price for a renewal of the truce. This pause gave King Charles time to assert his authority over his professed subjects, whose lukewarm loyalty had been the main obstacle to his exploiting the full resources of his country against the invader, and a number of measures to organise his forces were put into effect. Thus when the English sack of the Breton town of Fougères in March 1449 gave Charles good cause to reopen the war, he was ready to attack Normandy with overwhelming might.

Through the summer and autumn of this year the list of disasters reported in England lengthened at a horrifying pace, with the news that Rouen had fallen arriving at the time parliament was assembling. The members' feelings of alarm and shame inevitably bred anger against those responsible for the direction of the country's military and diplomatic policies. The charges against Suffolk concerning his relations with the French were clearly far-fetched and they have been shown to be untrue.[5] Less intemperate critics, however, could still have laid much of the blame for the loss of Normandy on Suffolk's head, for the superficial diplomacy which yielded the asset of Henry's bachelorhood in return for a treaty which merely postponed the settlement of basic issues, for his complicity in the action which renewed the war, and for the lack of preparation to withstand its consequences. Yet once the French monarchy had realised its potential strength, England's defeat was certain: in both money and manpower her resources were inadequate, and for many years waning enthusiasm for the war had reduced the number of recruited contingents and the incidence of parliamentary taxation. Suffolk alone could not be held responsible for the disastrous end of the Hundred Years War. His prominence in Henry's council made him an obvious victim for wounded national pride which felt that only treason could account for the recent débâcle. This, undoubtedly, was an important motive for his prosecution, but it does not fully explain his unpopularity.

On 28 November a murderous assault was made on Lord Cromwell, a veteran councillor and former treasurer of England. Suffolk's patronage of the assailant, William Tailbois,* naturally suggested that he was the real instigator of the attempted crime. The attack was the more outrageous as it happened in time of parliament, to one of its members, and thus violated the dignity and security of the

---

* Tailbois had been an esquire of the king's household for at least seven years.[6] See also p. 53 below.

whole body. The outcome was a sharpening of the hostility against Suffolk. When, three months later, the commons decided to initiate judicial proceedings against him, the immediate excuse offered for his arrest was the alleged plot to assist a French invasion and depose the king. This charge can easily be dismissed as preposterous, but that the rumours of treason to which the commons referred were not their invention can be proved.

In the previous May, the chief justice examined one John Mettingham, an officer in the king's household, about a conversation he claimed to have had when riding with John Hartlepool. The latter had boasted of the value of his friendship, and on being told bluntly that his purse was not equal to his ambitions, hinted that there would soon be violent changes in the country. He asserted that he had heard it being said about the court that there would soon be a new king, and this was shown to be true by Henry's planning to bury his jewels. The details of this alleged plot are obscure but it seems that Suffolk was involved. Hartlepool had already arranged for one man to take the duke's livery and he advised Mettingham to look for a new master because the king's servants would be in danger when he fell.[7] The statement of one man is not proof of a conspiracy, but talk of this kind is obviously what the commons had in mind when they spoke about "a heavy rumour and noise of slander".

There are, moreover, scattered notices among the records of King's Bench and elsewhere which point to increasing tension in the past few years. Allegations of seditious talk were becoming more frequent, and there were one or two cases of accusations of treason leading to trial by battle.* Instances of talk about Henry VI have already been noticed. One or two others followed the death of Humphrey, duke of Gloucester, on 23 February 1447. Thus an approver claimed that the keeper of Gloucester Castle told him, on 17 June following, that the duke had been murdered, and the same man heard another lament the coming of the queen to England.[9] Gloucester had been arrested on charges of treason and had died within a few days. Although there is no evidence that he was secretly put to death by his captors, rumours to this effect received wide currency and Suffolk was regarded by many as "Good Duke Humphrey's" murderer. Guilty

---

* The trial by battle in *King Henry VI, Part II* (Act II, scene iii), was based on a real case in 1447. Shakespeare's Horner was actually John Catourer, an armourer, and his apprentice was John Davy.[8]

or not, he and the court party can be blamed for encouraging an atmosphere in which talk of treason was rife through their initial proceedings against Gloucester and the earlier condemnation of his duchess on a charge of attempting to bring about Henry's death by witchcraft.[10]

The first of the charges made against Suffolk on 9 March opened by declaring that from the sixteenth year of the reign (1437-8) he had been "next and priviest of your counsel and steward of your honourable household". It was his conduct in this capacity which formed the grounds for the accusation, but this statement does provide a clue to the attitude of an influential section of his opponents. We have already seen how Suffolk and a few other men in regular attendance on the king despatched his official business and thus, for all practical purposes, exercised crown patronage and such prerogatives as the granting of pardons. The members of the formal king's council attempted to restrain this monopoly of influence enjoyed by Suffolk and his associates, and when he was abroad on embassy in 1444 they enacted a number of regulations designed to provide that royal grants made by the king's grace should receive their approval. These regulations soon became a dead-letter after Suffolk had resumed his place at court. The council sank into obscurity. Meeting at Westminster when the king was elsewhere, its members found themselves entrusted only with business of a trifling nature. As the system of salaries also broke down, several members inevitably decided that it was not worth their while to attend at all. In 1447, a special summons had to be sent when a good attendance was required, even though it was the duty of councillors to attend regularly without citation. Suffolk himself did not trouble to show himself at the council with any frequency: he preferred to stay with the king, at the seat of royal influence.

The decline of the council was accompanied by a narrowing of the ruling circle. When Cardinal Beaufort was the leading figure in the government, he could count on the support of a number of the lords, his kinsmen the Beauforts and the Nevilles, the archbishops of Canterbury and York, and other experienced administrators. Suffolk himself was initially a member of this group, but when the cardinal passed from the scene, his "party" did not stay intact. Stafford of Canterbury, the chancellor, and Beaufort's nephews retained their place in the court circle, but others broke away. Lord Cromwell became a personal enemy of Suffolk, while Cardinal Kemp of York probably took offence when Suffolk prevented his nephew's promotion to the see of London in 1448 and tried to obtain it for Bishop Lumley of Carlisle, the treasurer.[11]

In the heyday of Suffolk's supremacy, the peers generally were excluded from a place in royal councils. They would have been assembled during the protracted parliamentary sessions of 1445, but in the three years following there was only one short parliament, early in 1447; and only one reference has been found of the lords being called to a great council in the same period.[12] This treatment of the lords is referred to in a poem of about 1449 which laments that the dukes of Buckingham, Norfolk and York, as well as a number of earls, no longer had prominence in national affairs.[13] The same complaint appears in the statement of an approver in 1447, who said that in the previous year he heard a gentleman from Northamptonshire say that the king ignored the counsel of the lords spiritual and temporal and other magnates and barons of noble blood. Like another approver already noticed, he reported an alleged declaration that the king was ruled by Suffolk and the bishop of Salisbury "and other sons of beggars".* Again, in the first parliament to meet after Suffolk's death, the commons declared that he had estranged the great lords from the king.[15]

Here was one cause of Suffolk's unpopularity: people resented the denial to the lords of their traditional right to be the king's natural councillors. There is no record of the lords in the parliament of November 1449 renewing this ancient rallying cry for opponents of an unpopular ministry. We cannot expect to find the peers of Henry VI's time speaking with one voice as their forbears had done. That a good proportion was disposed to be critical of Suffolk, however, is revealed by their insistence that he should answer the commons' indictment despite the king's readiness to exonerate him. Suffolk obviously could not command a majority of the lords, and a fundamental reason for this was their resentment of his jealously guarded monopoly of influence in "the great business of the king and the kingdom".

It was in the manner Suffolk exercised this power that the commons found grounds for their complaints. For the past twelve years, they said, he had caused the king to give away a great part of his possessions,

---

* The conversation was said to have occurred in *Le Belle* in Fleet Street.[14] There still is a public house of that name there.

so that from a state of prosperity the crown's revenue had been so
reduced that it could not meet its expenses, and in consequence the
commons of the realm had been overburdened with taxes. This was
both an exaggeration and a distortion of the facts. The crown's debts
had amounted to £164,815 in 1433, the year Suffolk became steward,
and its revenues then were estimated to leave a credit balance of only
£8,000 after meeting the ordinary expenses of the king's household
and administration, the wages and pensions due at the Exchequer, and
the defence of Calais, Gascony, Ireland and the Scottish marches. The
treasurer had not included receipts from direct taxation in assessing
revenue at nearly £65,000 a year, but neither did he include the cost
of military operations in Normandy.[16] With the addition of the
proceeds of such direct taxes as the tight-fisted commons were persuaded to grant the gross total rose to about £70,000 a year after
1437, but from then the revenues diminished annually until the gross
receipts in 1450 were less than £50,000.

Economic causes partially explain the falling income from crown
lands and customs charges for the export of wool.[17] At the same time
there was an increase in the expenses classed as ordinary in 1433: thus
the average annual expenditure by the treasurer of the king's household which had been £10,800 in the six years 1431-7, became
£13,500 in the similar period following.[18] The arrival of a dowerless
queen worsened the position. The expenses of bringing her to
England amounted to £5,500, and a revenue of £6,700 was assigned
for her household.[19] As for the French wars, full figures of expenditure have yet to be calculated, but the lieutenant-general engaged in
1440 was promised £20,000 from the Exchequer each year,[20] and
other substantial issues were made to purchase ordnance and to assist
captains to pay ransoms for their release from the French. Even had
the country been at peace, however, it is unlikely that Henry's
government would have been able to pay its way. In 1449 its debts
amounted to £372,000.[21]

The general condition of the royal revenues was not discussed in
the indictment of Suffolk. Obviously he cannot be held entirely
responsible for the deterioration of the crown's revenues and it is
hard to believe that the flow of royal grants more than marginally
aggravated their already desperate condition. Yet if the commons
wanted a scapegoat for the king's bankruptcy as they did for the
disasters in Normandy, Suffolk had eminently qualified himself for

the role. While the king's poverty was notorious, the wealth of his favourite was equally flagrant. His collegiate church at Wingfield, the church and almshouse built by Suffolk and his wife at Ewelme, were visible signs that he was making handsome profits in the service of so poor a master as Henry VI. The charges against him specified some of the grants he had obtained from the king. The wardship of Margaret Beaufort was one. The commons claimed that Suffolk had gained £1,000 a year from this grant, and he had as much, they said, from the earldom of Pembroke. He had a second wardship, that of the duke of Warwick's heiress, which would have been more valuable still, and other offices and perquisites, some valued at a total of £400. All these sums could have been applied to the king's needs.[22] The number of offices of profit which accumulated in his hands show to what account he turned his influence with the king.[23]

This was but one side to Suffolk's control of crown patronage. It is not possible to assess how much he gained by less direct means. His position at court ensured that other applicants for the royal bounty required his goodwill if their petitions were to succeed, and the indictment alleges that it was "for covetise of great lucre of gold singularly to himself" that he obtained the royal assent to grants to other persons. An instance of his influence over crown appointments can be cited.

Master John Somerset was appointed chancellor of the Exchequer and warden of the Mint in 1439. Some eight years later, word went round that he was ready to sell the reversion to these offices, and several men tried to persuade him to do so. These suitors were not so much inspired by political ambition as a desire for a good investment, for the offices were sinecures, the duties attaching to them being performed by deputies. Somerset himself was actually the king's physician, and no doubt he had been given these offices of profit in payment for his professional services. One of his would-be successors, John Lemanton, tried to gain preferential treatment by enlisting the aid of the duke of Suffolk. For this favour he paid the duke an hundred marks. Suffolk then called Somerset to him and urged him to accept Lemanton's offer: Somerset "dared not say nay". Lemanton paid Somerset a thousand marks and, thanks to Suffolk, obtained royal grants of the offices to be effective after Somerset's death. Suffolk, however, now arranged the disposal of the reversion after Lemanton's death, so that the latter was unable to recoup any of his costs by selling it himself. In wrath, he demanded that Somerset should repay him some of the thousand marks. But the money had been spent on good works, said Somerset, and even if he had been paid double he would still not have returned a single penny, "to teach men to buy reversions by maintenance of lords".[24]

Two of the commons' charges stated that Suffolk had tampered with the king's revenue from direct taxation. One is made in general terms, with the burden of complaint being that taxes granted for the prosecution of the war had been applied to other uses and not to the king's profit. The second article declared that there had been a total of £60,000 in hand at the Exchequer when a new treasurer was appointed in 1446, the greater part of which "by labour and means of the said duke of Suffolk hath been mischievously given and distribute[d] to himself, his friends and wellwishers". Now it is on record that the Exchequer held £10,721 10s. 8¾d. in cash and bonds at the time in question and the roll of issues in this term fails to lend substance to the accusation.[25] It would not be easy to find proof of peculation in the Exchequer records now available, but one or two of the warrants for issues do indicate that Suffolk's associates gained some direct financial benefit from their position at court.*

The chancellor, Archbishop Stafford, was given £500 as a gift in December 1448. The warrant cites as the king's reason for the grant his desire that Stafford's diligent services and his attendance on the king in London and elsewhere, even during vacations, should not "pass unremembered"; he had received no reward for his services, it was said. Another of Suffolk's colleagues, Bishop Lumley, received a reward of £600 six months after his appointment as treasurer in 1446; this was in return for his previous services as warden of the west march and for his earlier attendance of the council. In 1449, Lumley had a further reward of £1,000.[26] Both men were in fact paid salaries for their employment as chancellor and as warden and treasurer. These "rewards" were presumably, like other acts of the king's grace, prompted by petitions advanced through the usual channel, and this was scarcely a hazardous passage in the case of either minister. It is small cause for wonder that one of Stafford's last acts before resigning his office was to seal royal letters pardoning all his misdemeanours.[27] Another way of manipulating the king's favour for direct financial gain was to obtain his pardon from statutory impositions. In 1446 Suffolk obtained a licence to export two thousand sacks of wool

* For Ayscough's profits, see p. 66 below.

without paying customs, and he had similar exemption on five hundred fothers* of lead in 1449.[28] Concessions of this magnitude – the first was worth £3,333 6s. 8d. – in the existing state of the king's revenues cannot have escaped hostile comment or failed to confirm the belief that Suffolk was enriching himself to the "over great impoverishing and hurt of this your realm".

A consequence of the crown's impoverishment was that its creditors generally had difficulty in obtaining early payment. They were provided with tallies of assignment† on certain revenues, but they then frequently found that others had prior claims on these issues and so they had to wait, sometimes for years, before their claims could be satisfied. The duke of York, for instance, was given tallies in 1446 which were still unredeemed in 1450.[29] The leading ministers, however, saw to it that they did not suffer similar embarrassment. Bishop Moleyns, the keeper of the privy seal, was notably adroit in this respect. He incurred heavy expenses in embassies to France but he made sure that these as well as his wages as keeper were paid speedily, either in cash or as the first charge on a new and therefore unencumbered source of crown revenue.[30] As the necessary warrants were written in his own office, he had no difficulty in safeguarding his interests. Moleyns was of course entitled to his wages and expenses, but other royal creditors would have felt aggrieved that he should make so quick an escape from their ranks while they remained unpaid: whoever lost by service to Henry VI, it was not Suffolk and his friends. Some of the largest creditors were reduced to making bargains with the crown, allowing part of their debts to be written off in return for sure payment of the remainder.[31] Others resorted to expedients like selling their tallies to brokers at a loss. The situation allowed more opportunity for profit to those who could bring influence to bear in the right quarter. Creditors who petitioned the

---

* An indeterminable measure, equal to a little less than a ton.

† These tallies were short wooden sticks, cut with knotches of varying sizes according to the sums of money involved, which were written on the tallies. They were issued by the Exchequer in pairs, one to the creditor, the other to the officer who was to pay him; this might be a collector of customs in one of the ports, a tax-collector, a sheriff or some other local officer responsible for collecting some of the king's revenues. The creditor, in person or through an agent, could now go to the stipulated officer, who would compare the former's tally with his duplicate. If it matched, and funds were available, the officer would pay the creditor, retaining his tally. The system may be likened to our method of payment by cheque, with the king having accounts in numerous banks.

king for assignment on an encumbered source would pay for the good offices of a courtier. A group of London brewers was able to recover a debt of £612 by enlisting the help of William Lumley, the treasurer's brother; this cost them £132.[32]

Four other articles in the indictment relate to the administration of justice. One will not stand up to close examination. This was the charge that Suffolk, for his own profit, had procured grants of privileges for various persons, ecclesiastical as well as secular, whereby the normal legal machinery of the national courts of law was not allowed to operate in their territories. The charter rolls do show that a number of grants of this nature were made to religious houses and boroughs in this time, but the total is not large nor were the privileges in question extensive. A second general accusation was that Suffolk had controlled the appointment of sheriffs. He had nominated candidates to the king and had secured the choice of men agreeable to himself; some had paid him for this favour, while others were chosen because of their readiness to serve his private interests, "whereof ensued that they that would not be of his affinity in their countries were overset, every matter true or false that he favoured was furthered and sped, and true matters of such persons as had not his favour were hindered and put back". Thus crimes of all kinds were multiplied, and murderers and other notorious wrongdoers, "seeing his great rule and might in every part of this your realm, have drawn to him, and for great good to him given have been maintained and supported in suppressing of justice and to open letting of execution of your laws".

Two specific instances were cited of Suffolk's intervention in legal processes, both concerning Lord Cromwell's assailant William Tailbois. One stated that Suffolk had ordered the sheriff of Lincolnshire to refrain from executing judicial writs issued to bring Tailbois to trial on a charge of murder, the other that he had obtained the king's pardon when Tailbois should have forfeited his bail for not appearing before the judges.* These were obvious charges. Naturally the choice of sheriffs and grants of franchises could easily be laid at Suffolk's door because of his nearness to the king. The two cases concerning Tailbois were probably brought to the commons' notice by Lord Cromwell, who took an active part in the proceedings.[34] Like most other articles of the indictment, there was enough foundation in fact to support the more general allegations. Yet their charges

* This pardon was granted on 8 November 1448.[33]

under this head of perversion of justice suggest that Suffolk's opponents had prepared their brief hastily, in a superficial manner, and
without spending much effort in the collection of suitable evidence.
We can ignore the articles of the indictment and still find sufficient
material to make a case against him.

   Suffolk's shadow had fallen on the administration of justice at two
points, at the centre, through his manipulation of the king's executive
and prerogative powers, and in those districts where he had territorial
interests. The most substantial bloc of his estates was in the counties
of Norfolk and Suffolk, and here he and his minions had, according
to their enemies, imposed a reign of terror, using forcible methods
to extort money and gain possession of land, yet contriving to deny
their victims the means of lawful redress. The poor people of Norfolk
and Suffolk, wrote Sir John Fastolf, "have lived in misery and great
poverty by many years continued". He himself claimed to have lost
vast sums through the extortions of Suffolk and his officers; they had
wrongfully expelled him from a manor and held it for three years
before he regained possession by legal action. In 1448, Margaret
Paston had written that it was being said in Norfolk that no man
dared to do or say anything which might offend the duke and his
clients, and that those who had been so foolhardy would "sore repent
them". A claimant to the Pastons' manor of Oxnead boasted that he
would have it for "he hath my lord of Suffolk's good lordship, and
he would be his good lord in that matter".[35]

   Suffolk's "good lordship", or favour, was indispensable as a
guarantee of immunity from vexatious suits or extortion by his local
followers. The citizens of Norwich tried to gain this goodwill and
seemingly paid his officers heavily for a promise to obtain it.* A local
squire said that he was threatened by Suffolk that "if he would not be
ruled by him, he should be so heavy lord unto him that he should
not be able to bear it".[36] This was no empty threat. As a great landowner, the duke had the means to intimidate his weaker neighbours,
but his position at court reinforced the conventional resources of local
power. As parliament had pointed out, Suffolk was able to influence
the king's choice of sheriffs. After his fall, a King's Bench judge wrote
that the victims of Suffolk's officers in Norfolk "may have remedy
now by the order of law" if a "good" sheriff and undersheriff were
appointed.[37] For several years past the sheriff of Norfolk and Suffolk

* See p. 218 below.

had been an officer in the royal household and presumably a willing tool of the duke. As it was the sheriff or his deputy who selected the juries, the chances of a man winning an action against a client of Suffolk were slender indeed. Abuse of legal procedures was of course already an evil of long standing, and other magnates besides Suffolk as well as lesser men were no less culpable than he. Victims of oppression who had no confidence in their local courts could apply for a remedy from the central government, to the king, his council or Chancery; but Suffolk's influence here could again be employed to frustrate petitions for redress against those who had his "good lordship".

Suffolk however was not immediately responsible for many of the extortions perpetrated in East Anglia during his period of power. Like other great lords, he engaged a number of lesser landed gentry and lawyers who formed a council of management for his estates and to uphold his local interests. Sir Thomas Tuddenham of Oxborough, near Norwich, was the foremost of his ministers, probably his steward. In 1443, Suffolk had Tuddenham appointed as his partner in the office of steward in the northern territories of the duchy of Lancaster;[38] as there were duchy lands in Norfolk, this position enhanced Tuddenham's authority in the county, where he had been a justice of the peace since 1434. To Suffolk also Tuddenham presumably owed his appointment by the king as keeper of the great wardrobe in 1446, a crown pension, a grant of the king's protection, and exemption from the burdens of local office generally laid on men of his class;[39] this last concession did not weaken his influence, indeed it left him freer to attend to his master's interests. John Heydon, an attorney, and John Ulveston of Henham were two other members of Suffolk's council who held the commission of the peace, the first in Norfolk from 1441, the latter in Suffolk from 1443. Whatever the truth of the charges brought against these men, there is little doubt that they roused the most bitter hostility of a substantial section of the society of the two counties. *The Paston Letters* include a list of twenty-two men "mischievously oppressed and wronged" by Tuddenham and Heydon, but as it also notes that "many men" had been prosecuted through their agency this is obviously not the sum total. A second memorandum quotes a number of misdeeds by Suffolk's councillors and their adherents, one, for instance, the case of a murderer who had escaped prosecution because he enjoyed

Tuddenham's patronage; and eight instances were given of people being drawn into litigation against each other to their mutual loss.[40] These lists again are not exhaustive, for many other charges are to be found in the file of indictments made in 1450.

Tuddenham and company lost their immunity from legal prosecution when Suffolk fell. On 2 August 1450, the crown appointed a commission to hear and determine all trespasses, oppressions and perversions of legal procedure in Norfolk and Suffolk. This was done on the advice of the great council in order to still local agitation.[41] New commissions of the peace for the two countries were issued on 9 October which excluded Tuddenham, Heydon and Ulveston.[42] Meanwhile their enemies were fearful lest the opportunity for vengeance should be lost; they compiled lists of cases to be presented before the expected commissioners, and anxiously debated the all-important question of who would be the next sheriff when the annual appointment was made. Their doubts on this score were set at rest, for on his arrival the new sheriff "swore by great oaths that he would neither spare for gold, nor love, nor fear, but that he would let the king have knowledge of the truth".[43]

The jurors he empanelled on 2 December were certainly no friends of Suffolk's men. They opened their presentments to the justices with a general charge. On 1 December 1435, they declared, Thomas Tuddenham, John Heydon, John Ulveston and John Bellay made a compact to maintain quarrels in Norfolk and Suffolk to the end that they might rule the entire countryside; they would choose all jurors in suits, and they would control all appointments of sheriffs, bailiffs and other officers, so that they could extort money at will; they would harry all those jurors and others who refused to comply with their wishes, causing them to lose their lives and property if it were possible; and they had sought out men of ample means and brought fictitious suits against them for purposes of extortion. By such methods they had amassed great sums of money. More detailed charges followed in an almost exhaustive catalogue: the acts of violence even included a case of cruelty to children, while blackmail, fraud, forgery, intimidation and maintenance of other men's quarrels were but selections from their misdemeanours.[44] Some of the accusations are palpably tendentious: where the reported victims of oppression were Suffolk's tenants it may be suggested that Tuddenham and his associates were not acting illegally but upholding their employer's interests with heavy-handed zeal. In other cases, however, most notably that of the city of Norwich, their activities cannot be so easily provided with a less sinister interpretation; here the motives for their intervention appear to combine a policy of promoting the duke's local dominance with the pursuit of profits for themselves.* Tuddenham was found guilty of a great number of misdemeanours and was condemned to pay more than three hundred fines which totalled £1,396.[45] He would presumably have also been liable for damages, and these might well have been assessed at several times the amounts he had been fined.

The exploits of the Tuddenham gang inevitably tarnished Suffolk's reputation, and they help to account for the bitterness against him in the parliament of 1449-50. The shire knights and burgesses from East Anglia, and the peers with interests there, could have provided damaging evidence of how the king's chief councillor manipulated the local administration of justice. Elsewhere, in parts of the country where Suffolk had no immediate stake as a landowner, his intervention was less flagrant than it was through the agency of men like Tuddenham and Heydon, yet it was no less serious in its consequences in at least one case.

On 22 May 1448, Sir Humphrey Stafford of Grafton, his eldest son Richard and a number of servants, were making for their inn at Coventry when they met Sir Robert Harcourt and his attendants. Humphrey had already passed by when Richard came alongside Harcourt. They immediately fell to blows: Harcourt struck Richard on the head with his sword, not seriously, for the young man then made at Harcourt with his dagger. He stumbled, and one of Harcourt's men stabbed him in the back, mortally. Sir Humphrey was also struck from behind when he returned, so that he fell from his horse. "And all this was done, as men say, in a Pater Noster while." Then there was a general mêlée in which Stafford's servants killed two of Harcourt's men. On the following day, the city coroners indicted Sir Robert as principal in the murder of Richard Stafford. He was placed under arrest and for a time detained in Chester Castle,[46] but he had still not been brought to trial almost a year after the affray. Harcourt applied to the king for a stay in proceedings, and consequently the chief justice was directed by a writ of privy seal to restrain the local sheriff from taking the usual measures to bring him

* See Appendix III.

before a court of law. This information comes from a petition to the king from Humphrey Stafford: he had hoped to see his son's death "by the course of your law duly punished", and now he asked that the chief justice should be instructed to proceed. This plea was likewise granted, on 22 March 1449,[47] but in fact Harcourt continued to evade the law. At length the Staffords tired of waiting for satisfaction by judicial means. They assembled some two hundred of their Warwickshire friends and tenants on 1 May 1450 and travelled by night to Stanton Harcourt in Oxfordshire. Sir Robert had enough warning to make for the tower of the parish church. Stafford's little force laid siege to the church for six hours, firing, it was said, more than a thousand arrows; one killed a Harcourt retainer. They threatened to burn the church if their quarry did not come out, and they did fire the room under the tower; but Harcourt held out and his assailants had to abandon their attempt to avenge Richard Stafford.*

This incident appears the more dramatic when we recall that it took place on the very day that Suffolk was murdered. The two events are closely linked. Humphrey Stafford, now Sir Humphrey's heir, was a member of the commons which impeached the duke. He would have immediately learned of the sentence banishing Suffolk from 1 May. It is almost certain that this sentence was taken into account when the Staffords made their plans to attack Harcourt. They may well have felt that Suffolk's removal would have weakened the court, and that until a new regime established itself circumstances would favour the begetters of bold and lawless measures. There most probably was a further consideration in their minds. Presumably it was Suffolk who had furthered Harcourt's attempts to evade justice.† With Suffolk gone, the Staffords had no need to restrain their desire for vengeance through fear that Harcourt had a protector able to direct the crown's resources against them.

The parliamentary impeachment of Suffolk raises the constitutional problem of ministerial responsibility. The right of a medieval king to select his councillors and officers of state was unquestioned, and they were in principle responsible only to him for their conduct. There

---

* Sir Humphrey was killed in an encounter with the Kentish rebels in the following month. Harcourt received a general pardon on 25 May, and his surviving attackers were pardoned on 23 November 1450.[48] Harcourt was killed by Humphrey's bastard son in 1469.

† Harcourt was a member of his company when he escorted the queen to England in 1445.[49]

was no law or convention which bound a king to dismiss a minister
even when all parliament spoke against him. A king would sometimes respond to remonstration and seek to placate critics by discard-
ing an unpopular adviser, but no such concession could be looked for
from a king as devoid of political sense, if not oblivious to the realities
of his time, as the unfortunate Henry VI. Here is the real explanation
of the preposterous charges of treason made against Suffolk. His
enemies wanted to have him adjudged guilty of offences which
carried a capital sentence because there was no other way of breaking
his influence over the king. It was a just irony, and wholly in tune
with the prevailing attitude to the law, that Suffolk's opponents
should propose to destroy him by means of a feigned and malicious
indictment.

The second set of charges "touching misprisons which be not
criminal" lead us to the root causes of the hostility to Suffolk's regime
among the politically articulate members of English society. Of all
his malpractices in office, none was more damaging to both crown
and country than his perversion of legal processes in favour of his
local interests and those of his clients. The other misdemeanours
imputed to Suffolk, peculation and the like, were serious enough, and
the supporting evidence does confirm that his regime was marked by
a low standard of public morality. It may be questioned, however,
whether Suffolk and his associates were much more corrupt than
other prominent men of this time: the councillors of Henry's
minority had not hesitated to advance their own interests. What
distinguishes Suffolk from the colleagues of his earlier days is not
ambition but achievement, for since they shared power so also did
they share its perquisites; while Suffolk had no rival in the manipulation of crown patronage. But a minister of the king who perverted
the course of justice threatened the whole fabric of society. The same
house of commons which indicted Suffolk declared:

> The honour, wealth and prosperity of every prince reign-
> ing upon his people standeth most principally upon con-
> servation of his peace, keeping of justice, and due
> execution of his laws, without which no realm may long
> endure in quiet nor prosperity; and for lack hereof many
> murders, manslaughters, rapes, robberies, riots, affrays
> and other inconveniences, greater than before, now late
> have grown within this your realm.[50]

This passage provides a text for the study of the collapse of Lancastrian government. The crown's failure to uphold the law was a major cause of the civil warfare which led to Henry's deposition. His poverty, his want of material resources to enforce respect, was a contributory factor, but this would not have been a fatal weakness had his government retained the loyalty of his subjects. This it forfeited when the image of the king's impartiality in his subject's private quarrels was destroyed. By the same token, the law itself came into disrepute when it was seen to be loaded in favour of those with connections in the royal household. Aggrieved subjects could have no confidence that the king's courts would remedy their injuries. Naturally they tended to seek alternative means of redress. We have seen how the Staffords tried to exact vengeance by their own efforts when the normal processes of justice were not allowed to take their proper course. Here is a striking illustration of the truth of the commons' declaration, and other cases will be observed later. Those who succeeded to Suffolk's place in the king's favour failed to restore the crown to a position above the disputes of his subjects. They did not heed the warning of the two violent acts of 2 May 1450, when the banished favourite went to his death as the outcome of his abuse of power, and the public consequences of this misgovernment were revealed at the siege of Stanton Harcourt church.

III

Cade's Rebellion

There is a superficial resemblance between the closing stages of Suffolk's career and that of George Villiers, duke of Buckingham, who enjoyed almost as long a period of favour in the courts of James I and Charles I: both escaped the fury of the house of commons only to become the victims of self-appointed executioners. The judicial murder in 1641 of Thomas Wentworth, earl of Stafford, however, is a more appropriate parallel. In both cases, the removal of the king's leading minister ended a period in which the government had been carried on in his name by a small group of personal advisers and was followed by a series of crises which resulted in civil war. There had been opposition before, mostly in the form of critical talk which could be countered by prosecuting the individuals concerned, but the fall of the favourite, the first objective of the court's enemies, seemed to act as a signal for the outburst of long-pent feelings of protest and desires for reform. The banishment of Suffolk is another example of the crown sacrificing a minister and finding that, far from appeasing its critics, it had only encouraged them to press for further concessions. The commons were not satisfied and went on to urge new measures of retrenchment. But the most dangerous threats of 1450 and the following years came from other quarters than parliament. The greatest magnate in the kingdom, Richard, duke of York, made a forceful entry into national politics and assumed the leadership of the government's critics. The first challenge to the crown's authority, however, was made by people who usually took little part in matters of state.

From the first weeks of 1450, indications that public dissatisfaction with the government was taking a dangerous turn began to multiply. On 9 January, Adam Moleyns, bishop of Chichester and until recently keeper of the privy seal, was murdered at Portsmouth by mutinous soldiers.* Three days later, there was a riot in Dowgate ward, London, when a crowd chanted the refrain;

> By this town, by this town,
> For this array the king shall lose his crown.

Those concerned were quickly brought to trial,[2] but the attempt against Suffolk on the night of his release from the Tower showed that the London mob was still in an ugly mood. Seditious libels were being distributed in the city and attached to church doors.[3] At Eastry, in Kent, some two hundred men began a demonstration against the king which rapidly attracted thousands of recruits; they were reported to have elected captains who took names like the king and queen of Fairyland, "Jenessay", "Haveybynne" and Robin Hood.[4] This movement was speedily suppressed, and one of the ringleaders "feigning himself an hermit cleped Bluebeard" was executed at Canterbury on 9 February.[5] The recent history of Kent had been marked by a series of disturbances regarded as treasonable by the authorities. Five men from Tenterden were executed as traitors in 1438, and later that year some seventy men were accused of assembling at Rainham and plotting to destroy the king.[6] Continuing unrest is disclosed by the appointment of judicial commissions to visit the county and try cases of treason and insurrection in 1443 and 1445, while in 1448 a number of men accused of treason were arrested and taken to the king.[7]

In the last week of May 1450, large bodies of men from the towns and villages along the great highway from London to Dover, and also from the Weald, came to Blackheath, where they were drawn up in battle order. In its early stages, this host was well-behaved; those members who looked for plunder were put on trial and executed. It was not a rabble. The rapid concentration and generally good discipline reveal not only leadership with the marks of authority and

---

* Cuthbert Colville, esquire, who was indicted of the murder with some three hundred others (unnamed), had been engaged in the previous autumn for service in France.[1]

capacity for organisation, but also a strong common purpose. The majority came from the land, but agricultural grievances had not brought them out: there were less of the usual reasons for peasant revolts in Kent than in any other English county, for much of the land was held by small, free tenants, and labour services had been commuted for rents in most of the larger estates. Moreover, large numbers of those involved were craftsmen and tradesmen from the towns: those dependent for a living on the trade route from London to the Channel ports, and the weavers and others concerned with the manufacture of cloth, had been hard hit by the drastic fall in exports and the vagaries of the Flemish market in recent years. Still less likely to be drawn into a peasant movement were a number of men of property: one was a knight, eighteen more were esquires, and seventy-four described themselves as gentlemen; some clergy also took part.

The identity of the rebel commander is an unsolved mystery. He is known to us as Jack Cade. The official order for his arrest states that he was born in Ireland, served in the household of a Sussex knight, and fled to France after murdering a pregnant woman. If his background was so disreputable, it is remarkable that he was accepted as a leader by Kentish gentry; the royal councillors who met him were impressed by his bearing and intelligence. Cade assumed the name of John Mortimer, claiming kinship to the duke of York; an Irish origin would lend credence to an imposture whereby he could hope to attract the duke's sympathisers.[8] One of the rebels' demands was that York should be recalled from exile in Ireland and given his rightful place near the king, and the king's council apparently claimed that their object was to put York on the throne.[9] Was there a still closer link with the duke? Was his the hand behind Cade? Hall, and after him Holinshed and Shakespeare, put forward the opinion that York enticed Cade to adopt the name of Mortimer in order to gauge how much support he could expect. A Suffolk jury actually alleged in 1453 that the Kentish rebellion was the outcome of a Yorkist conspiracy,* but York's own conduct in this year hardly supports this assertion.†

Cade's leadership was founded on his skill as a propagandist. His manifesto – "the complaint of the commons of Kent" – embraced the grievances of several levels of society and thus called them together

* See p. 79 below.   † See p. 75 below.

in a common enterprise, while issues of a national and political nature appealed to a wider public. The first article referred to a rumour that the county was to be turned into a "wild forest" as punishment for the murder of Suffolk: the fear aroused by this supposed threat may well have provided the stimulus to turn discontent into revolt. The main burden of "the complaint" was the corrupt and oppressive conduct of the officials responsible for the king's administration in the county – the extortions by sheriffs and their underlings, their persecution of "simple and poor people" by false charges in the courts, and by causing them to travel to distant parts of the county by holding courts far from their homes. The parliamentary elections were not free, for the magnates of the county, at the prompting of "divers estates", forced their tenants and other voters to elect candidates not of their choosing.

Other complaints were made about the king's council and household. Lords of the blood royal had been excluded in favour of men of lower degree, who abused their position by preventing subjects who sought legal redress from approaching the king unless they were given gifts. Household servants, it was said, obtained grants of property belonging to men accused of treason and then endeavoured to bring about their conviction and execution in order to gain these goods; they also dispossessed men of their rightful estates through false legal actions, for "the true owners dare not hold claim nor pursue their right". People were not paid for food and other articles taken for the king's household by his purveyors. Indeed, it was alleged, "the king is stirred to live only on his commons"; officials embezzled the revenues of the crown while the people were oppressed with taxes. Collectors of these parliamentary taxes obtained their offices by bribery, and they both defrauded the king and robbed his subjects. Only one of the fifteen articles relates to the defeats in France: this refers to rumours that the English losses were due to treason, and it calls for a national enquiry to establish whether this was the case and, if so, to find these traitors so that they could be punished by law, "without any pardon".

The moderation of the last article says much for the temper of the rebels. Likewise in their demands to the king and "the true lords" of the council they urged him to resume possession of his alienated estates, dismiss and punish "all the false progeny and affinity of the duke of Suffolk", and retain about his person the true lords of the blood royal – the dukes of York, Exeter, Buckingham and Norfolk – "and all the earls and barons of this land: and then shall he be the richest king Christian".[10] Another statement of the rebels' aims which was probably circulated in their camp at Blackheath also makes declarations of loyalty to the king, and expresses the desire to see him rid of evil councillors and enriched by a resumption of crown lands. This manifesto is less concerned with local grievances, although it does call for an impartial judicial entry into corrupt legal practices in Kent. The traitors in the council, it said, had tried to pervert the king, telling him that good was evil and evil good, that he was above the law and could break it at his pleasure, and that by himself he could say who were traitors; they had corrupted the law and plundered the king.

> We say that our sovereign lord may well understand that he hath had false counsel, for his lords are lost, his merchandise is lost, his commons destroyed, the sea is lost, France is lost, himself so poor that he may not [pay] for his meat or drink; he oweth more than ever did [any] king in England, and yet daily his traitors that be about him wait where ever [any]thing should come to him by his law,* and they ask it from him.[11]

Political reform was the rebels' desire: their sufferings under oppressive and corrupt sheriffs and other local officials were due to the corruption of the kings' council and household, and the remedy they put forward was that the king should recall his "natural councillors", the great peers of the realm. Rebels though they were, the men of Kent were far from being revolutionaries: their solution for the country's ills was that of all baronial movements against the crown in the past two hundred years.

"The complaint" was submitted to the council in the second week of June, as the king and lords returned from Leicester after the dismissal of parliament. The rebels were ordered to disperse. They fell back, but an advance party from the king's forces was destroyed in an ambush at Sevenoaks. This repulse led to unrest in the royal camp, and to stave off mutiny, Lord Say, the treasurer, a former sheriff of Kent and one of its most hated landowners, was sent to the Tower along with William Cromer, the equally unpopular present sheriff of

---

* *I.e.* as forfeitures of the lands and/or goods of condemned felons.

the county. The king's unreliable troops were dismissed and he withdrew to Kenilworth. The citizens of London, left to defend themselves, admitted Cade and his host on 4 July. Say and Cromer were taken from their prison and executed.

The government's collapse encouraged other malcontents. At Edington, in Wiltshire, Bishop Ayscough was dragged from the church by a mob six hundred strong and beheaded. They called him a traitor. He had been Suffolk's closest associate in the royal court, and a close runner-up in popular odium. His murderers were said to have plundered his baggage and removed his episcopal insignia and other articles valued at £1,000 as well as £3,000 in cash, a sum double his bishopric's annual revenue. If these figures are not too exaggerated, they suggest that the king's late confessor had not wasted his opportunities at court, and they bear out the allegations of peculation made against Suffolk and his cronies. On the day of the murder, 29 June, there was a rising in Salisbury directed, it would seem, against the church authorities, and a little later this mob destroyed the bishop's records kept in the palace there. The oppressive secular authority of the bishop in his cathedral city was probably a major cause of this outburst, and his neglect of his spiritual duties may have added to the local resentment.[12] Other riots took place at Sherborne and at Devizes and elsewhere in Wiltshire later that month,[13] and there was a further revolt on the Isle of Wight.[14] Two other bishops, Booth of Lichfield and Lyhart of Norwich, were threatened by angry mobs after their flight from court to their neglected dioceses, and the people of Gloucester plundered a manor of Abbot Boulers because of his employment by Suffolk in his unpopular diplomacy.[15] In Essex, there was a considerable rising, and a force advanced on London to join Cade's men there.

Meanwhile, in London, the disorderly behaviour of some of Cade's followers alienated the citizens, and on the night of 5 July they cleared the streets of rioters and, aided by the garrison of the Tower, won control of London Bridge. This seemed to the council a good opportunity to come to terms with the rebels. A free pardon was offered and accepted. Cade and his followers departed. Many went home, but he retained an armed band and attempted to take Queenborough Castle. On the 12th, he was mortally wounded while resisting arrest, for his renewal of operations put him outside the scope of the pardon. The council, however, continued to allay unrest. A judicial commission was appointed on 1 August to try cases of trespass, oppression, extortion and other abuses of the law in Kent.[16] At its head was the chancellor, Kemp, himself a native of the county and for this reason probably likely to lend a sympathic ear to local complaints. With the archbishop of Canterbury, the duke of Buckingham and a number of professional judges, he presided over sessions held intermittently at Rochester, Maidstone, Canterbury and Dartford from 18 August until the middle of December.

The record of these proceedings shows that the people of Kent were far from cowed after the disintegration of their great host. The men indicted by the local jurors were all members of the royal household or of the county administration. Some of those charged, such as Lords Dudley and Rivers, Sir Robert Wingfield and Thomas Daniel, were accused of taking horses and money in the previous June; it is more likely that they were in fact being held responsible for pilfering by their followers as they were making the initial attempt to suppress the rebellion. It was held against Alexander Iden, the new sheriff, that he had arrested and robbed Henry Wilkins, a henchman of Cade. Most of the charges were made against previous sheriffs and their officers. Stephen Slegge, undersheriff to James Fienes (later Lord Say) in 1442, had extorted ten marks by promising to arrange for the acquittal of a man falsely indicted. He was sheriff himself in 1449, and further charges were laid against him for his conduct then, while his deputy was described as a common extortioner and oppressor of the people; so also were the deputies of William Cromer. Slegge had assisted Lord Say in expelling Humphrey Evias from his property and with so threatening Reynold Peckham with threats of imprisonment and the gallows that he agreed to exchange land with Say, wherein he was defrauded; and, while sheriff, Slegge had helped to compel Say's tenants to pay more than their customary rents. Robert East, the keeper of Maidstone gaol, had deceived the king's justices by denying that he had a certain prisoner, and he had detained a woman until her husband came to terms with him. More examples of his misdeeds were quoted and these, like the rest on this roll,[17] lend substance to "The complaint of the commons of Kent".

There was a fresh wave of outbursts in the last week of August and throughout September in Sussex, Wiltshire, Essex and Kent. Large numbers were involved, but those risings which did not fade away were soon dispersed by a show of force.[18] Rumblings of discontent on an ever decreasing scale persisted in Kent; the last rising, when the name of Cade was invoked, was the fiercely anti-clerical demonstration at Hawkhurst in 1456.[19] The majority of those who had followed Cade refrained from further adventure. They had their pardons and no legal proceedings were taken against them. It was only those who had caused further trouble after the grant of the pardon on 8 July 1450 who were brought to trial. After each rising a strong judicial commission was sent into the county, sometimes accompanied by the king. One batch of convicted rebels was led to him, naked to the waist and with cords round their necks; after prostrating themselves to the ground, they received his pardon. Others were executed, the largest number to be condemned by one tribunal being the forty-one victims of "the harvest of heads" in February 1451. Magnates of opposing factions were at least united in their attitude to rebellious commoners: the duke of Somerset commanded the royal forces and presided over the tribunal in the autumn of 1450, York was appointed to a judicial commission in the following December, and the earl of Salisbury, now his ally, was in charge of the proceedings in 1456.[20] Even the commons in the parliament of November 1450, despite their hostility to the court, showed their dislike of base-born rebels by bringing in a bill of attainder against Cade, so that he might be called "false traitor for evermore".[21]

IV

Richard of York

The great wave of popular disturbances in the summer of 1450 had barely begun to recede before a fresh crisis faced the council of Henry VI. Once again its authority was challenged, this time by the most powerful magnate in the realm, Richard, duke of York. He had estates in most English counties, the chief loose concentrations being in north Hertfordshire and to the east in Essex and Suffolk, and in the east midlands and southern Yorkshire, with castles at Sandal, Conisborough and Fotheringay, but his most important holdings were in central and south-east Wales and in the adjacent English counties.* In Ireland also he held vast territories, among them the earldom of Ulster and half a dozen other lordships. These extensive possessions had come to him by the union of several great inheritances. His father, the condemned traitor Richard, earl of Cambridge, had married the daughter and eventual heiress of Roger Mortimer, earl of March. To Richard of York had descended the Mortimer lands in the marches of Wales, and also the earldom of Ulster which had come into the family through the marriage of Earl Roger's father to a granddaughter of Edward III. His title was inherited from his paternal uncle, the duke of York killed at Agincourt, the son of Edward III's fourth son, Edmund of Langley. Richard thus had a claim to be the heir to the crown should the house of Lancaster, sprung from Edward's third son, fail for want of direct heirs. Through

---

* Their value was about £3,500 p.a.[1] For their distribution see Map II pp. 96-7.

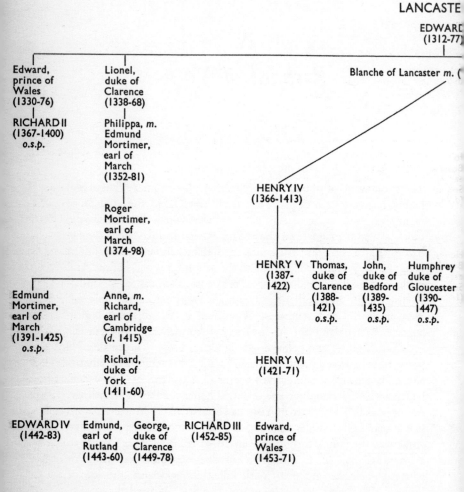

Edward,
prince of
Wales
(1330-76)

RICHARD II
(1367-1400)
o.s.p.

Lionel,
duke of
Clarence
(1338-68)

Philippa, m.
Edmund
Mortimer,
earl of
March
(1352-81)

Roger
Mortimer,
earl of
March
(1374-98)

Blanche of Lancaster m. (

HENRY IV
(1366-1413)

HENRY V
(1387-
1422)

Thomas,
duke of
Clarence
(1388-
1421)
o.s.p.

John,
duke of
Bedford
(1389-
1435)
o.s.p.

Humphrey
duke of
Gloucester
(1390-
1447)
o.s.p.

Edmund
Mortimer,
earl of
March
(1391-1425)
o.s.p.

Anne, m.
Richard,
earl of
Cambridge
(d. 1415)

Richard,
duke of
York
(1411-60)

HENRY VI
(1421-71)

EDWARD IV
(1442-83)

Edmund,
earl of
Rutland
(1443-60)

George,
duke of
Clarence
(1449-78)

RICHARD III
(1452-85)

Edward,
prince of
Wales
(1453-71)

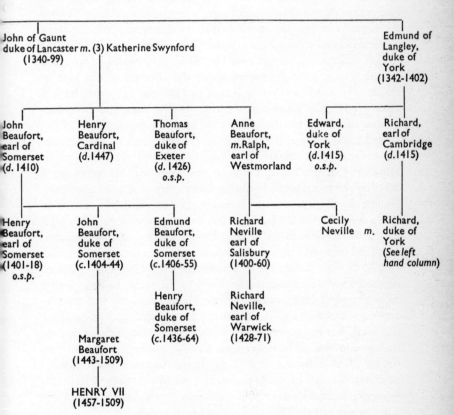

John of Gaunt
duke of Lancaster m. (3) Katherine Swynford
(1340-99)

Edmund of
Langley,
duke of
York
(1342-1402)

John
Beaufort,
earl of
Somerset
(d. 1410)

Henry
Beaufort,
Cardinal
(d.1447)

Thomas
Beaufort,
duke of
Exeter
(d. 1426)
o.s.p.

Anne
Beaufort,
m.Ralph,
earl of
Westmorland

Edward,
duke of
York
(d.1415)
o.s.p.

Richard,
earl of
Cambridge
(d.1415)

Henry
Beaufort,
earl of
Somerset
(1401-18)
o.s.p.

John
Beaufort,
duke of
Somerset
(c.1404-44)

Edmund
Beaufort,
duke of
Somerset
(c.1406-55)

Richard
Neville
earl of
Salisbury
(1400-60)

Cecily
Neville   m.

Richard,
duke of
York
(See left
hand column)

Henry
Beaufort,
duke of
Somerset
(c.1436-64)

Richard
Neville,
earl of
Warwick
(1428-71)

Margaret
Beaufort
(1443-1509)

HENRY VII
(1457-1509)

his mother's family, however, Richard was descended from Edward's second son, but until 1460 he refrained from stressing this link and the arms he bore were those of Edmund of Langley. Since Humphrey of Gloucester had died in 1447, Henry VI was the only surviving male descendant of Henry IV. As his marriage seemed to be barren, York could feel he was well placed in the line of succession. As both heir presumptive and overmightiest of subjects, he inevitably claimed for himself a leading role in national affairs, nor would contemporary opinion generally consider this claim unreasonable.

This position was denied him. He had become estranged from the Suffolk group over differences about the conduct of the war in France. He was lieutenant in France in 1436 and 1437, and he was again engaged, in 1440, for five years as lieutenant and governor-general of France and Normandy. In 1442, the main weight of the French royal army was flung against Gascony, and by the summer the situation was critical. The English also lost some ground in Normandy, and the king's council was faced with the problem of whether reinforcements should be sent to either or both provinces. Despite the objections of the treasurer, Cromwell, it was decided to raise a second army for Gascony. Its command was entrusted to John Beaufort, earl of Somerset and nephew of the cardinal. Negotiations about the terms of his commission went on for months, for Somerset wished to make a number of conditions. One, obviously, was that he should not be subordinate to York. In the event, he was given a more extensive commission than York's, as lieutenant and captain-general of Gascony and France "in the parts where . . . York actually exerciseth not the power that we have given unto him". His contingent also was to be larger than York's[2] and, as if to remove all doubts of his relationship with the latter, Somerset was created a duke on the day of his appointment, 30 March 1443. Moreover, Somerset received preferential treatment at the Exchequer. While York was urged to "take patience and forbear him for a time" if his wages fell into arrears, Somerset was paid £25,000 as an advance on his wages.*[3] His expedition was a dismal failure, and he came home, to die, early in 1444.

York had thus been wounded in both pride and pocket. He was reduced to serious financial straits: by the end of his term in France,

---

* Lord Cromwell had resigned as treasurer on 6 July, doubtless because he objected to the issue.

the crown owed him almost two year's wages and he became unable
to pay his captains and garrisons.[4] Yet he was still eager to keep the
principal command in Normandy and the king's council apparently
agreed to his reappointment by July 1446.[5] Then York had a violent
quarrel with Adam Moleyns, the keeper of the privy seal, whom he
accused of bribing his troops so that they would charge him with
peculation. The result was an open breach with the court.[6] The
command was now given to Edmund Beaufort, Duke John's brother,
and York was appointed to the lieutenancy of Ireland for the unusually long term of ten years.[7] Suffolk, clearly, wanted him out of
the way: he was gaining too much familiarity with the forces in
France, and his employment there enhanced his reputation at home,
whereas in Ireland he would be safely and unprofitably employed in
yet another vain struggle to suppress rebellion. From his Irish exile,
York had the dubious satisfaction of observing a second of the
favoured Beauforts leading English armies to disaster.

The emergence of Richard of York as a political leader in the late
summer of 1450 appears to have been largely inspired by his animosity
towards Edmund Beaufort, duke of Somerset.* Certainly both then
and later York called upon the crown to prosecute Somerset for his
conduct of the war in Normandy. His persistence in urging this
action reveals a personal vendetta. No doubt Somerset by his military
incompetence and signal failure was a sitting target for York's
charges, but why had York taken it upon himself to make them?
He may well have been genuinely indignant about England's defeats
and really believed that Somerset was responsible. But given the
meagreness of England's war effort, the discontent among her
Norman subjects, and the great resurgence of French military
strength, it is unlikely that any English commander could have held
his position. York, as a former lieutenant-general, should have
realised this. Yet he was an arrogant man, and might have felt that
had he been in command in 1450 he would have flung back the
French. He did however have other motives for his campaign against
Somerset, and it is more reasonable to suppose that he was just
making capital of his opponent's military misfortunes; by so doing,
he could win the backing of his fellow-countrymen who were
shamed and astounded by the loss of Henry V's French conquests.
York was equally ready to put himself at the head of his compatriots

* He was created duke in 1448.

who demanded an end to abuses in the administration of the law. His sincerity in this is questionable. York wanted to be popular, and through the distribution of manifestoes and letters he strove to convince people that his demands on the king's court were made for the common good.

Abbot Wheathampstead of St. Albans, himself no partisan of the court, had no doubt of the true reason for York's pursuit of Somerset: it was because Somerset by his false insinuations had prevailed upon the king to have York's new appointment to France revoked and so secured the command for himself. Revenge for this affront was York's motive.[8] Beside this, however, there was the question of the succession to the crown should Henry die childless. The first Beauforts were the prenuptial offspring of John of Gaunt and Katherine Swynford. They were legitimised by Richard II, but in confirming this decree Henry IV had barred the family from the succession. Yet what one king could forbid of his own motion, another could allow, and Henry VI's pliability was notorious. It was said in 1450 that Suffolk had entertained the idea of marrying his son to Margaret Beaufort, the only child of Duke John,* with the object of having her made queen and his son thereby king.† The rumour of this scheme, whether true or not, would certainly have made York and his well-wishers uneasy: he could not take his claim to be heir apparent for granted. As Edmund Beaufort came to entrench himself in the king's council, and in Henry's favour, there was good reason to fear that he might be officially recognised as the Lancastrian heir.

* Henry VII's mother.
† This was alleged at an inquest in London on 4 July 1450, presumably the same tribunal which condemned Lord Say to death. Among those accused of complicity were Thomas Kent, the clerk of the king's council, and Edward Grimston, a household official. The scheme was said to have been hatched on 20 July 1447; the king of France was to be called in to remove Henry VI and put the happy pair on their thrones. Commissions were appointed to examine these charges in March and April 1451. The trials in King's Bench ended in acquittals in the autumn of 1452.

Suffolk said in parliament in 1450, however, that he had intended to marry his son to Anne Beauchamp, the duke of Warwick's heiress. Anne's marriage was not at Suffolk's disposal for two years after he had been granted Margaret's custody in 1444. The queen was given Anne's custody in 1446 but Suffolk bought it from her within three months. Thus he may at first have planned to marry his son to Margaret and then discarded her in favour of Anne when she became his ward. Anne's inheritance was far greater than Margaret's, and if this was his reason for preferring her as a daughter-in-law, his interest in Margaret may equally well have been confined to her territorial assets.[9]

Like the commons of the previous parliament in their indictment
of the duke of Suffolk, York made charges of treason against a royal
favourite with the object of having him put on trial; arrested and in
detention, Somerset would no longer be in a position to influence
the king. But York's ambitions obviously did not stop here. His
purpose was to take Somerset's place as the dominant figure in the
king's council. He felt, no doubt, that this was his birthright. He also
had urgent personal reasons for wanting this position. One was to
ensure his standing as Henry's apparent successor to the throne, to
prevent any move to recognise another heir. A second pressing
motive was financial.

In 1446, at the end of York's term as lieutenant in Normandy, the
Exchequer owed him £38,666. He renounced £12,666 of this in
return for adequate provision for payment of the remainder. He was
given numerous tallies of assignment, but four years later a good
proportion of these had still not been honoured.[10] The crown then
owed him a further £10,000 for his wages in Ireland and as arrears
of his hereditary pension at the Exchequer.[11] Despite the nature and
extent of his services, York had to take his chance with the king's
numerous other creditors. Without court favour, he could not hope
that any preference would be given to his claims. He continued to
wait. In 1454, he stated that his great expenses in France had compelled him, for want of wages, to sell "a great substance of my
livelihood, to lay in pledge all my great jewels and the most part of
my plate"; he had also borrowed heavily from his friends.[12] This
burden of debt goes far to explain why in the years following 1450
York made increasingly desperate attempts to storm his way into
the king's council. The bankruptcy of Lancaster drove York to
rebellion.

The duke of Somerset entered London on 1 August 1450, bringing
with him from France a train of defeated soldiers in a state of near
mutiny. Within a fortnight, he was taking a seat in the king's council,[13]
and this was probably the reason why York decided to return from
Ireland. It is a more likely explanation than that he was somehow
involved in Cade's rebellion, as his traducers alleged; had he been
its instigator, it is curious that he timed his movements so indepen-
dently and came nearly two months after the dispersal of Cade's
followers, of which he cannot have been ignorant. York was still in
Ireland, at Trim, on 26 August,[14] but within a few days he was

landing in Anglesey. Some measures were put in hand for his arrest and to prevent his adherents from joining him; but these plans would appear to have been instigated from the court rather than by the council, for they were strangely desultory and there was no general mobilisation of the police forces at the crown's command.

York evaded these attempts at interception and by the time he reached London had a following some four thousand strong. About Michaelmas he seemingly forced his way to the king's presence to complain about the resistance offered to his journey, and to demand exoneration from the charges of treason which, he said, had been made against him. In reply, Henry denied that any formal indictments had been made, and he declared that he regarded York as a faithful subject. York now took up the cause of popular grievance: he referred to the widespread complaints "that justice is not duly administered", and he urged that those whom rumour had charged with treason should be put in prison and brought to trial. The king's answer was that he intended to correct the shortcomings of the legal system by setting up "a sad and substantial council", with unprecedented powers; York would be a member, but he was rebuked for presuming that he alone could counsel the king.[15] This promise was the sole fruit of York's direct approach to the king, and no record has been found to show that it was carried out. Frustrated at court, he now tried to achieve his aims through another constitutional channel.

On 5 September writs had been issued to call a parliament to meet on 6 November. The record of the commons in the last parliament must have suggested to York that here was a potential ally in his campaign for reform. The forces of opposition in the commons of 1449–50 had assailed both the leading persons and the practices of the king's administration. The removal of Suffolk, Moleyns and Archbishop Stafford was not enough. For months the commons refused to grant any subsidy. They said that the community was too impoverished by taxation, unpaid royal debts and lack of justice to give the king means to pay the costs of his household. These expenses should be met from the crown's permanent resources; that they were inadequate was the fault of the king in giving away so much of his "livelihood". To remedy this, the commons raised the call for a resumption of royal grants. A third session had to be held, in May, and even now, at Leicester, in the midst of the king's duchy of

Lancaster estates, the opposition held firm. The council had to give way. An act of resumption was passed, a second measure from the commons appropriating certain regular crown revenues to the household was accepted, before a subsidy was granted, and given in a form which disclosed the commons' continuing distrust of the government: instead of being paid into the Exchequer, the receipts were to be delivered to four treasurers appointed by parliament, and they were to issue the money in wages for the army.[16] It was more than forty years since a subsidy had been granted on terms so humiliating to the crown. Taxation, the commons felt, was an extraordinary measure, justified only by national emergency, and its issues should be applied only to defence: the king should "live of his own".

A still more pressing concern of the commons was the corruption of justice. The commons had voiced their disquiet on the general problem in the course of their proceedings against Suffolk and William Tailbois, but they had not offered any general remedy. It would have been a fruitless exercise. The statute book was full of measures against legal abuses. The problem was how to enforce them. The impeachment of Suffolk, like "the complaint of the commons of Kent", expressed the belief that the root of the evil was to be found in the king's household. Justice was being perverted from the centre, not only by the chief officers like Suffolk and Say, but by "menial servants" as well. The rebels demanded that the court be purged of these corrupt officials. Here was a cause in which York could join forces with the commons. Their motives might differ: York wanted his enemies removed from positions of influence so that he could take their place, the commons' demand was that the government should administer the law without fear or favour. That York did not share the commons' ardent desire for an impartial administration is suggested by later events, for when his opportunity came, he used the crown's authority on the side of his magnate adherents; nor was he less culpable than other peers of attempting to influence legal proceedings to the advantage of his clients.[17] Yet for the moment he seemed to be the man best-fitted to direct the popular cause. His birth commended him as a leader, his record in France and Ireland commanded respect, his treatment by the court gained sympathy; the manifestoes of the Kentish rebels show what hopes were put in him.

In the autumn of 1450, York took the part expected of him. His petition to the king that suspected traitors should be brought to trial was described as "much after the commons' desire", indeed it echoed the demands of the men of Kent. The publicity this petition received added to his reputation. The servant of John Paston who secured a copy advised his master to organise a demonstration in Norwich when York visited the city in October; he urged that the duke should hear a "hideous noise and cry" against Sir Thomas Tuddenham and his fellow "extortioners", otherwise they might escape their just deserts.[18] Clearly the author put a good deal of faith in York's sympathy and influence. For his part, the duke was anxious to enlist support and there could not have been more fertile ground for his purpose than the two counties where Suffolk and his minions had so recently held sway. With the assistance of the duke of Norfolk, he was trying to secure the election of knights who would uphold his cause in the forthcoming parliament.

York's following among the lords was small. His wife was a member of the numerous and well-placed Neville family, but these kinsmen were not at this stage prepared to accept his political leadership. The only notable peers who actively supported him in 1450 were the duke of Norfolk and the earl of Devon. Neither can be termed a "Yorkist": they did not persistently adhere to him in the following years, but for the present their interests inclined them to his side. Devon's real quarrel was with his local enemies, Lord Bonville and James Butler, earl of Wiltshire, whose standing in the court circle gave them what he doubtless felt to be an unfair advantage in any hearing of their dispute before the king's council. Norfolk was York's nephew by marriage – his mother was another Neville – but in the closely related state of aristocratic society this link was a comparatively tenuous one. Norfolk also had reasons of his own for opposition to the court. He was presumably aggrieved at his exclusion from the council, a fact not unknown to Cade's followers, who recited

> The White Lion is laid to sleep,
> Through the envy of the Ape's clog.*[19]

Suffolk's envy was no doubt sharpened by their rivalry for dominance in East Anglia: Norfolk made no secret of his intention to "have the principal rule and governance through all this shire of which we bear

---

* The allusions are to the white lion in the arms of Norfolk's family, the Mowbrays, and to Suffolk's badge.

our name".[20] The two dukes were also engaged in disputes over property rights which Norfolk continued to pursue against Suffolk's widow.[21] Norfolk had been detained in Kenilworth Castle and the Tower of London for some time, probably in 1440 and as a result of his threats to John Heydon: for this rigorous treatment he could blame the royal favourite who was Heydon's employer. A further cause of resentment arose from his quarrel with Sir Robert Wingfield of Letheringham, Suffolk, which led to his being confined in the Tower for a second period in 1448. Wingfield had a place at court, and to this he owed his protection from Norfolk and his immunity from prosecution for his own misdeeds.*

Norfolk's territorial resources in East Anglia and South Wales made him a formidable ally. He kept a considerable household of knights, esquires and other retainers in his well-fortified castle at Framlingham, Suffolk. The garrison of Framlingham was a force to be feared by the duke's enemies. One of his esquires, Charles Nowell, led an armed gang some two score strong which, it was said, held the counties of Norfolk and Suffolk in terror in the years 1450-2; even the clergy were not immune from their violence, and no royal officer dared to arrest them.[22] Sir William Ashton with Nowell and others of the garrison were accused of still more sinister activities. They were said to have plotted with York's chamberlain, Sir William Oldhall, on 6 March 1450, to depose the king and have York put in his place; they had published writings and ballads stating that Henry, by the advice of Suffolk, the bishops of Chichester and Salisbury, and Lord Say, had sold his realms of England and France to the French king, and so they urged the people to rise against Henry and call on York to accept the crown; and later, at Bury St. Edmunds, they proclaimed Jack Cade to be their leader, and on 26 May sent letters calling on the men of Kent to rise and join York on his journey from Ireland. This indictment was made in February 1453, by an extremely hostile jury,† and little weight can be given to it. But the local reputation of Norfolk's retinue must have been an embarrassment to a leader professing, as York did, a desire to restore order and cleanse the process of justice, and this may to some extent account for his failure to see all his nominees elected to parliament in 1450.[24]

---

* See Appendix IV.

† It included well-known partisans of the court like Sir Miles Stapleton and Edward Grimston.[23]

London was in a state of high excitement before parliament met. The city was swarming with discharged soldiers whose unruly behaviour prompted strong measures by the civic authorities. York's badge (a fetterlock) was displayed in many places; it was displaced in favour of the king's arms, and then restored by his friends. When York himself came for parliament on 23 November, two weeks after its formal opening, his sword was carried before him and more than three thousand men are said to have followed. With him were the duke of Norfolk and the earl of Devon. Other lords brought large companies; the earl of Warwick had "a mighty people arrayed for the war". A mob besieged Westminster Hall on 30 November, crying out to the assembled peers "Do justice upon the false traitors or let us be avenged". Next day, a rabble of ex-soldiers attacked Somerset's lodgings at Blackfriars. York and Devon intervened to save him from violence, and he made his escape in the earl's barge to the safety of the Tower. According to some London chronicle accounts, he was committed, as if for trial, but there is no evidence of any charges of a judicial nature being made against him and it is more likely that he was housed there for his own protection.

York and Norfolk seemingly took it upon themselves to restore order, proclaiming that looters would be punished with death, and that same day a man who ignored the order was executed in Cheapside. Three days later the king and all the lords and their arrays marched through the city, "which was one of the [most] glorious sights that ever any man in these days saw".[25] This was the court's response to York's declaration of martial law: this great demonstration of strength under the king's leadership was in fact a public rebuke for the duke's taking upon himself the crown's responsibility to preserve the peace. He was to do this again in the following summer. Whether genuinely or not, York posed as the champion of order, and even to his most bitter enemy he was scrupulously correct; his reputation would have been irreparably tarnished had he merely stood by while Somerset was butchered by the mob.

In parliament, feeling for York was strong among the commons. They elected his chamberlain as their speaker, and gave their support to a petition against the murderers of William Tresham, a member of his council, who had been the speaker in the previous parliament. The chancellor told them that their business was to provide funds to keep the seas and defend Gascony, and to pacify the populace rioting

in many parts of the country. The tax granted by the last parliament
had not been so much as assessed. The commons agreed that its
collection should be speeded. Otherwise they were more ready to
discuss financial reform than open their purse strings. They appro-
priated revenues from the customs for military expenses and introduced a second act of resumption, for the officers of the king's
household had prevented the previous act from harming their
interests.[26]

The first two measures were passed before the Christmas recess,
the last was the sole fruit of two further sessions in 1451. The commons
were more eager to attack the court. They asked that twenty named
persons should be banished to a distance of twelve miles from the
king by 1 December 1450, under pain of forfeiture, unless they had
to appear in a court of law. These people, they said, had so behaved
about the king that many of his possessions had been squandered and
the law subverted. Nearly all those named were in fact men who had
been indicted in the sessions at Dartford in the previous August,[27] or
in the supposed plot of the duke of Suffolk which had been unearthed
while Cade's forces were in London.* To the lists had been added
the names of the duke of Somerset and Norfolk's enemy Robert
Wingfield. The proceedings against Suffolk were resumed: he had
not answered the indictment of the last parliament, it was said, and
justice demanded his conviction; a petition was made for his attainder
so that his lands could be confiscated and his title extinguished. The
king refused this demand outright. The commons ultimately out-
raged the administration by permitting one of its members to present
a bill asking Henry to recognise York as his heir. Parliament was
dismissed towards the end of May 1451, and the member, Thomas
Young, a burgess for Bristol, was put in the Tower.†

The reply given to the petition for the banishment of courtiers
was an almost complete and barely courteous refusal. The king, it
was said, always desired to be surrounded by virtuous servants and
he knew of no reason why any of those named should be dismissed.
He would however retain with him only the lords and those others
necessary for his convenience; the remainder would be sent away for
one year, within which he would listen to any complaints which

---

* See note on p. 74 above.
† Young was a friend of Oldhall, who may have prompted him to put up
his bill.[28]

might be made against them. But this concession was made of the
king's grace alone "and by no other authority". The spirit of this
reply recalls the decision to banish Suffolk, made on the king's
motion only, and the answer given to York's demand for the reform
of the government. Underlying all three statements is a firm assertion
of the king's prerogative authority: he alone had the right to choose
his advisers and domestic officers, his alone was the supreme responsibility to see that justice was done. We can detect in these answers the
influence of an astute and resolute defender of constitutional pro-
priety. Twice if not on all three occasions the spokesman was the
chancellor, Cardinal Kemp. His also, we may feel sure, was the mind
which formulated these replies. It was the mind of a canon lawyer of
great distinction, subtle, therefore, but rooted in principles, and he
carried the experience of forty years in high office in Church and
state, in the king's council and in international diplomacy.

John Kemp was the last great civil servant of the house of Lancaster. That the crown had to turn to this septuagenarian was a
further legacy of Suffolk's jealous regime; there was indeed a dearth
of experienced talent at the king's command. Kemp brought to
Henry's council greater firmness of purpose, a desire for sound
administration and justice. He would no more than bow before a
parliamentary storm; he would not yield an inch on matters of
principle. Yet he appointed himself to a commission to hear the
grievances of the Kentish people against their local tyrants, and he
removed the notorious Tuddenham and Heydon from the Norfolk
bench and encouraged their victims to press for their punishment by
law.[29] One contemporary asserted that Kemp's integrity and fearless-
ness in the cause of justice were not likely to be surpassed in any
other age or land.[30]

While Kemp lived, the revived court faction under Somerset did
not enjoy a monopoly of influence in the government comparable
with that exercised by Suffolk. Tuddenham soon recovered favour
at court but he did not return to the commission of the peace until
after Kemp's death.* The chancellor's policy was doubtless seconded
by a man of similarly long administrative experience now in high
office in the household itself. Following Lord Say's death, Ralph
Cromwell had returned to court as the king's chamberlain.[32] That he

---

* He was pardoned all but £200 of his fines (see p. 57) on 4 July 1451. He
and Heydon were reappointed J.P.'s for Norfolk on 28 March 1455.[31]

did not thereby identify his interests with those of Somerset is shown by York's confidence in him.* In financial administration there was also a new sense of responsibility. The last act of resumption, unlike its predecessor, was vigorously put into effect, to the loss of household officers and great magnates, Somerset as well as York; by so doing, the government not only improved its revenues, it could also hope to earn the confidence of the commons in a subsequent parliament.[34]

* On 20 December 1451, York appointed Cromwell with others (including Oldhall) to settle a private dispute with one Thomas Brown.[33]

V

The Siege of Taunton

In the parliament of February 1449, the lords were asked to consider how troops could be raised in readiness for the approaching end of the truce with France. Their replies show that they were far more perturbed by the condition of England itself. Lords Sudeley and Cromwell "think that due justice might be had and a good accord amongst the lords first", and the majority of their colleagues gave the enforcement of justice at home precedence over the military problem abroad.[1] The commons in the following parliament shared the same anxiety, declaring that the number of crimes of violence had increased to an unprecedented degree in recent years, and if confirmation were needed, the records of the court of King's Bench provide ample evidence of a great wave of disorder. Naturally it was in those parts of the country most distant from the centre of government that lawlessness was at its worst, a danger not only to local society but a potential threat to the crown itself, for these were the conditions in which interested magnates were best able to recruit large followings of militant retainers. East Anglia, despite the oft-cited testimony of *The Paston Letters*, appears as a haven of law and order when compared with Devon and Cornwall and the lands beyond Severn and Trent. There can be little dispute that the northern counties were the most lawless part of England, a district where the normal processes of justice were held in utter contempt and almost entirely ignored.

The south-west was the north's closest challenger for such a reputation, with the difference that the inhabitants of Devon and Cornwall still resorted to the central courts in attempts to obtain the king's justice. Their disputes, therefore, remain on record among the archives of Chancery and King's Bench: nearly every file of indictments includes some tale of murder, abduction, or seizure of lands, by unusually large bands of armed men; every patent roll gives orders to investigate reports of piracy on the high seas or in coastal waters. Such evidence gives a picture of an area where brutal outrage was the common coin of daily life, so common, indeed, that there are indications of a more than usually callous indifference to human suffering. It is not surprising that some of the few allegations of torture in this period come from the south-west.[2] It was in this environment that there took place the best known of the private wars of Henry VI's later years.

The leading opponents represented different types of magnate. Thomas Courtenay was the twelfth earl of Devon. Probably created in 1141, the title had fallen into abeyance when the direct line of Redvers died out in 1262, but it was revived for their heirs the Courtenays in 1335. The earl's hereditary possessions included nearly forty manors and numerous rents and services in Devonshire, another dozen in Cornwall, and smaller numbers in Somerset, Dorset, Hampshire, Buckinghamshire and Berkshire. Unlike other surviving comital houses, however, the Courtenays were not growing richer from generation to generation; indeed, the ninth earl, who died in 1377, had reduced his heir's expectations by making provision for younger sons. Until his mother died in 1441, Thomas Courtenay's total annual income was barely £1,000.[3] His unsuccessful attempt in 1446 to be allowed precedence before the earl of Arundel reveals that pride of ancestry was an important feature of his character.

While Devon could think of himself as the traditional leader of society in the south-west, his enemy, William Bonville, had no hereditary claim to local eminence. The Bonvilles of Shute were a Devonshire family of respectable antiquity and several of its heads had been knighted, but until recent years their circumstances had been modest and only one had been thought worthy of appointment to the office of sheriff. This was another William Bonville, who was sheriff of Somerset in 1380 and of Devon in 1389. The family fortunes had then been improved by the marriage of his son to the heiress of John FitzRoger of Chewton, in Somerset. The social advance of the Bonvilles was emphasised when their son William, born in 1393, married the daughter of Lord Grey of Ruthin. After her death, he again found a noble spouse, none other than a Courtenay, the widow of Lord Harrington and the aunt of the twelfth earl.

This marriage may have lain at the root of the ill-feeling between the earl and Bonville. There may have been some disagreement about the lady's property, Devon's ancestral pride may have been offended by the connection with the rising member of an undistinguished family. But in this as in most private disputes of the time, we lack a clear pointer to the cause. When the consequences of these quarrels were so far reaching, it is a natural temptation to assume that their origins were serious issues – disagreements over political questions, for instance, or conflicting economic interests. This puts too high an assessment on fifteenth-century rationality. These people were violently emotional. The judicial records of the time show numerous prosecutions for murder and rape. A large proportion of the homicides were the outcome of sudden quarrels; all men carried arms, and hot words soon led to their use. The Stafford-Harcourt affray in Coventry indicates that the education of the knightly class did not curb hot tempers. The possibility cannot be precluded that baronial feuds such as that of Devon and Bonville were due in the first place to simple causes like personal antipathy, injured pride and jealousy. In this case, the most likely explanation is that the earl felt that the regional pre-eminence which was his birthright was being threatened by Bonville's growing influence in local government.[4]

Bonville was a capable and industrious man of affairs; although his background was undistinguished, he attained noble rank and responsible office by a talent for making himself useful and an equally necessary political opportunism. He served in France under Henry V, where he was knighted, and again in 1424, when he provided a contingent of forty men to the expedition sent to recover the vital fortress of Le Crotoy,[5] at the mouth of the Somme. He had been sheriff of Devon in the previous year and on his return from France he became one of the most active country gentlemen in the south-west, often being charged to investigate reports of lawless enterprises on land and sea. He was appointed a justice of the peace in Devon in 1431, and later in Somerset and Cornwall also. These useful honorary services did not escape recognition and in 1437 Bonville was described as the king's knight. This was on the occasion of the grant of the office of royal steward in Cornwall. The duchy of Cornwall, the traditional appanage of the heir to the crown, was at this time held by the king. As the senior office in the duchy's administration, the stewardship was both influential and lucrative; to the salary of £26 13s. 4d. could be added the perquisites to be obtained when presiding in his court or granting leases. Bonville persuaded Sir John Courtenay to resign the office and, presumably through the influence of friends at court, secured his own appointment as steward. The previous steward was presumably John Courtenay of Powderham, a descendant of the earl of Devon who died in 1377. His son, Sir Philip Courtenay, was a close associate of Bonville. They are often to be found serving on the same commission or witnessing a private charter. In 1440, the two knights were employed at sea in an effort to suppress piracy.[6]

It is in this year that we first hear of the bad relations between Bonville and the earl of Devon leading to hostile demonstrations by armed bands. Two royal letters were sent to the earl in October, calling him before the council and requiring him to stop these unlawful gatherings. Bonville obeyed a similar order and promised to accept the king's ruling. Devon was excused from coming to Westminster as he had fallen ill, and Sir John Stourton, a member of the council, was sent to take security from the earl that he would keep the peace.[7] In the following May, Devon petitioned the king for the office of steward of the duchy of Cornwall. Now, Bonville already in effect held this office, although his letters of appointment described him as steward of the king's lands in Cornwall. There is no more flagrant instance of Henry's generosity in granting the favours for which he was constantly being solicited, without any apparent consideration of the consequences, than his assenting to the earl's request. Two days later, on 7 May, Devon's patent was sealed in Chancery. A week passed before the king's council realised that it had permitted a stupendous administrative blunder and that if Devon's grant were put into effect there might be "great trouble" in Cornwall. He was therefore instructed to make no attempt to perform the office of steward.[8]

The earl seems to have ignored this command and the situation now went from bad to worse. There was an outbreak of disorder in Devon and Cornwall, with both sides assembling friends and adherents, and some fatal casualties ensued. Sir Philip Chetwynd, a friend of Bonville, was attacked on his way from Bristol to London by men whose livery was identified as the earl's. In November, the council called Devon and Bonville before it to put an end to these disturbances. As the stewardship was now the main cause of their dispute, both had to agree to its being put in the hands of a third party, while arbitrators determined who had the better title to the office. All disputes between them, "from the beginning of the world until now", were to be settled by agreement. Both the earl and Bonville took the chancellor by the hand and promised to ensure that no injury was done to the other. The decision about the steward-ship was to be made by 1 March 1442 but no trace of the sentence, if it were made, has been found. The earl was still styling himself, and giving orders, as steward of the duchy in May 1444.[9]

The quarrel now lapsed while Bonville was engaged as seneschal of Gascony. His appointment was not inspired by the council's wish to keep him and Devon apart, for he was its reserve candidate for office.[10] It was, however, nearly twenty years since he last had experi-ence of warfare in France, and obviously other qualifications beside military ones were considered. Presumably it was believed that Bonville would be a congenial subordinate of John Beaufort, duke of Somerset, who was to command the main force being raised, despite some opposition, for the relief of Gascony. Bonville's own contingent was to consist of twenty men-at-arms and six hundred archers, and he recruited some of these men in Devonshire, one of them being Walter Ralegh. Bonville reached Bordeaux towards the end of June 1444, and he remained in Gascony for three years,* during which he took part in some fighting and received serious injuries.[12] On 10 March 1449, he received a writ of summons to parliament and thus became Lord Bonville of Chewton. His faithful services both at home and abroad fully merited this distinction, but his elevation is a further indication that the duke of Suffolk regarded him as a useful supporter who would strengthen his party among the peers.†

While Bonville was occupied overseas, the earl of Devon had been, so far as is known, quietly occupied on his own affairs at home. He had turned a deaf ear to a royal request in 1443 that, "following the steps of his father", he should "put to his mighty hand" and lead an

---

* Although he remained seneschal until 1450, he was seemingly in England from 1447.[11]

† Suffolk's henchman William Tailbois was Bonville's son-in-law.

expedition to relieve Avranches.[13] Devon preferred to do his soldiering in England. For some time after Bonville's return there was no known outburst between him and the earl. Devon's hostility still smouldered, but with his powerful connections Bonville was a more formidable rival than he had been in 1440. Suffolk's fall deprived him of his most influential patron, but he soon attached himself to another leading figure in the royal circle. This was James Butler, son of the earl of Ormond, who had married a west country heiress and was raised to the English peerage, as earl of Wiltshire, in the same year as Bonville. Wiltshire had fallen out with one of his neighbours, Edward Brook, Lord Cobham* and it is therefore hardly remarkable that from this time Cobham became closely associated with the earl of Devon. Devon himself now made common cause with the duke of York, the natural focus for men with enemies in favour at the king's court. He took part in York's shows of strength in London in the autumn of 1450. His appearance in a demonstration against the so-called betrayal of Normandy[15] seems hypocritical in view of his refusal to serve in 1443. This new found concern for the fate of the French territories says much for the nature of his connection with York. The only political aim they had in common was a desire to dislodge the ruling faction of the day.

The failure of York's demonstrations and of the pressure of his adherents in parliament left Devon's enemies in possession of their privileged position at court. The earl resolved, therefore, to strike against Wiltshire and Bonville with the only means left to him. In August 1451, he mobilised his retainers. It is possible that Wiltshire took similar measures, for both earls were sent orders to appear before the council.[16] Devon was not to be deflected from his purpose, and on 22 September he was in Taunton with a large concentration of followers of his own and of Lord Cobham and a number of less eminent adherents. This gathering, later to be described as an act of rebellion, was estimated to number between five and six thousand men. The leaders issued a statement that their only purpose was to

---

* Despite his Kentish title, Cobham's principal estates were in Dorset and Somerset. That the earl of Wiltshire was his enemy is suggested by an indictment that on 24 October 1451, and again on 8 January following, he attempted to kill Wiltshire's servant Robert Cappes.[14] This supposition seems to be confirmed by the fact that Cobham became a steady adherent of York and fought at St. Albans (1455) and Northampton (1460); this loyalty is to be explained by Wiltshire's remaining a leader of the court group.

further the common good, "although in their hearts they thought otherwise". Thus, it was said, they induced many innocent people to take part in a campaign which had as its true purpose the murder and spoliation of the earl of Wiltshire and Lord Bonville. Similar high-sounding declarations were made at Bridgwater, but at Glastonbury the appearance of the host, with its five carts loaded with

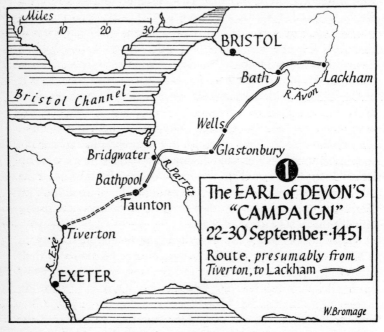

The EARL of DEVON'S "CAMPAIGN" 22-30 September · 1451
Route, presumably from Tiverton, to Lackham

W. Bromage

guns and other weapons, caused general alarm, increased when Devon's followers billeted themselves there for the night and helped themselves to food and drink. The march was resumed on the following morning. On reaching Wells, they were met by Bishop Beckington, a retired diplomat doomed to plead lost causes, who, with the dean of Wells, made a brave attempt to urge Devon to keep the peace. He replied roughly that "he would not discuss the matter until he had avenged himself on the earl of Wiltshire".

Devon was now nearing this enemy. Before entering Bath, he drew up his forces in the usual three divisions as if he were preparing for battle. The earl of Wiltshire was then only eight miles away, at Lackham. As Devon and his followers were settling down for the night in Bath, Wiltshire was warned of their approach and he hurried away to join the king at Coventry.* He was said to have been ordered to depart by the king but it is unlikely that he required such instructions. Wiltshire was to distinguish himself in the Wars of the Roses by running from every battle in which he took part.† Devon's army arrived at Lackham on 24 September to find the house empty. Further pursuit was out of the question and Bonville remained to be dealt with. The host turned back towards Bath and for the next three days its members dispersed all over eastern Somerset and some far into Wiltshire to plunder the houses of the earl of Wiltshire's tenants as well as those of persons not involved in the quarrel.

Devon now learned that Bonville had slipped behind him and had taken possession of Taunton Castle. Hastily recalling his forces, he reviewed them at Bathpool on 28 September, when their numbers were checked. After they had been drawn up for battle, he led them into the town and began a regular siege. For three days the castle was encircled while siege engines were being made. The government, however, was now preparing to intervene. The duke of Buckingham and the earls of Salisbury and Shrewsbury were called upon to join the king in the midlands with such strength as they could muster,[18] but before a royal army was sent against the earl of Devon, the duke of York arrived to bring the siege to a close. On his approach with Lord Moleyns and Sir William Herbert, Devon was persuaded to call off his forces and Bonville yielded the castle to his deliverer.[19] York induced the enemies to depart in peace and Devon, "as if he were enjoying the king's good-will", made terms with Bonville.[20]

York seems to have taken it upon himself to put down disorder in the west country. A London chronicler reported that he arrested Wiltshire and Lord Berkeley and put them in custody on 12 October.[21] If this statement is correct, it would indicate that York had also been busy in Gloucestershire, where the Berkeleys, at a severe disadvantage, pursued a quarrel with the countess of Shrewsbury.‡ York had no

---

* Henry was in the Midlands from 27 September to 12 October.[17]

† St. Albans (1455), Mortimer's Cross and Towton (1461).

‡ In 1466, however, Berkeley's son said that it was the countess who captured his father (on 4 September 1451) and held him prisoner for eleven weeks. She denied this but said that Berkeley Castle was a den of thieves and had been entered in pursuit of wrongdoers; Lord Berkeley was not detained, she said, but was indicted of various crimes. Berkeley and his sons received a general pardon for all their offences before 29 September 1451 on 20 November following.[22]

formal commission from the king to suppress these disturbances. He had, apparently, acted on his own initiative, forestalling direct intervention by the crown. By so doing, he had shown himself as a peace-maker, as a public spirited man with a greater sense of urgency than the king's immediate advisers, able to take effective action to disperse private armies and restore order to a terrorised countryside. The gain of such a reputation would have great value. York had a further motive. Devon was one of his few political allies. Had he not acted before the council did, Devon might have been placed under arrest and Bonville would not have failed to benefit. York could not afford to see his ally weakened, if not destroyed.

In the event, Devon suffered no immediate consequences for his warlike operations. He was dismissed from the commissions of the peace for Devon and Cornwall in November, but no judicial proceedings were taken against him until 11 January 1452. He was thus still at liberty then, and making ready for a yet more daring enterprise. His indictment before the Somerset justices on that day no doubt helped to strengthen his resolution. Its details of the campaign of September 1451 are circumstantial enough to appear true; but as in so many of these judicial proceedings we are left with the feeling that the misdeeds of only one side to the quarrel are put on record. Wiltshire and Bonville were not free from suspicion – they both obtained pardons on 19 February 1452[23] – but as they were members of the faction in favour no formal charges were made against them. This unequal treatment, causing a belief that the scales of justice would always be tilted in his enemies' favour, explains why Devon was prepared to follow York to any extremity in his opposition to the court.

VI

"The Field at Dartford"

In 1450, Richard of York had employed the constitutional means at the disposal of a great magnate critical of royal policy. He had made a direct appeal to the king and he had enlisted the commons in parliament. His failure had been complete. No concession had been made to his demands that the king's council should be re-formed, that he should have a place on it, and that Edmund, duke of Somerset, should be dismissed, perhaps even put on trial for his conduct as lieutenant in France. Somerset, indeed, was still on the ascendant. His appointment as captain of Calais in 1451 was not merely an enhancement of his power, giving him command of the largest military establishment at the king's disposal; it was a public affirmation that the king rejected the allegations that Somerset was a traitor. As for York's call for the cleansing of the administration of justice, Chancellor Kemp may have taken up this cause but at the king's court there was no sign that the worst features of the Suffolk regime had been abandoned. The men who were the subject of popular outcry in 1450 retained their places about the king. With Somerset's backing, Tuddenham,* Heydon and Daniel again became men to be feared in Norfolk; when John Paston brought an action against Lord Moleyns, a private royal letter was sent to the sheriff ordering him to select a jury that would acquit Moleyns.[1]

The government did show firmness in the task of restoring the crown's authority in the areas of popular discontent. Throughout

* See also p. 82, note.

1451 the king was taken on a tour of southern, central and eastern England, and with him went the royal justices and Somerset* and other councillors commissioned to try those implicated in the recent disturbances. Henry could still command the loyalty of a formidable section of the great nobility, as the muster of forces, probably for employment against the earl of Devon, bore witness. Yet despite the odds York continued to nourish his ambitions. He could place no more hope in parliamentary pressure. No future house of commons could be more ready to assist him than that of November 1450, and it had been unable to shake the government. Parliament, in any case, could only be assembled when the crown chose to call it. As for his magnate allies, Devon still had strong cause to support him, but Norfolk's friendship had waned. The collapse of the administration before the great Kentish rising, however, may well have convinced him that popular unrest might provide him with enough support to overawe the court.

York's attempted coup in 1452 was preceded by months of planning and the dissemination of propaganda designed to attract the active sympathy of the common people. In September 1451, he wrote to various towns and men of influence in Norfolk – and possibly elsewhere – to solicit their aid in his schemes. Edmund Clere of Stokesby, a "cousin" of the Pastons and probably a connection of Sir John Fastolf, brought copies of these letters to the mayor and citizens of King's Lynn.[3] Others were active in York's cause, like John Deeping, a Dominican friar of Stamford, who in the course of sermons in various churches of Lincolnshire urged his congregations to support the duke.[4] The details of the plot appear to have been arranged in the following November; the evidence for this, however, comes from the indictments presented when those concerned were put on trial by York's enemies. York himself was never named as a principal in these charges, probably because of his subsequent pardon by the king. His direct part in the preparations is thus unrecorded. The formal accusations were confined to his adherents, with pride of place being given to his chamberlain, Sir William Oldhall, and others of the duke's council like Sir Edmund Mulsho. On 3 Novem-

---

* A warrant dated 24 September 1451 shows that Somerset had charge of the arrangements for this progress. It ordered his repayment for issues made on the king's behalf, including sums given to judges at Salisbury and to a man sent from Northampton to the earls of Devon and Wiltshire.[2]

ber, it was said, Oldhall arranged with various men of Hitchin, Hertfordshire, that they should rise against the king, and eight days later he was at Fotheringay making similar plans with Mulsho. He had presumably called at Royston, Cambridgeshire, on his way north, for on the 10th a rising was organised there, and at Grantham and Stamford on the 11th and 12th. His plans laid, Oldhall made for London, and on 23 November he began his long, voluntary confinement in the sanctuary of St. Martin's-le-Grand.[5] This suggests that his movements had aroused the suspicions of the government and that he felt himself to be in danger of arrest.

At this time York was apparently in his estates in the Welsh Marches, while the court was moving between Coventry and Kenilworth. The continuing attendance on the king of the duke of Buckingham and the earls of Salisbury and Shrewsbury, and their retinues, must have given him cause for disquiet. He was aware that the blackest of interpretations were being put on his conduct and that Henry was "my heavy lord, greatly displeased with me". He invited two peers to Ludlow so that he could make a solemn declaration of his loyalty to the king, and on 9 January 1452 he wrote that he was ready to make a similar oath in the presence of such lords as Henry might send to him.[6] If we consider what plans York's officers had been making on his behalf, this profession appears shamelessly cynical, but it must be borne in mind that York consistently asserted that he had no intentions against Henry himself: Somerset was the target of his schemes. His declaration was presumably ill-received at court. His enemies there could remark upon the arrogance of this subject who asked that an embassy should be sent to him, as if he were an independent potentate.

York obviously had no desire to venture into the royal camp. In his next encounter with the court, he was determined to negotiate from a position of strength. On 3 February he revealed his intentions to the citizens of Shrewsbury in a letter which he signed as "your good friend". Recalling how he had put various articles for the reform of the government before the king in 1450, he said that it was through the sinister influence of the duke of Somerset that these had been set aside. Somerset was now supreme over the king and thus the country was in danger of destruction. York therefore intended "to proceed in all haste against him" with the help of his kinsmen and friends. His object was to bring peace and safety to the kingdom,

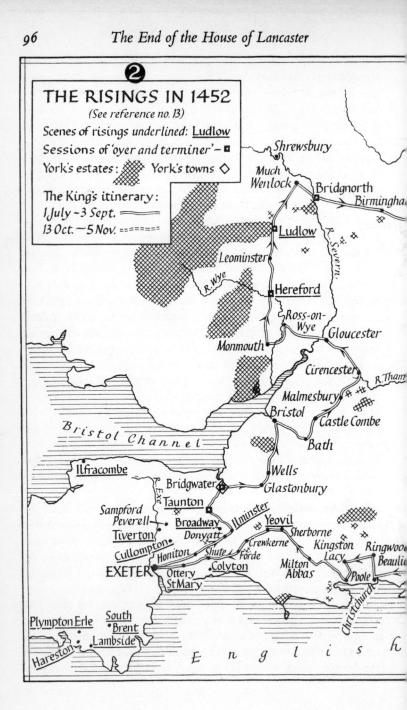

2

THE RISINGS IN 1452
(See reference no. 13)

Scenes of risings underlined: <u>Ludlow</u>
Sessions of 'oyer and terminer'– ▪
York's estates: ▨ York's towns ◇

The King's itinerary:
1 July – 3 Sept. ━━━
13 Oct. – 5 Nov. ═══════

W. Bromage

and again he protested that in so doing he would be acting according to his duty as a loyal subject.[7]

York and the king's advisers had simultaneously decided to break the deadlock due to his reluctance to come before Henry in person. At the same time as York was mustering his retainers and writing to solicit assistance from the Salopians and, apparently, the citizens of other towns in the midlands and south-east, the clerk of the council was bringing him a summons to attend that body at Coventry. When the clerk returned* to Westminster on 12 February, he brought news of the duke's martial preparations.[8] From the south-west there also came reports of armed risings, and on the 14th the duke of Buckingham, Lord Bonville and others were commissioned to proceed against the rebels there.[9] Here the leaders were York's ally the earl of Devon and his henchman Lord Cobham; the latter was sent a peremptory order on the 17th, bidding him attend the king without delay.[10] On the same day the council learned of letters which York had sent to a number of towns which, under pretence of "intending to the common weal", were incitements to rebellion. The civic authorities in these places – Canterbury, Maidstone, Colchester, Sandwich, Oxford, Winchelsea and Sudbury – had been prompt in forwarding these messages to the council.[11] Further commissions were issued for the arrest of those conspiring against the king in Kent, Norfolk and Suffolk.[12]

The king and his magnate supporters moved into the midlands to oppose York's march, but he took a less direct route, probably southward down the Severn valley so that he could join Devon and Cobham before turning east. His immediate purpose was to enlist a larger following before he encountered the royal army. He made for London but the city authorities, in obedience to royal letters, refused him admission. He had perforce to cross the Thames at Kingston and then followed the south bank to Dartford, where he drew up his troops in order of battle. The royal army, meanwhile, had returned to London on 27 February, and then followed York into Kent.

As the duke's army was crossing the south midlands, there was a series of demonstrations in his favour in a number of towns in eastern and western England. The first, not remarkably, was in his stronghold of Ludlow, where Edmund Mulsho, Roger Eyton and

* He had set out from Westminster on 1 February.

others held the town in arms from 10 February to 3 March. Between 19 and 23 February other assemblies numbered in hundreds declared their support for York in Cambridge, Chelmsford, Hitchin, Grantham, Stamford and Fotheringhay. A number of risings occurred at various places in Somerset and Devonshire at the same time. The last of these demonstrations was in Hereford on 3 March. In most of these towns either York or Devon was the local overlord. Hereford was an exception. Here the rising seems to have been organised by York's retainer, Sir Walter Devereux of Weobley, who had skilfully exploited the unrest of the unfranchised tradesmen against the civic oligarchy.*

The so-called assemblies in Yeovil and Ilminster on 19 February were in fact Devon's army as it advanced to meet York. The Devonshire men charged with rebellion on the following day do not appear to have joined their earl; some, indeed, were driven back at Sampford Peverell by Bonville, who took an active – and interested – part in the suppression of the revolt in this part of the country. None of those later indicted, however, either here or elsewhere, were charged with any more serious act of treason than announcing their readiness to assist York, Devon and their forces in Kent. They were not accused of going after the duke to join his army.[13] The purpose of these local risings is therefore by no means obvious. Possibly the original plan had been that these men should reinforce York and they had been thwarted by the unexpectedly rapid movement of the king's forces into the midlands; these were at Northampton on 22 February,[14] and thus ready to oppose any attempt by York to reach his adherents in the east midlands.

The revolt however had been planned by former members of York's general staff in France. Presumably the first object of their battle plan had been the junction of York and Devon, and this would have precluded an eastward march to collect forces in Northamptonshire and Lincolnshire. The organisers would also have aimed to secure lines of communication for their own benefit and to hamper the movements of the royal army and its reinforcements. This was probably the first purpose of the risings in the east midlands and at Hereford. The rising at Chelmsford, however, indicates a different objective, for there could be no question of York going out of his way to recruit its militant artisans, nor did the town command any

* See Appendix V.

vital internal line of communication. The revolt here suggests that York's staff had considered the psychological effect of these local risings: they may well have thought that the court's resistance to York's open military demonstration would have been undermined when it learned that throughout the country urban centres were being held by York's professed adherents. The impact of such reports would certainly have been alarming had all the cities and towns solicited by the duke made declarations in his favour. What had been planned, in fact, was a widespread civil rebellion against Henry's government as well as an overt military revolt.

York had overestimated the strength of his appeal to the commons. In Kent, his miscalculations proved to be disastrous. Here he had hoped for the active assistance of those who had rallied to Cade, *alias* Mortimer, in 1450. The men of Kent did not stir, and instead of having a great gathering of Kentish men behind him, York was cornered, with the royal army and London blocking any retreat to his strongholds in the Welsh Marches. On 1 March the king's forces followed him, pitching their camp on Blackheath. The two armies were probably fairly well matched: York's was presumably the smaller, but he had the time to establish a good position behind the River Darent. It is questionable, however, if either he or the king's council had any desire for a military action. York's warlike attitude was apparently only part of a larger plan to intimidate the court by raising the country, and in this he had partially failed.

In the royal council, the conciliatory duke of Buckingham, and York's kinsmen the Neville earls of Salisbury and Warwick, would have spoken against any proposal for an immediate attack; since they had contributed more than half the strength of the king's army, their counsel could not be ignored by Somerset and others more hostile to York. Consequently the council opened negotiations and sent a delegation to York, both the Nevilles being members, as was another relative, Thomas Bourchier, bishop of Ely. York stood by his original purpose: Somerset should be placed under arrest and put on trial for his conduct in Normandy. Only if this demand was met would he dismiss his troops. The delegation agreed, and seemingly the king also gave his verbal assent. York's army then disbanded.

York was an honourable man, and he did not doubt the word of the king's envoys. But when he went into the king's tent, he encountered Somerset at his accustomed place beside Henry. It was not

Somerset, but York, who found himself detained as a prisoner. He was taken to London and confined to his house there. He had indisputably committed high treason by raising an army against the king, but the council as a whole was obviously reluctant to bring him to trial. Somerset and his other enemies may well have doubted if York's peers would convict him. He had consistently protested that it was not the king but Somerset who was the target of his attacks, and he had prepared a formidable list of charges giving details of Somerset's incompetence as lieutenant in France. A formal trial of York might well turn into a trial of Somerset. The royal envoys who saw York at Dartford had apparently been impressed by his arguments against Somerset; they had agreed that there was a case to be answered. Those councillors would certainly not have consented to any extreme measures being taken against York; having accepted his terms for the dismissal of his army, they would have damned their own fame had they pledged themselves only for the purpose of betraying York to the vengeance of his opponents. He was accordingly set free on 10 March after making a solemn affirmation of his loyalty to Henry in St. Paul's Cathedral.* His quarrel with Somerset was treated as a private matter and submitted to the arbitration of nine spiritual and temporal peers.[16]

King Henry's heart, reports the abbot of St. Albans, was now moved by the spirit of mercy to offer a general pardon† to all who required one.[17] In fact, 2,430 people did purchase the pardon in the following twelve months, among them York, Oldhall, and Bristol's audacious burgess, Thomas Young. But the pardon was not given as freely as the abbot had supposed it would be. York's adherents in Hereford, Stamford, Grantham and Hitchin did not benefit until the autumn, after they had been brought to trial. Neither the earl of Devon or Lord Cobham was able to obtain a copy.[18] Cobham was kept imprisoned in Berkhamsted Castle for at least two years,[19] and it is likely that Devon was detained for some time: he was formally charged with treason for his part in the rebellion and he had to wait two years for his trial and subsequent acquittal by the lords.[20] Nor

---

* The London chronicles said that York was released because of a report that his son was leading 10,000 Welshmen on London. The indictment of John Sharp (see note on p. 102 below) suggests the source of this information, but it is unlikely that the king's council was afraid of the ten-year-old Edward, earl of March.[15]

† General pardons are discussed in Appendix II.

did Oldhall's pardon save him from prosecution and forfeiture of his estates, and he thought it best to remain in sanctuary.[21]

Once again the king was taken on a tour to lend the dignity of his presence to the proceedings of the commissioners appointed to try those involved in the local risings. Setting out on 1 July, they reached Exeter on the 17th, then travelled northwards through Bristol, Gloucester, Hereford and Ludlow, where the court spent three days (12-14 August). This was no "domiciliary visit to the duke of York", with the kindly Henry dispensing goodwill and forgiveness,[22] for here in York's stronghold Somerset presided over the trials of his retainers and tenants, at least one of whom was subsequently hanged at Tyburn.* Having thus put the seal on York's humiliation, the court returned to London. The east midlands received a similar visitation in the autumn. The formal records of these sessions do not suggest that York's adherents were treated with the severity appropriate to charges of high treason. The purpose of these progresses was to enforce respect for the crown, not to punish. After their indictment before the commissioners, the offenders submitted to the king and received his pardon.†

The court's triumph was reflected in the next parliament, which met at Reading on 6 March 1453. It need not be supposed that the commons had been packed, although their readiness to take a lead from the government shows a spirit very different from that in the previous parliaments. It would seem that the members were fearful of the recent trend in public affairs: they had seen how narrowly the country had escaped civil war, and despite their general agreement with York's demands for good government they could not approve of the lengths to which he had pursued his quarrel with the court. Moreover, there were reasons for a more appreciative regard of the present administration. The last act of resumption had been enforced

---

* This was John Sharp. He was indicted at Ludlow for plotting in London on 6 March 1452 to bring forces from Wales to depose the king in favour of "him who was the rightful heir". Subsequently Sharp went to Ludlow, where he was involved in the killing of a yeoman of the king's chamber on 20 April. His victim was said to have been his wife's lover. As Sharp was hanged, and not drawn and quartered, he was presumably condemned for murder, not treason.[23]

† Thus those indicted at Hereford received general pardons within a few days. One chronicle alleges that Somerset ordered the execution of men pardoned by the king after they had knelt before Henry in the snow. The author's persistent "Yorkist" bias makes the statement highly suspect, and since these proceedings took place in the summer the climatic detail is obviously fanciful.[24]

and was bearing some fruit. What is more, an English army was again in France and Bordeaux had been recovered, and a fleet had been raised for safeguarding English vessels from pirates. The commons were therefore disposed to assist rather than criticise the government. They chose a speaker agreeable to the court, and granted the crown subsidies and a force of 20,000 archers for six months' service "for the defence of the kingdom". The last concession, it has been suggested, could only have been made "in contemplation of civil war", but this seems most improbable as the communities providing these troops were to have four months' warning to make them available.* The commons were more obviously furthering partisan ends in two of their petitions. They asked that crown grants made to "any person or persons . . . that were assembled in the field at Dartford" against the king should be revoked, and that Sir William Oldhall should be attainted for his traitorous conduct in aiding and advising these people as well as Jack Cade and other Kentish rebel leaders.[26]

Thus in the summer of 1453 Richard of York was utterly isolated. He had lost the goodwill of the country gentry who provided the house of commons with its more active members. The people of south-east England had turned a deaf ear to his appeal: the average townsman or peasant was not prepared, now or later, to let his political sympathies cause him to be involved in the dangerous quarrels of magnates. Politics, "the great business of the king and kingdom", was the concern of the lords alone. Even the shire knights in parliament did not want any position in government for themselves. They wanted "good and abundant governance", but the responsibility to give it belonged to the king and his councillors, among whom the lords could be trusted to act as guardians of the true interests of the nation. As for the lords, York's small following among their ranks had disappeared. Cobham, probably Devon as well, were in prison, while Norfolk had abandoned him.† The latter, indeed, was even appointed to one of the commissions to try York's

---

* A suggestion that the counties should raise archers for the French war had been made by the lords in the parliament of February 1449. Commissions to organise the raising of the archers (the total had been reduced to 13,000) were in fact issued in December 1457, when French naval activity was threatening the south coast.[25]

† The king gave him £200 and a gold cup in recognition of his good services, on 26 May 1452.[27]

adherents, and among his colleagues were the earls of Warwick and Worcester and Lord Cromwell.[28] These men were to become York's allies, but at present they stood behind the crown and upheld its authority against the perils of civil war. Even at this time there was no such thing as a "Yorkist party". The duke was banished to private life; on 6 March 1453, his lieutenancy of Ireland was taken from him and given to the courtier earl of Wiltshire.[29] But the magnates whose loyalty to the crown had frustrated his schemes were divided among themselves over personal issues. In northern England the quarrel of its two greatest families was approaching a climax. With this new development, and the simultaneous collapse of the king's sanity, York's position was completely transformed.

VII

Richard Neville and the West March

"People born near the sun in southern or eastern climes have less blood than others, for they are the more dried up by the sun, and so their physique is more delicate, and in consequence they are less fit to fight their enemies at close quarters." With this quotation from Vegetius' *De Re Militari*, the learned Abbot Wheathampstead accounted for the victory of the north country men at the second battle of St. Albans. Likewise in the first battle outside his cloister, victory went to the northerners because their opponents were effeminate, more like Paris than Hector in their bearing.[1] The superiority of the northerners in arms does not require an explanation drawn from a Roman work of the fourth century A.D. The forces which triumphed at these two battles did not owe their military qualities so much to the climatic rigours of their native soil as to the conditions in which they and their ancestors had lived in the last century and a half. Ever since Edward I had attempted to impose his suzerainty over Scotland, northern England had known no peace. Full-scale wars were infrequent, but with no lasting settlement ever concluded between the two kingdoms their border subjects engaged in incessant strife. The two kings appointed wardens to defend their marches and restrain their subjects from violating official truces. The borderers, however, did not depend on their governments for protection nor did they pay over much regard to their treaty obligations in the quest for plunder. Every landowner built his own little fortress, a stone pele tower where he and his dependants could take refuge during enemy raids. The condition of life in the Border counties demanded constant vigilance and a skill in arms essential to defend one's home and to ride in pursuit of marauders and recover losses at the expense of their fellow countrymen.

The qualities which made the men of the Border hardy warriors also made them difficult subjects. Accustomed to reliance on their own efforts in self-defence, they were little inclined to obey a king who was unable to protect them; with robbery, arson and man-slaughter the constant hazards of daily life, they had little respect for the laws of their own land. The problem of keeping order in the north remained with English governments until the end of the sixteenth century. These districts were too distant from the capital to be ruled directly. The three hundred miles from London to Carlisle required a journey of several days, possibly as much as two weeks,* and, even today, severe winters can make the major roads from the south and east impassable. The Norman kings chose to delegate responsibility for ruling border counties, creating franchises of which the Bishopric of Durham and the lordships of Tynedale, Redesdale and Hexhamshire survived in the fifteenth century. In Cumberland and Westmorland the territorial lords enjoyed less extensive liberties but some retained a number of legal privileges: the Cliffords, for instance, were hereditary sheriffs of Westmorland, and the sheriff of Cumberland was not permitted to act in the honour of Cockermouth. The legacy of a policy of government by delegation was the enhancement of the authority of the local lords over their tenants. This posed an even more serious problem for the central government than the lawlessness of the north. The northern mag-nates were formidable obstacles to royal authority for it was they, not the king, who commanded the devotion of these unruly people. From the twelfth to the sixteenth centuries, the most dangerous rebellions began in the north.

The gap between lords and other tenants-in-chief of the crown was probably deeper in Cumberland than in most other English counties. In 1429, when an inquisition was held into the number of knights' fees in the county, it was reported that only two crown tenants under baronial rank held as much as half a knight's fee; all other land held directly from the king was divided into properties so small that the duties owed to him were less than a quarter of the

* A royal warrant of 1447 described Cumberland as a "far country".[2]

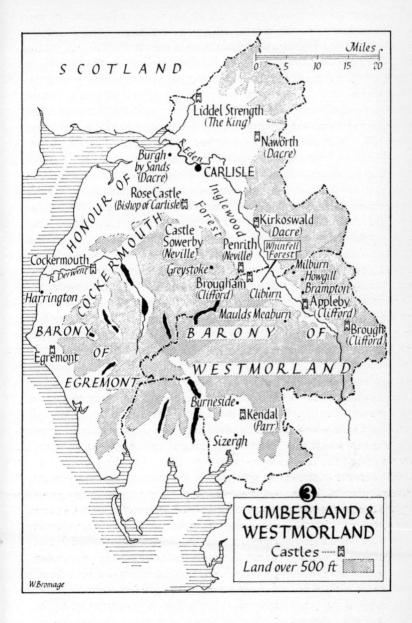

Miles
0   5   10   15   20

SCOTLAND

Liddel Strength
(The King)

Naworth
(Dacre)

Burgh
by Sands
(Dacre)

R. Eden

CARLISLE

Rose Castle
(Bishop of Carlisle)

Inglewood Forest

HONOUR OF

Kirkoswald
(Dacre)

Castle
Sowerby
(Neville)

Penrith
(Neville)

Whinfell
Forest

COCKERMOUTH

Cockermouth

R. Derwent

Greystoke

Milburn
Howgill

Brougham
(Clifford)

Cliburn

Brampton
Appleby
(Clifford)

Harrington

Maulds Meaburn

BARONY

OF

BARONY

OF

Brough
(Clifford)

Egremont

WESTMORLAND

EGREMONT

Burneside

Kendal
(Parr)

Sizergh

③
CUMBERLAND &
WESTMORLAND
Castles ····· ⌂
Land over 500 ft

W. Bromage

service of a knight. Society was dominated by a few great houses. Foremost were the Percies, whose castle at Cockermouth was the centre of an honour comprising most of the western half of the plain between Carlisle and the sea to Caldbeck and Uldale on the northern fells of Lakeland, and also embracing Bassenthwaite, Buttermere and Loweswater. Henry Percy, earl of Northumberland, also shared the castle and barony of Egremont, which included Wastwater and Eskdale, with the first countess of Westmorland and Lord Harrington; Sir Richard Huddleston was their sub-tenant for the whole lordship. Lord Dacre of Gilsland held the barony of Burgh-by-Sands and the districts around his castles at Naworth and Kirkoswald to the east and south-east. Baron Greystoke was the only other prominent tenant-in-chief[3] with the wide tract of fell country between Saddleback and Ullswater as his patrimony. He would have been a less substantial figure without his lands in Yorkshire, where his principal residence was Henderskelfe, now long buried under the gardens of Castle Howard. The Dacres also had lands outside Cumberland, while the Percy estates in Northumberland, Yorkshire, Sussex and several other counties made their lord one of England's foremost peers. Lord Clifford held the northern portion, the "barony" of Westmorland, with castles at Appleby, Brougham and Brough; he likewise had property elsewhere, notably in Worcestershire and Yorkshire, where Skipton Castle was his chief stronghold. Southern Westmorland – the barony of Kendal – was divided: half was held by John, duke of Bedford, until 1435, and was granted to John Beaufort, duke of Somerset, in 1443; the remainder was split between the Parrs, who occupied Kendal Castle, and the Lumleys, a Durham family which had forfeited its baronial rank by rebellion against Henry IV.

At the beginning of the century, the Percies' supremacy on the Border had been confirmed by the appointment of the earl of Northumberland as warden of the west march and of his son Hotspur as warden of the east march.[4] The office of warden had originally been established to provide the Border counties with military guardians, but political developments in the reign of Richard II led to the conversion of the office into a most desirable prize for ambitious nobles. Wardens were from this time engaged for a term of years at rates of payment higher than any other royal officer in England received. The annual salary of the warden of the west march was

£1,500 in times of truce and £6,000 in wartime, in return for which he undertook to defend Carlisle at his peril and do his best to protect the march, that is, Cumberland north of the River Derwent and the barony of Westmorland. The wages of the warden of Berwick-on-Tweed and the east were double those of his western colleague. As a warden was allowed to decide how many troops he need employ, his opportunities for making a sizeable profit are obvious. Such troops as he did retain were his own men, not the king's, and the wardens of the marches were thus able to raise private armies at the crown's expense. It is clear that Richard II regarded the appointment of wardens as a valuable form of patronage, by which he could reward or hope to win a supporter. Although in wartime it was preferable to have as warden a magnate with estates, and thus tenants, in the march counties, in the more settled international situation prevailing in his last years Richard granted the wardenship of the west march to near relations without any private interests on the Border.

There is little doubt that the earl of Northumberland furiously resented the grant to royal kinsmen of an office to which he aspired. This feeling was probably his chief motive in joining Henry of Lancaster and helping him to seize the throne in 1399. Recovery of the west march was the price of his treason, and this Henry paid two months before his accession by a grant under the seal of the duchy of Lancaster. With Roxburgh added to Hotspur's wardenship of the east march, the Percies' hegemony on the Border was complete and guaranteed for ten years by indentures with Henry IV: it was to last for less than four. Hotspur was killed in rebellion in 1403 and his father was dismissed from his wardenship. Hotspur's son, the second earl of Northumberland, became warden of the east march in 1417 and held the office until 1434, and his son and heir was warden from 1440 to 1461. The wardenship of the west march, however, became the equally hereditary property of the Neville family, with the first earl of Westmorland (1403-14), his eldest son, John (1414-20), and another son, Richard, earl of Salisbury (1420-35, 1443-60), maintaining a continuity broken only when the last went to fight in France and Marmaduke Lumley, bishop of Carlisle, secured a grant for seven years by offering to accept reduced rates of payment.

Richard Neville was one of the outstanding political figures of his day, a man with solid qualities to match the eminence which birth

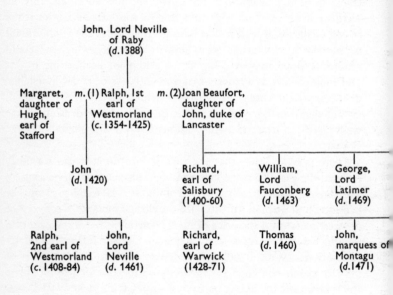

John, Lord Neville
of Raby
(d.1388)

Margaret,   m. (1) Ralph, 1st   m. (2) Joan Beaufort,
daughter of   earl of   daughter of
Hugh,   Westmorland   John, duke of
earl of   (c. 1354-1425)   Lancaster
Stafford

John   Richard,   William,   George,
(d.1420)   earl of   Lord   Lord
                      Salisbury   Fauconberg   Latimer
                      (1400-60)   (d. 1463)   (d. 1469)

Ralph,   John,   Richard,   Thomas   John,
2nd earl of   Lord   earl of   (d. 1460)   marquess of
Westmorland   Neville   Warwick   Montagu
(c. 1408-84)   (d. 1461)   (1428-71)   (d.1471)

* Actually the youngest of Ra■

ND PERCY

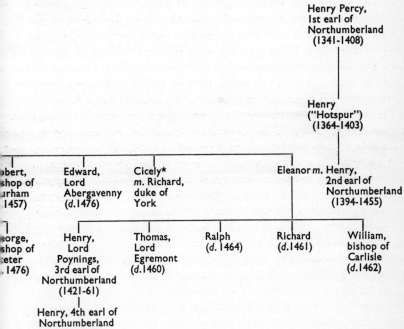

Henry Percy,
1st earl of
Northumberland
(1341-1408)

Henry
("Hotspur")
(1364-1403)

| obert, shop of urham 1457) | Edward, Lord Abergavenny (d.1476) | Cicely* m. Richard, duke of York | | Eleanor m. Henry, 2nd earl of Northumberland (1394-1455) |

| orge, shop of eter , 1476) | Henry, Lord Poynings, 3rd earl of Northumberland (1421-61) | Thomas, Lord Egremont (d.1460) | Ralph (d. 1464) | Richard (d.1461) | William, bishop of Carlisle (d.1462) |

Henry, 4th earl of
Northumberland
(c.1449-89)

d Joan's fourteen children.

and great estates assured him. As the father of Warwick "the King-maker", his reputation has long been overshadowed by the more spectacular achievements of his son. Richard inherited from his father the earl of Westmorland the role of Lancaster's watchdog in the north of England. The policy of using Neville to balance Percy had in fact been initiated by John of Gaunt, when he was Richard II's lieutenant in the marches. The Lancaster-Neville association had been confirmed by the marriage of Earl Ralph to Gaunt's daughter, Joan Beaufort, and its strength was proved when the earl supported Henry's bid for the crown and played a major part in defeating the rebellions of the Percies and Archbishop Scrope. The union was also remarkably fruitful in its domestic consequences. Ralph already had nine children by his first wife and Joan gave him fourteen more. Richard was the eldest of the second family, and shortly after his birth Ralph provided for him by settling a large part of his estates, principally in the North Riding of Yorkshire, on Joan and her children by Ralph. He was able to do more by exploiting his connec-tion with the royal house and its debts for his services. No family ever made as many desirable marriages in a single generation: four sons became peers in right of their wives, while several daughters were married to prominent nobles. As firstborn, Richard naturally made the best match, to the daughter and, eventually, sole heiress of the earl of Salisbury. A proper balance was maintained by assigning one of the youngest, Robert, to the Church; he began to collect benefices before entering his 'teens until, at the early age of twenty-three, he inevitably received a bishopric.

Henry V chose Richard Neville as warden of the west march in 1420. At twenty, Richard probably already had a few years' military experience and he must have shown a capacity for command. He now became one of the most influential men in northern England, for at the same time he was appointed a justice of the peace in Cumberland, Westmorland and Durham. In addition, he was called upon to serve on embassies to negotiate with the Scots. His private standing was improved when his mother made a grant to him, for the term of his life, of the lordships of Middleham (Yorkshire) and Penrith (Cumberland) at the favourable annual rent of £400.[5] In 1429, he succeeded to the title and estates of earl of Salisbury. The lands of his wife's inheritance gave him a revenue of at least £1,240 *per annum*[6] to add to the £1,250 he drew for his salary as warden.

The wardenship did not demand Richard's full-time service and his brother George, Lord Latimer, was engaged as lieutenant while he was in London attending parliament and the king's council. Salisbury attended the king when he went to be crowned in France in 1431, taking a retinue of 800 men. After his return, he undertook the command of the east march as well, for one year, and then, in 1435, resigned both wardenships when his contracts expired. In the following year, Salisbury made an indenture with the king to serve in France with the duke of York, his brother-in-law, and take a contingent of 1,300 men-at-arms and archers.[7]

Salisbury was back in England in the autumn of 1437, attending meetings of the king's council; he was appointed a member, with a salary of £100, on 13 November. Early in the following year, he was asked to become a warden, presumably of the east march, where the then warden was due to retire on 31 March.[8] This offer Salisbury refused: he was too deeply involved in family affairs which later led to the assembly of "great routes and companies upon the field". The first earl of Westmorland's provision for Joan Beaufort and her children had been made at the expense of John Neville, his son and heir by his first wife. John had died in 1420 and his son Ralph, the second earl, did not come of age until 1429, when he entered a patrimony shorn of the bulk of the great Yorkshire estates and throughout charged with providing Joan with a third part as her dower. Ralph not unreasonably wished to upset a settlement which was both disastrous to him and contrary to the established rule of descent by primogeniture.

The king's council made continuous efforts to induce the two branches of the Nevilles to settle their differences by arbitration. From 1430 to 1441 they were from time to time constrained to make bonds to refrain from entering each other's lands except by process of law. With Salisbury a member of the council, it is not likely that the earl of Westmorland put much faith in its impartiality. After the outbreak of violence in 1438, royal letters were sent ordering the opponents to keep the peace, but it was not until 1443, three years after Joan's death, that accord was reached. The settlement was very much in Salisbury's favour: Westmorland succeeded to nearly all Joan's dower, as was his due, but he was obliged to admit Salisbury's title to the lands she had held by her husband's gift and to grant Salisbury and two of his brothers annual pensions totalling nearly

£400, which they undertook not to claim as long as Westmorland
made no further attempts to reverse the settlement.⁹ Salisbury was
not subjected to a similar form of restraint, presumably because he
had convinced his colleagues in the king's council that Westmorland
was the aggressor.

He had already taken possession of the lands his mother had held
by Earl Ralph's grant. In 1441, he leased his castles of Sheriff Hutton
and Penrith, with five other manors in Yorkshire and Cumberland,
to his uncle Cardinal Beaufort and a group of his own retainers;
the lease was for three years, at an annual rental of 1,000 marks
(£666 13s. 4d.).¹⁰ This was not the sum of his Neville lands: he still
retained Middleham Castle and other Yorkshire estates. The king
had also given him the third part of Egremont, which Joan held for
life, although he was not permitted to succeed to her life-interest in
Liddel Strength, on the Scottish Border.¹¹ The total value of Salisbury's lands at this time cannot have been much less than £3,000 *per
annum*; only a handful of bishops and secular peers had more. He
lived in great state, with a large household which included eight
domestic chaplains.¹² In December 1443, he again became warden
of the west march, a grant he had secured four years earlier by
petitioning the king. As Bishop Lumley was serving for £1,050 *per
annum*, Salisbury offered to take only £1,000. He wanted the
wardenship for ten years, from as soon as the bishop would give it
up. The king's council granted the ten-year term, but beat the salary
down to £983 6s. 8d. and rejected Salisbury's request for another
£200 to repair Carlisle Castle. He had obtained the longest grant
made of a wardenship since 1399, when the Percies were given ten-
year terms. For many years, successive governments had shown that
they considered these long grants to be undesirable, and indeed it was
dangerous to give extensive tenures of important and lucrative
offices. Lumley had shown the way to reverse this policy by exploiting the crown's financial weakness. He held on to the office to the
end of his seven-year term.

In 1443, Salisbury also received a grant to himself and his heirs of
the office of justice of the royal forests north of Trent; in Cumberland,
this gave him charge of Inglewood Forest. In Westmorland, he held
the office of steward of Kendal, presumably of the "Beaufort fee";
as this belonged now to the king's ward, Margaret, the young
daughter of the late duke of Somerset, the office made Salisbury a

leading figure in southern Westmorland. In 1445, he was granted various revenues in the honour of Richmond to compensate for the surrender of a church in his wife's inheritance, another useful addition to his northern interests.[13] Salisbury knew how to exploit his standing as a trusted and valued officer of the crown. His close kinship to Cardinal Beaufort, the king's banker, was also a profitable asset. He was, in fact, an intimate associate of the faction in control of the royal government, as was revealed by his presence in the party which arrested Humphrey of Gloucester in 1447.[14]

Salisbury was equally successful in pulling the strings of family affection in Durham, where Bishop Robert Neville was persuaded to consider his extensive temporalities as a suitable source for the further enrichment of his brothers. Richard was given a pension of £100; Thomas, and after him William, were stewards of the Bishopric, George, chamberlain, and John his deputy; and all five regularly assisted their episcopal kinsman by serving on his commissions of the peace, assize and array. In addition, Salisbury had acquired the custody of Barnard Castle, thus gaining command of another route over the Pennines.[15] While Robert lived, the Bishopric was as much part of Salisbury's empire as the west march, and with his estates, justiciarship of the forests and stewardship of Pontefract (since 1425), the earl was a dominant figure in Yorkshire also. Wherever he could, he tried to ensure that the various offices forming this powerful concentration should become part of his heir's patrimony. His greatest coup was in the west march: in 1446, the king granted the office to Salisbury and his son Richard, or whichever of them lived the longer, for twenty years from 1453.

Neville had by now converted the wardenship from a lucrative and honourable office into a principal buttress of his dynastic policy. When he first became warden in 1420, his position in the march was by no means comfortable, for more than half the lands there were held by the closely linked houses of Percy, Clifford and Dacre. The Nevilles' only territorial footholds were the manors of Penrith and Castle Sowerby and, until 1440, Liddel Strength. A warden's commission empowered him to call out all men of military age to serve under him whenever invasion threatened, but without the goodwill of their lords he could be seriously hampered; his march jurisdiction could likewise be obstructed. Yet from the first years of his wardenship Richard Neville began to entrench himself as if he meant to stay.

His mother gave him a lease of Penrith and he made it his personal headquarters. As warden he was of course captain of Carlisle Castle, but the city was too close to the frontier: it could quickly be cut off by a Scottish force. Penrith, on the Westmorland border, served better as a base and was useful as a centre for gathering reinforcements. A sizeable market town, it lay on the Roman road from the south-east to Carlisle, and although it had occasionally been sacked by the Scots, its less exposed position led the royal justices of assize and gaol delivery to prefer to hold their sessions there in times of hostilities.[16]

Neville's possession of Penrith was an important asset, and he improved it by building a castle,* one of the last private fortresses to be raised in England. Penrith Castle is a small version of the compact style of castle built by the northern magnates in the later middle ages, with a high wall embracing all the domestic offices, and which dispensed with the earlier-favoured curtain wall and turrets. As far as the defence of the English border was concerned, Penrith Castle was superfluous, for the Cliffords' greater fortress at Brougham, less than two miles away on the farther bank of the Eamont, still commanded the main road to the south. The square red sandstone ruins of Penrith Castle are as much a monument to the divisions of fifteenth-century England as a reminder of her wars with Scotland; while those who saw it being built would have adduced that Richard Neville intended his family to be a permanent power in the west march.

The financial value of the wardenship was considerable, even though the Exchequer was often unable to pay the warden's wages as they fell due. When Neville went to France in 1436, the government, as a special concession, arranged for arrears of £1,100 to be paid. His employment of this money shows how little he had been embarrassed by the Exchequer's failure to give him full regular payment, for the arrears were not required to pay his soldiers' wages: £250 went to pay a debt to his brother Fauconberg and £750 to the earl of Warwick as part of the cost of purchasing from him the marriage of his daughter to Salisbury's son.[18] There is a more specific indication of the margin of profit the wardenship yielded. In 1457, Salisbury and his son Richard, as joint wardens, engaged a second son, Thomas, as their lieutenant to hold Carlisle Castle and defend

---

* Penrith Castle is not mentioned in the survey of Neville's father's lands in 1425 and the earliest reference to it appears to be one of 1437.[17]

the marches when necessary. His annual wages in time of peace or truce were to be £333 6s. 8d. and in wartime £500. The wardens' salary from the Exchequer was then £1,250 *per annum* or double this figure in wartime, and in addition they estimated their annual receipts from the local perquisites of the office at £66 13s. 4d. Thomas, in fact, was to carry out the wardens' duties for less than a quarter of their official salary. Their profit was a real one, for since Salisbury resumed the office in 1443 his payment had been secured on regular sources of crown income, so that instead of receiving tallies,★ which might have been worthless, to meet wages as they fell due, he could collect his money from the assigned sources on fixed days without prior application to the Exchequer. In 1459, this arrangement for "surety of payment by patent" was described as a special favour, "not accustomed before".[19] He was certainly very much better treated than the warden of the east march, who was not given a similar concession and was owed two and a half years' wages by 1455 and apparently received nothing at all between then and 1459.

The financial aspect of a wardenship was a secondary consideration. The office was even more valuable for the opportunity it gave the warden to raise a personal following among the best natural source of fighting men in the country. In his long period of office, Salisbury attracted to his service a valuable number of men living in the two counties of his march. His success in this field may be considered as a classic example of "bastard feudalism", for he had to overcome the handicap of having a very small landed interest in the district: the men who came to regard him as their "good lord" and protector were not his tenants. His position as warden helped in developing these relationships, for some who served under him against the Scots may have been won by respect for his martial qualities, or by the liberality or charm he may have displayed. A more potent attraction, however, was his undeniable ability to "maintain" his clients, through both his private resources and his good standing with the king's council.

Salisbury's opportunity to build a party among the ranks of the landed gentry was provided by their own divisions. All over England men were seeking the patronage of influential magnates who could "maintain" them in their quarrels as the ordinary course of the law

★ Explained on p. 52, note.

failed to provide justice or protection. Nowhere did it appear more ineffectual than in the counties of the marches towards Scotland which were so far distant from the capital. An instance is known of a Westmorland litigant who had difficulty in avoiding his enemies when he went to Westminster to present a petition to the chancellor. A few such petitions from Cumberland and Westmorland do survive from the first forty years of the century,[20] but after about 1440 resort to Chancery appears to have ceased. The same is true of criminal proceedings in the court of King's Bench: the Border counties are almost entirely unrepresented in its records. An itinerant royal commission of assize and gaol delivery was sent to visit the northern counties every summer, and it held sessions in Newcastle-upon-Tyne, in Carlisle five days later, and in Appleby on the second day following. Only a handful of prisoners, usually cattle-thieves, would be produced before them. In some years,* the justices abandoned their visits to Carlisle and Appleby because of the state of war with Scotland.[21] It would be absurd to attribute the dearth of legal records concerning the district in the middle years of the century to a blissful absence of strife, for the earlier evidence indicates that in the Eden valley the legal bonds of society were already wearing dangerously thin. There are tales of bands of armed men, one or two hundred strong, trampling down corn "as if they were making a foray into Scotland in time of war" or laying siege to houses in attempts to kill their occupants. We must not be too ready to accept the complaints of litigants at face value, but the incidence of a group of alleged misdemeanours in a limited area, in this case the vicinity of Appleby, does at least suggest that the relations of the closely neighbouring families concerned were hardly cordial. There were, moreover, at least two feuds in which certain of the stages are known to have been accepted as proven by contemporaries; they are also significant as illustrations of the strain placed on the local administration of the law.

There were in northern Westmorland a number of offshoots of the former baronial house of Lancaster of Kendal. The most substantial of these branches in Henry V's time was headed by Sir John, tenant of the Cliffords in Milburne and other manors, for many years a justice of the peace and twice a knight of the shire in parliament. The second time he was at Westminster, John Lancaster reported a narrow

* 1449 and 1455-7.

escape from assassination in the summer of 1421, when he was visiting Roland Thornburgh's widow at Mauld's Meaburn. Five sons of William Thornburgh then came to the house with the worst intentions, bringing with them swords and Carlisle axes, those indispensable instruments of north-country homicide. These weapons they hid under their beds in the chamber where they were to spend the night with Sir John, but he was able to frustrate their plan to kill him as he slept. The Thornburghs next took some of Lancaster's cattle and in September disturbed a session of the peace at Appleby, effectively threatening the jury with death if any charges were made against them.[22] Sir John died in the following year and his estates were divided among his four daughters, one of whom brought to her husband, Robert Crackenthorpe, the manor of Howgill.[23]

Crackenthorpe became a justice of the peace for Westmorland in 1424, and for ten years his life passed without any notable recorded incident. Then he and his colleagues, Hugh Salkeld and Sir Christopher Moresby, had to intervene in an ugly private fracas. Dame Katherine Lancaster had a disagreement with John Cliburn, a modest freeholder, and she enlisted the support of a number of the local gentry, among them Sir Henry Threlkeld and William Thornburgh. A large force was collected and led to Cliburn's house at Cliburn for a dawn attack. Cliburn was still holding out at midday, after a thousand arrows "or more" had been fired, and the justices then came and persuaded Dame Katherine to call off the siege. She continued to persecute Cliburn and eventually had him imprisoned.[24] It was probably these disturbances which prompted the county magistrates to hold a special enquiry into recent breaches of the peace. Crackenthorpe, as a member of the quorum, was present at this session in Appleby. It was abortive, for Threlkeld and Thornburgh intimidated the jurors so that they were afraid to speak the truth about the riots. Dame Katherine was incensed against Crackenthorpe for holding this investigation, and with her husband Sir John planned with William Thornburgh and other members of their families to kill him as he made his way homeward through Whinfell Forest. He escaped, but by continuing their attempts against his life his enemies prevented him from holding any more sessions. Crackenthorpe's plea to the lord chancellor to take measures against his enemies did not save him, and in August 1438 he was killed at Brampton, Westmorland. The Lancasters and Thornburghs maintained the quarrel against his widow, taking her cattle and burning a barn full of corn.

These events were confirmed by a commission of enquiry appointed by Chancery, but the ringleaders once more suffered no penalty. William Thornburgh was dismissed from the commission of the peace, to which he had surprisingly been appointed in 1437, but in 1442 he obtained a royal pardon from all charges of murder and felony. His sons Roland and Oliver persuaded the king that they were innocent of Crackenthorpe's murder and that their indictment for it was procured by malice; they were pardoned in 1443. The Thornburghs probably owed their escape from justice to Salisbury's mediation, for in 1454 the earl described William as his servant.[25] There was, however, more to this quarrel than Crackenthorpe had suggested: it was not only his zeal as a justice that roused his enemies. That the Thornburghs had a long standing feud with the lord of Howgill was shown by Sir John Lancaster's petition in 1421. The enmity of the second Sir John Lancaster and his formidable wife doubtless arose from similarly private causes: it is likely that they had a claim to the Howgill property, and their continuation of the quarrel against Crackenthorpe's widow, another Lancaster, seems to bear this out. If it is true that Salisbury "maintained" the Thornburghs, we can attribute to this feud one reason for the Crackenthorpes becoming staunch "Lancastrians"; two members of the family were killed at Towton.

Shortly after Robert Crackenthorpe's death, there was an outburst of violence in the southern half of the county. Here the protagonists were Sir Thomas Parr and Henry Bellingham. Bellingham was the first to complain to Chancery: he said that Parr brought a great "multitude of people" to destroy his house at Burneside but was diverted "through treaty of good gentlemen of the same country". Parr continued to menace Bellingham, and was in a very advantageous position, being deputy sheriff to Lord Clifford, and "the coroners of the same shire be his menial men". Bellingham thus had no hope of redress at common law and asked the chancellor to have Parr dismissed from office. This was not done, for it did not lie in the chancellor's power to choose Lord Clifford's deputy. Bellingham's family now sought their own remedy. When Parr was in London in 1446 to represent Westmorland in parliament, Robert and Thomas Bellingham, with three servants, made a murderous attack on him as he was leaving his lodgings in the city. The house of commons regarded this as an affront to their body and petitioned the king for stern measures. A proclamation was issued to cite the would-be assassins to King's Bench, threatening that if they failed to appear they would be attainted felons, and that they would not be allowed the benefit of any royal pardon or letters of protection. The Bellinghams later said that they were so alarmed by the tone of this proclamation that they dared not come to stand their trial. Three years later, although he was presumably an attainted felon, Thomas Bellingham was elected to parliament by the Westmorland free-holders. He reported that his family and Parr now "be accorded" and he successfully petitioned in parliament for a pardon.[26]

The reconciliation was not lasting, and the Parr-Bellingham quarrel does much to explain Parr's future career. His grandfather William had been a landless younger son in the service of John of Gaunt; a valiant warrior, he must have owed his marriage to the heiress of Kendal Castle to the good offices of his master.[27] We have already seen that Thomas enjoyed the confidence of Lord Clifford, but he became a stout supporter of the earl of Salisbury and later of Edward IV; after being attainted for his part in the skirmish at Blore Heath in 1459, he gave services amply rewarded in his own lifetime and thus laid the foundation for his family's high rank in the sixteenth century. Henry Bellingham became no less prominent in the "Lancastrian" camp.

If the accounts of these two Westmorland feuds tell us anything, it is that by 1440 application to the central courts was entirely useless, and that the local judicial machinery commanded little or no respect. As the Tudors realised, local government had to be entrusted to the county families, but the crown had to keep tight control over their operations. Without strong central restraint – and backing when required – private interests too easily perverted the administration of justice. How, then, was society saved from complete anarchy in Henry VI's later years? We can trace one or two indications that alternative methods of settling private disputes were adopted in the counties of the west march. It is an outstanding feature of a number of collections of family records that almost every one contains an arbitration award dating from the middle years of the fifteenth century.[28] Thus Sir Thomas Harrington was called upon in 1447 to adjudicate between the Threlkelds and the Thornburghs. He firstly decreed "that rest and peace, full friendship, good love and true accord be had and kept among the said parties for all the said variances, quarrels and debates". Then he stated that the evidence he had seen proved that the Thornburghs owed a rent for certain property.[29] The issue was trifling and might easily, in happier times, have been settled in a court of law, but there is a suggestion that the parties had resorted to force before submitting their dispute to mediation. In another case, a petition was sent to the earl of Salisbury; this was from John Cliburn, after the attack on his house. Salisbury's court, whether as warden of the march or lord of Penrith is not clear, was used by some litigants to secure the enforcement of a bond for an hundred marks.[30] These scraps of evidence bring us back to the central theme of "maintenance". It was to the greater figures in their society that men turned for redress or mediation. Prudence demanded, as a form of insurance, that a small landowner should seek the patronage of a powerful lord.

There is no contemporary list of Salisbury's retainers in the west march, but two of his indentures with local men still exist. Before going to France in 1431, he engaged Sir Henry Threlkeld to accompany him with eight men-at-arms and twenty-two archers,[31] a temporary arrangement which suggests a more lasting understanding; as we have seen, Threlkeld on his return took part in dubious enterprises with William Thornburgh, who was a client of Salisbury. The second indenture was between Salisbury and Walter Strickland of Sizergh, who in return for a pension of £6 13s. 4d. paid from the revenues of Penrith, was retained "for term of his life, against all folk, saving his allegiance", and engaged to follow the earl in England and abroad, in peace and war. As Strickland could muster a total of 290 armed followers, he was a useful adherent. He was, however, by no means one of the most considerable tenants in Westmorland, and the size of his company hints at the county's wealth in reserves of manpower. This indenture was sealed in 1448, when Salisbury was preparing to defend the border, but Strickland's allegiance survived his patron's death: in 1461, he was appointed to a commission to arrest Edward IV's enemies in Westmorland.[32]

Some of Salisbury's other retainers can be identified from an unusual source. When he became chancellor, he admitted his clients to the customary privilege of Chancery officers of prosecuting their debtors in his court. Some prominent figures in Cumbrian society are accordingly described as "the chancellor's servants" in 1454. There was Ralph, Baron Greystoke, one of the poorer peers, but a useful adherent in Yorkshire as well as in Cumberland. Three esquires – Roland Vaux, John Skelton and Thomas de la More[33] – each represented Cumberland in various parliaments between 1449 and 1456, the last two serving twice. These three men each held the office of sheriff of Cumberland several times: the shrievalty was occupied by one of this trio in six of the ten years following 1443,[34] when Salisbury again became warden.

The lists of justices of the peace in the years 1454-71 shows that heads of other prominent Cumbrian families, such as Sir Richard Musgrave and Hugh Lowther, received commissions in the earlier years of this period, were dismissed when Richard of York and his associates were proscribed in 1459, and reappointed by Edward IV in 1461. These men were not "Yorkists" but Neville retainers, for they remained as justices after the restoration of Henry VI and were dismissed by Edward when he recovered the throne. On the other hand, the Parr and Huddleston families were more consistently loyal to York, but they were adherents of Salisbury in the 1450's. The great baronial families of the west march, the Cliffords, Dacres and Percies, were to fight against York, but they could not secure the loyalty of local society to the Lancastrian dynasty. Salisbury had won over an important section of the landed gentry. His control, through his retainers, of the shrievalty of Cumberland suggests that his influence here was comparable with that of the duke of Suffolk in East Anglia; whatever his other attractions were, this was a formidable reason for seeking his patronage. Inevitably, this local dominance by an "outsider" with little territorial interest in the Border country provoked opposition from the family with the greatest stake in the region.

VIII

"The Beginning of Sorrows"

The outbreak of war with Scotland in 1448 marked a turning point in the development of the Neville "interest" in the north-west. Hitherto there had been no hint of strain in the earl of Salisbury's relations with the great landed families of the English border counties. After a brief period of hostilities with the national enemy, however, there can be traced the first stages of a quarrel which had the direst consequences for England itself. While the Scots were giving fresh proofs of their "evil will, malice and untoward disposition",[1] the English magnates worked together to defend the Border. Salisbury and the earl of Northumberland's heir, Lord Poynings, both made forays into Scotland from their respective marches. Salisbury was supported in the west march by Lords Clifford, Dacre, Scrope of Bolton and FitzHugh; he engaged Dacre as his lieutenant to hold Carlisle.[2] There is a hint that Salisbury was not an ideal military commander in a royal letter thanking these peers for their services, for it states that he had been charged to confer with them and disclose the king's instructions that he was "to do that he goodly may to your ease and pleasure".[3] It would seem that Salisbury was too imperious to consult his colleagues. His age, probably, made him a less effective warrior, for Poynings came over from the east march to invade Dumfriesshire, where he was defeated and taken prisoner. The war came to an end on 11 August 1449.

With the war, a new figure appeared in Cumberland. Thomas Percy, the earl of Northumberland's second son, was born in 1422.

He epitomised the problem of the younger son, for no heiress was found for him and he became a charge on his father's estates, with pensions totalling £74 *per annum*.[4] Quarrelsome, violent and contemptuous of all authority, he possessed all the worst characteristics of a Percy for which his grandfather Hotspur is still a byword. He had already given proof of his mettle by gathering a band of ruffians whose misdeeds led to their being flung into gaol at York in 1447.[5] The Scottish war temporarily solved the problem of finding Thomas suitable employment. He was sent into Cumberland to look after the family estates and to lead their tenants against the Scots. He also received the king's thanks for these services and soon after the end of the war, on 16 November, he sought his reward in a petition that he should be raised to the peerage with the title of Baron Egremont. Henry granted this request and a pension of £10 from the royal issues in Cumberland.[6] Four years later, Egremont was told that the true reason for his creation as a peer was not gratitude for his past services, which were slight, but the king's expectations of his future conduct, particularly in keeping the peace and suppressing the disorderly.[7]

Egremont remained in the north-west after the conclusion of the treaty of truce with Scotland. Early in 1450, he was at Cartmel to mediate in a private quarrel which arose from the killing of a doe. A little later, he arbitrated between the widow and the heir of Sir Henry Threlkeld. On this occasion a list of witnesses was recorded: there were three knights – Thomas Curwen, John Pennington and William Martindale – and five esquires, among them Henry Bellingham and John Broughton.[8] These five men, at least, were Egremont's followers and drew pensions from the revenues of the honour of Cockermouth. The pensions were recent grants, part of a general policy of the earl of Northumberland to strengthen his following.[9] Egremont had been charged with the task of recruiting supporters in Cumberland. As tenants of the earl, Curwen and Pennington would have required little inducement to engage themselves; in the case of Henry Bellingham, whose estates were in southern Westmorland, the explanation for his seeking the patronage of the Percies is to be found in his feud with Thomas Parr. His choice of protector was to lead to his attainder by Edward IV in 1461. Another Bellingham became a member of Egremont's garrison at Cockermouth, as did Henry Kipping, also a Westmorland man by name, who was one of the gang imprisoned at York in 1447. One instance is known of this garrison's activities: they captured a man and held him in the castle for six months.[10]

Egremont's operations were an open challenge to the Neville "interest" in the west march. It is in this competition for influence, and possibly in a legacy of friction from the war of 1448-9, that we must look for the causes of this feud with his uncle Salisbury and the earl's sons John and Thomas Neville. The quarrel did not arise, as so many others did, from conflicting titles to land, for Egremont had none, and his father and elder brother were not at first principals in the conflict. Some differences may have arisen from the division of the barony of Egremont until Salisbury gave up his share in April 1449, seven months before Thomas Percy took his title from that lordship. The king had compensated the Nevilles for this surrender with a grant of land and the greater part of Richmond Castle, in Yorkshire, with the reversion of the remainder. There had been disorders in Cumberland before this arrangement was made, for a commission was appointed to enquire into treasons, unlawful gatherings and other felonies, on 6 May;[11] no record of its proceedings have been discovered.

The Percies' influence in the west march was augmented in 1452 when William, Egremont's brother, was appointed bishop of Carlisle, with a special dispensation from the pope as he was only twenty-four years of age.[12] While one may wonder what spiritual gifts this young prelate brought to his diocese, his family benefited by gaining control of Rose Castle, the episcopal seat. Bishop Percy's first year at Carlisle was marked by such "great dissensions, riots and debates" among various people in Cumberland "that one half of the shire was divided from that other". The sheriff, a protégé of Salisbury,[13] fell foul of Egremont, who swore that he would have his head, and sent some of his followers to waylay and assault him.[14] If this description of the state of Cumberland in 1453 is not too exaggerated, we might presume that Egremont had succeeded in grouping under his leadership all those who were at odds with the Nevilles and their adherents.

The scene of the feud was now transferred to Yorkshire, the Nevilles' home ground. With nearly fifty manors in the county, they were far stronger here than in Cumberland. Many of Salisbury's properties were scattered, but there were two large concentrations, Wensleydale and the lands centring on Middleham Castle, in the north-west, and a rich group round Sheriff Hutton, the great fortress eight miles north of York City. Four other manors lay along the Derwent to the east of York.[15] At this time, the estates of the Bishopric of Durham could be considered as Neville property, and in Yorkshire these consisted of Howdenshire in the south, Allertonshire in the north, and, near Sheriff Hutton, Crayke Castle, which Bishop Neville had recently rebuilt.[16] Salisbury's authority in the county had been further enhanced by royal patronage, to which he owed the offices of steward of Pontefract and justiciar of the northern forests. The Percy lands in Yorkshire were also considerable, although less extensive than the Nevilles'. Leconfield Castle near Beverley was one centre, another was Topcliffe, at the north end of the vale of York, but the largest compact group was in lower Wharfedale. The earl of Northumberland's principal Yorkshire residence was here, at Spofforth, an early fourteenth-century mansion more distinguished for domestic amenity than military strength. One of the manors of this estate, Healaugh, was Egremont's own headquarters.

Between Healaugh and Sheriff Hutton lay York City. It did not escape involvement in the conflict of its hostile baronial neighbours. Its internal affairs gave Egremont an opportunity to recruit followers and possibly even to gain control of the city. At this time York's principal industry, the manufacture of woollen cloth, was declining in the face of competition from the new centres in the West Riding. There had also been a sudden decrease in the foreign trade of the city's merchants, and records of smaller numbers of admissions of freemen and declining rents show that the 1450's were a period of growing hardship. There were, no doubt, many idle craftsmen ready to listen to Egremont's offers of employment. He was also assisted by the divided state of the city's society. Its most recent historian has observed dissension between the ruling oligarchy and unfranchised commons in the 1460's but has concluded, for want of evidence, that there was no such strife before this time.[17] The events of 1453 and 1454, however, give us cause to suspect that there was already a severe cleavage. Egremont's success in winning popular favour was presumably due in part to his exploiting the grievances of the lesser tradesmen and craftsmen against their civic rulers, who were inclined to sympathise with the Nevilles.★

Egremont did not attend the second session of the parliament of

★ For a similar development in Hereford, see Appendix V.

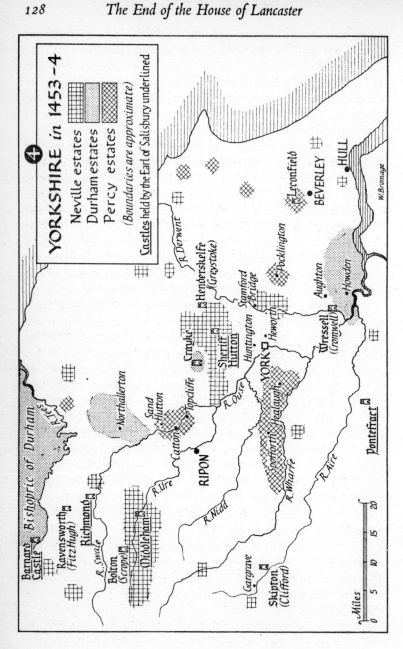

YORKSHIRE *in* 1453–4

Neville estates
Durham estates
Percy estates

(Boundaries are approximate)

Castles held by the Earl of Salisbury underlined

W. Bromage

Bishopric of Durham

R. Tees

Barnard Castle

Ravensworth (Fitz Hugh)

Richmond

R. Swale

Bolton (Scrope)

Middleham

Gargrave

Skipton (Clifford)

R. Nidd

R. Wharfe

R. Aire

R. Ure

Catton

RIPON

Northallerton

Sand Hutton

Thopcliffe

Crayke

Sheriff Hutton

Henderskelfe (Greystoke)

R. Derwent

Stamford Bridge

Huntington

Heworth

YORK

Spofforth (Healaugh)

Pontefract

Aughton

Howden

Wressell (Cromwell)

Pocklington

Leconfield

BEVERLEY

HULL

Miles
0   5   10   15   20

1453. He was at Healaugh on 12 May, distributing his livery of red and black to eight York tradesmen.[18] There was nothing very sinister in this, or, so far as is known, in his other activities at the time, but on 7 June the king sent him an order to come to him at once. To Henry's wonder and displeasure, Egremont paid no heed to this summons, or to a fresh order on 26 June. A third letter was sent on 7 July which indicates why he was sought: the king entreated Percy to enlist "to do us service of war" in Gascony, raise a retinue for this purpose, and come to the capital in all haste, promising that "you shall, with God's grace, receive payment soon after your said coming".[19] We can well believe that at least one member of the king's council, namely Salisbury, must have considered this an excellent idea. Once again, Egremont took no notice. A small contingent was in fact raised, but it never sailed. Gascony was irretrievably lost on 17 July, when the last English army was destroyed at Châtillon.

Meanwhile, the drift to a new war was gaining momentum in the north. John Neville, the best soldier in Salisbury's brood, had gone in pursuit of Egremont. Believing his quarry to be at Topcliffe, he went there on 29 June, but despite his threats of violence to the Percy tenants he was unable to find his enemy there.[20] This was three days after a letter had been sent to call John to the council to answer for the "divers things and novelties" against the peace occasioned by his dispute with Egremont.[21] Elsewhere in the county, at Sandal, Northumberland's retainer Sir John Salvin forcibly expelled Sir John Clarvaux's widow from the manor on 12 July.[22] That same day the government took action to deal with the deteriorating situation by appointing a commission of oyer and terminer to go into Yorkshire to try all cases of insurrection, felony and grants of livery. As if to ensure the commission's impartiality, the earls of Northumberland and Salisbury were put at its head. Although this commission was renewed on 25 July, the government was having second thoughts about the suitability of its leading members, and two days later an independent commission of three judges led by a councillor, Sir William Lucy, was appointed to investigate all reports of riots and other disturbances in Yorkshire, Northumberland, Cumberland and Westmorland. At the same time letters were sent to the two earls, urging them to do their utmost to disband their sons' followers and so prevent any fresh tumults. More letters were directed to Egremont, John Neville, and eight other knights and esquires, ordering them to keep the peace and co-operate with Lucy in his work of pacification; they were threatened with forfeiture of lands and goods if they disobeyed.[23] These letters also were to be solely of historic value. Far from being impressed, Egremont was now planning an assault more outrageous than any of his earlier misdeeds.

The last day on which the earl of Salisbury is known to have been in London this summer was 18 July, when he was present at the king's council.[24] He now went into Lincolnshire, to attend the marriage of his son Thomas at Tattersall Castle, Lord Cromwell's seat. The bride was Lady Willoughby, a well-dowered widow who was also one of Cromwell's nieces and heirs. She had been free for only a few months before this alliance was arranged and received the royal licence on 1 May.[25] The lady's private inclinations are unknown, but her timorous old uncle was anxious to gain a protector and Salisbury welcomed the opportunity of having another son amply provided for. We may imagine with what pride Ralph Cromwell conducted his guests through his new castle, pointing out the spaciousness of its apartments, the handsome, decorated fireplaces, and the broad windows. The Nevilles, for their part, would have thought how feebly Tattersall's brickwork splendour compared with the cliff-like masonry of Sheriff Hutton and the sturdy keep at Middleham behind its turreted curtain-wall.

As the bridal party set out for Sheriff Hutton, Lord Egremont prepared his own reception. He called together a large assembly of his followers, tenants of the Percy estates in Yorkshire, a score more from the honour of Cockermouth, and some like Thomas Crackenthorpe and Richard Bellingham from Westmorland who had no territorial association with the Percy family. He was joined by several knights who were family pensioners, John Salvin of Duffield and Henry Fenwick and John Pennington from Cumberland, and one most important ally, John Clifford,* the son of Lord Clifford of Skipton and Westmorland. Egremont was also able to call on a considerable following in York City, mostly members of the crafts, tailors, weavers, and the like. Nor was his assembly lacking in spiritual comforters: the rectors of Leathley and St. Wilfrid's, York, the vicars of Otley, North Cave and Middleton-in-Teesdale, three unbeneficed chaplains and a summoner came to do their part. Some of the York craftsmen met on 23 August and promised to follow

---

* Later known as "Butcher" Clifford.

Egremont and his brother Richard Percy as their captains, and on the following day John Burn of Bainton was sent to call out the Percy tenants. The combined force, said to be five thousand in number, assembled on Heworth Moor, on the north-east outskirts of York. Later that day Salisbury and his countess, Thomas and his bride, and John Neville, passed through the city and took the road northward to Sheriff Hutton. As they came to Huntington, Egremont and his army were waiting for them with the purpose, it was later alleged, of killing all five. Salisbury cannot have been unprepared and his retinue must have been formidable enough to make Egremont hesitate. There were altercations and threats, doubtless a fair amount of rough play,* but the Nevilles reached home without bloodshed.[27] It had been an ugly incident, and the one chronicler who recorded it regarded this encounter as the opening round of the civil wars.[28]

The tension was maintained in the two months following. Large bands of partisans of both families moved round the county, attacking their enemies' tenants and property: John Neville broke into Northumberland's house at Catton, smashing doors and windows; Richard Percy led some of Egremont's henchmen to Gargrave where they attacked the bailiff of Staincliffe in the parish church, pursued him over the altar, and would have killed him there had not the vicar, holding the Host, bade them desist; and Sir John Salvin with about fifty Percy tenants was passing through Aughton when some of his followers stole wine and other articles from the vicarage.[29] Salisbury moved on to Middleham and here the recorder of York and three of the city's legal counsel visited him on 28 September with a message from the mayor, who was attempting to mediate between him and Egremont. A second mission was sent to Middleham and then went to Spofforth to speak to Lord Poynings, Egremont's elder brother.[30] The archbishop of York, Bishop Neville of Durham and the earl of Westmorland also intervened, striving to appease the two factions.

Royal letters in identical terms were sent to Salisbury and Northumberland on 8 October, the king† telling each "that at all times before this you have been held [to be] a sad, a sober and a well ruled man, as it sitteth you in all wise so to be"; such a duty their high estate required of them "to the service and support of us in keeping

---

* One man who was injured sued Egremont and Richard Percy for damages of £66 13s. 4d., with what result is not known.[26]

† More nominally than ever, as Henry was then insane.

of our peace and of our laws". As members of his council, they had sworn to submit their disputes to the council. They had ignored letters ordering them to dismiss all gatherings of followers and indeed were known to have planned to make "the greatest assembly of our liegemen . . . that ever was made within this our land at any time that man can think". The earls were warned against carrying out these plans under pain of degradation from their rank. Letters in equally stern terms were also directed to Egremont and John Neville.[31] Neither party took any heed of these royal commands. The two families had assembled in strength and on 20 October their concentrations were complete, the Percies – Northumberland, his sons Poynings and Egremont, with Lord Clifford – at Topcliffe, and the Nevilles – Salisbury, Warwick, and their allies Lord Fitzhugh and Scrope of Bolton – at Sand Hutton,[32] only four miles distant, to the north. No estimate of numbers has been recorded, but if we recall that Egremont's forces were said to be five thousand strong in August, doubtless an exaggeration, and also consider the potential strength of Poynings in the east march and of Warwick on his estates in the midlands, it is not likely that either party had less than ten thousand men in the field. For at least three days they lay in such dangerous proximity, while the mayor of York's agent in Thirsk tried to discover Salisbury's intentions. Nothing happened. The enemies apparently agreed to call a truce and dismissed their forces. But there was no reconciliation; the day of reckoning had merely been postponed.

IX

The Genesis of "York"

When parliament was prorogued on 2 July 1453 to leave the lords free for their summer recreations and the commons to bring in the harvest, the chancellor announced that the king intended to visit various parts of the country in order to suppress maintenance, extortion, oppression, riots and other long standing evils.[1] It is most likely that the "north parts" were included in the proposed royal itinerary: most of the southern and midland counties had seen royal progresses in the two previous summers and the critical situation north of Trent obviously called for the strongest measures that the crown could attempt. The intended visitation did not take place, and the great northern families were not diverted from their particular choice of seasonal sport. Neville and Percy came to the brink of war, and though they parted without bloodshed there was no guarantee that a similar crisis might not again develop and bring about a real trial of strength. There was in this situation the most pressing danger, not merely to the society of northern England, but to the crown itself. The earl of Devon's dispute with Lord Bonville had led to his alliance with the duke of York and so to the military demonstration of 1452. If their quarrel persisted, either Northumberland or Salisbury would sooner or later come to associate himself with the court's chief opponent.

Before the autumn of 1453, it was still an open question which northern earl would take this step. York, no doubt, was Salisbury's brother-in-law, but so also was Northumberland. History would suggest Northumberland as York's natural ally. His father, the celebrated Hotspur, had denounced Henry IV's usurpation and perished in a scheme to put York's Mortimer uncle on the throne. In contrast, Salisbury's father and grandfather had been Lancaster's staunchest lieutenants in their conflicts with the Percies. The Lancaster-Neville accord had been ratified by marriage, and Salisbury was the first-fruit of that union. He was a kinsman of the king, therefore, and first cousin to the duke of Somerset. There was no reason to suppose that these links had worn thin. On the contrary, recent additions by the crown to Salisbury's authority and possessions bore witness to his remaining in favour, and his loyalty survived the crisis of 1452, when he brought a large contingent into the field against York. Salisbury was also a member of the king's council, although his attendance was infrequent owing to his commitments on the Border. On the other hand, there were no similar indications of Northumberland's standing at court. He had been appointed constable of England on 25 May 1450, but he was replaced by Somerset four months later.[2] He had not the Nevilles' success in tapping the king's bounty. While they had preferential treatment in the payment of their wages as wardens of the west march, his son, Lord Poynings, had to take his chance at the Exchequer for remuneration of his services in the east. Northumberland's name does not appear in the surviving lists of councillors. If he were called upon, he did not provide a contingent to the royal army in 1452. His unreliability, indeed, had been amply demonstrated in 1436, when he abandoned the defence of Berwick-upon-Tweed even though it was in immediate danger of Scottish attack, because his contract as warden had expired.[3] Chancellor Kemp had his own reasons for distrust, for he had accused Northumberland of organising attacks on his Yorkshire tenants in 1443.[4]

It was not however the heads of the two families who were to determine their allegiance. Salisbury's son and heir, the earl of Warwick, had become a member of the king's council in 1450 and his name appears among the lists of witnesses to royal charters* up to 20 June 1452.[5] He brought forces to the army facing York at Dartford and on 6 July he was appointed to one of the ensuing commissions to try York's supporters.[6] He was not similarly employed

---

* These "witnesses" were not necessarily present when a charter was granted but the inclusion of their names indicates that they were members of the council at the time.

again for nearly two years after this, nor is he shown as a member of the council or as a witness to charters in the same period. This negative evidence suggests that Warwick had disassociated himself from the court. In fact, he had quarrelled with Somerset. Somerset was no magnate in his own right* and, like Suffolk, he did not scruple to augment his fortune by the opportunities his position allowed him. According to a contemporary French observer, Somerset's character was marred by extreme avarice.[8] He joined in a suit to deny Neville the "Warwick" chamberlainship of the Exchequer, and he may have gone further, to scheme the annexation of some of the earl's lands to his own wife's inheritance: this is far from certain, a possible interpretation of some ambiguous royal letters, but Warwick had some cause to suspect his intentions.

Then, in 1453, Somerset obtained a royal grant making him the custodian of lands in Glamorgan which Warwick already had in his charge.† Warwick instantly prepared to oppose this attempt to oust him. There were "great gatherings, congregations and assemblies unlawful" in Cardiff, and Cowbridge Castle was strongly manned "as it were in land of war". Somerset and Warwick were cited before the king on 21 July and ordered to surrender the disputed lands to a temporary keeper until the council could determine who was entitled to have their custody. When the council gave this order in writing, Somerset was one of the six members present,‡ and the keeper they chose was Lord Dudley, the treasurer of the king's household.[9] Yet another quarrel of great lords had thus developed to the brink of private war, and once again one of the contestants had ample reason to believe that the king's council was disposed to favour his adversary.

Warwick's breach with Somerset prepared the way for the alignment of the Nevilles with York. Salisbury might have been reluctant to join the opposition to Somerset had it not been for his own dispute with Northumberland. He may well have feared that Somerset's hostility to his son and heir might influence any action the council took to resolve the northern problem, and that he would find himself at the same kind of disadvantage as the earl of Devon did in his

* His income from land was little more than £300 a year. Crown pensions and offices gave him nearly £2,000 more.[7]

† See Appendix VI.

‡ The others were the chancellor, the treasurer, the prior of St. John's, the dean of St. Severin, Bordeaux, and Thorp (the first speaker in the parliament of 1453).

quarrel with Lord Bonville. There were, indeed, signs of some understanding between Somerset and the Percies at this time. The election of William to the see of Carlisle in 1452 was one. Another was the appointment of Egremont to a judicial commission otherwise heavily manned by peers connected with the court, in January 1453.[10] These considerations doubtless made the Neville earls more ready to form a close association with York, but an occasion for their coming together did not arise until the autumn of 1453. The hard-headed Salisbury, moreover, would have seen little profit in an alliance with York when the latter was virtually an outcast from the governing class; while York would scarcely be prepared to undertake any fresh move against the court in the company of men who had played a large part in thwarting his previous attempt.

A catastrophe now entirely altered the political situation. Early in August, the king suffered a shock which prostrated both his body and his mind. Of the nature of this "sudden fright" we have no information. It might have been some alarming spectacle, for such had been the occasion of his French grandfather's first breakdown. For the result there are three reports which concur in saying that Henry was deprived of his senses and memory, unable to speak or use his limbs, incapable even of moving from the place where he sat.[11] In this condition he was to remain for nearly eighteen months. The tainted evidence of two approvers from Southwark reflects the reaction of Henry's subjects. Both men attributed the collapse to necromancy: one blamed a group of Bristol merchants for working on books of sorcery for this end on 12 July 1453, the second confessed to casting a spell over a cloak belonging to the king on 28 July at the instigation of Lord Cobham who, he correctly said, was then in prison.[12] Obviously Henry was suffering from some form of mental illness which would have been recognisable today, and this could have been of long standing,* thus accounting for his apparent detachment from temporal affairs and the contemptuous remarks made about him by some subjects. But our information about Henry VI is insufficient to enable us to trace the development of a mental disease over the course of his life. All that we may legitimately infer is that the balance of his mind was not strong enough to sustain the stresses to which he was exposed at this time. The revolts and

---

* Henry's condition after his breakdown bears a fair resemblance to a period of stupor in a case of katatonic schizophrenia.[13]

plots of the last three years had led to unwonted physical exertion on his part, as he was taken round the country to restore order, and in recent months he would have been alarmed by the reports of baronial wars in Yorkshire and south Wales, with the news of Shrewsbury's defeat on 17 July and the loss of Gascony probably coming as the final, unsupportable blow to the king's reason.

Henry's breakdown had occurred when he was visiting the royal hunting lodge at Clarendon, in Wiltshire, and here he was kept for two months while the administration of his government went on as if nothing had happened. The pretence could not be kept up indefinitely; the council could hardly claim to be acting in the king's name once it became known that he was completely incapacitated, and in pressing questions like the pacification of magnates' disputes it was imperative that its authority should be beyond question. A great council was accordingly summoned to meet at Westminster though even now the fiction was observed that it was Henry who called it: "among other things that moved his highness, one was to set rest and union betwixt the lords of this land".

The king's council, no doubt at Somerset's wish, did not invite York to attend this meeting, but the lords of the great council would not allow him to be excluded and a belated summons was sent on 23 October.[14] Apart from the impropriety of his exclusion, there was now less ambiguity about his status. A son had been born to Queen Margaret on 13 October, and York could no longer be regarded as an immediate claimant to the royal succession. York behaved with punctilious restraint when he took his place in the great council. He told the lords on 21 November that he had been ordered some time ago to dismiss certain of his private advisers, which he found a great inconvenience, and he asked for permission to recall them.[15] This moderation reveals his uncertainty about his position.

Now that York had been admitted to the council, a number of the peers began to seek his friendship. His understanding with Salisbury and Warwick probably dates from this time. The earl of Worcester, the treasurer since 1452, came over to him.* The duke of Norfolk, again in trouble with the court,† returned to his side. It cannot be

---

* This is shown by his dismissal at the end of York's protectorate. For his previous attitude, see p. 104.

† His retainers were accused of trying to intimidate a parliamentary election for Suffolk in 1453.[16]

presumed, however, that these peers became his staunch allies immediately, in this autumn. Even in the case of the Nevilles, it is as likely that York's relations with them gradually developed into closer associations during their continuing contact throughout the following year. By January, he had also gained support from the king's half-brothers, the earls of Pembroke and Richmond,[17] and his relations with them certainly did not ripen into lasting friendship. His oldest ally, the earl of Devon, was rescued from the oblivion which had followed his appearance at Dartford in 1452, and he could now look forward with confidence to the trial of his indictment for high treason.* When the great council set up a temporary king's council, York, Norfolk, Warwick, Salisbury, Worcester, Devon and Salisbury's dependants Lord Cromwell and Baron Greystoke formed the majority of its known lay members.[19] York was at last in a position to take action against his principal enemy. Shortly before Christmas, Somerset was confined to the Tower, and the charges about his conduct in France were revived, with Norfolk assuming the office of chief prosecutor.[20]

This complete swing of the political pendulum inevitably alarmed those who had now lost the amenities of royal favour. As the date for the next session of parliament drew near, there was great apprehension in London lest the assembly of peers might lead to violence. The courtiers Wiltshire, Bonville and Beaumont, with the northern lords Poynings, Clifford and Egremont, were "making all the puissance they can and may to come hither with them". York, Salisbury, Warwick, Pembroke and Richmond were all expected "with a goodly fellowship". Somerset, from his prison, was said to be planning some mischief, sending spies into all parts of the land and organising demonstrations in his favour. Cardinal Kemp, fearing for his safety, was arming his household, and the duke of Buckingham, another not directly involved in the feuds of his peers, was reported to have made two thousand badges.[21]

In this disturbed atmosphere it is hardly surprising that the lords were unable to come to a decision on how parliament was to be conducted without the king's presence. When it reassembled at Reading on 11 February 1454, the treasurer had to be sent down to adjourn it for three days, to meet again in Westminster. In the

* He was reappointed a J.P. on 15 December. The lords acquitted him on 14 March 1454.[18]

interval, it was agreed that York should act as the king's lieutenant in parliament. The commons were incensed by the arrest of their speaker as a result of York's legal proceedings against him for seizing some of his property, and they showed their displeasure by refusing a request for subsidies. Instead, they asked for information about the formation of a council and pertinently urged York and the lords "to have specially and tenderly recommended the peace of this land". The death of Cardinal Kemp on 22 March forced the lords to make some less makeshift arrangements for the conduct of government during the king's incapacity; it was beyond the customary competence of the council to appoint a chancellor. Still uncertain, the lords sent a delegation to discover Henry's wishes about the choice of Kemp's successor. It is possible that this meant no more than obtaining Henry's assent to their nominee, for they had prepared a list for membership of the king's council, for which his approval was to be sought. Despite repeated interviews, when the delegates exhausted their ingenuity in trying to communicate with the stricken king, "they could get no answer nor sign". The responsibility could not be avoided. The lords had to choose between at least two possible courses. One had to be proposed by the queen: this was that she should be appointed regent, with full control of crown patronage and seemingly free of any conciliar restraint.[22] Only the most committed members of the court could approve of this solution, alien as it was to all constitutional precedents. The measures actually adopted recalled the arrangements during Henry's minority. York was appointed protector – not, he protested, at his own seeking – and his position was defined as being that of chief councillor, with special responsibility for the country's defence and the suppression of treason.[23]

Other precedents from the minority were observed when a council was appointed. It is possible that the 1423 ordinance for the council was adopted, for the members now signed council warrants.[24] To ensure regular attendance, councillors were to be paid salaries, and the scale of payment was that established in 1424.[25] The new council was comparatively large and comprehensive of baronial interests, including friends of Somerset like Wiltshire and Viscount Beaumont as well as York and the Nevilles; while several bishops, the duke of Buckingham and some other lay peers held the balance. The appointment of Salisbury as chancellor on 2 April therefore cannot be considered as a purely private act of patronage by York, for the agreement of the neutral group of councillors, if not of all, would have been necessary. It was undoubtedly unusual to appoint a layman to this office,* but there was no bishop who had risen from office in the royal administration who would have been a natural choice as Kemp's successor. With over thirty year's experience as a councillor, justice of the peace and warden of the marches, Salisbury cannot have been considered incapable of the highest administrative office.

The Nevilles did make some profits from their favourable position. Warwick recovered possession of his wife's hereditary Exchequer office, and his younger brother Master George was commended to the pope for his "blood, virtue and cunning" as worthy of appointment to the next vacant bishopric. Again, this was not an act of unfettered patronage but done with the approval of twenty-six spiritual and temporal lords.[26] York also had a dispute settled in his favour. He had seemingly opposed Wiltshire's appointment as lieutenant of Ireland in March 1453, and on 1 December obtained an official confirmation of his own appointment for ten years from 1447. Wiltshire now objected, and on 6 February 1454 the Irish revenues were put in cold storage until the council could determine who should be lieutenant. This it did on 15 April, and its decision was attested by fifteen signatures, Wiltshire's among them.[27] York was in a good position to prevail but the legal merits of his case were strong.

He was less successful with regard to Calais. Although he was appointed and engaged as its captain, the garrison refused to admit his authority while their wages were not paid to date. York's interest in wresting control of this great fortress from Somerset was obvious enough, for the captaincy would have considerably enhanced both his authority and his income, but once more he appears to have had the full backing of the council, and Buckingham's half-brother, Viscount Bourchier, was employed in the negotiations with the soldiers.[28] The general feeling in the council may have been that, with a strong likelihood of a French attack on Calais, it was essential that its captaincy should be held by a proved soldier, as York was, and that Somerset, imprisoned on suspicion of treason, should be removed from this command. On 18 July, the council upheld York's refusal to release Somerset on bail, and the names of those present once more show that this was not a narrowly partisan body.

* The last occasion was in 1411.

The earl of Northumberland attended this meeting of the council.[29] Two weeks later, he successfully applied for temporary relief from judicial proceedings;* the council's grant of his request amply demonstrates that its membership was wide enough to make it reasonably impartial. No doubt there were tensions between individual members, but these could be contained by the remainder of their colleagues. For the internal peace of the realm, it was highly desirable that these private enemies should come to the council. The appearance of Northumberland at the same session as Salisbury was a most promising development, and it did at least suggest that he did not fear that the Nevilles were sufficiently influential to do him any harm by conciliar action, and it might have been a first step towards reconciliation. But Northumberland's son, Lord Egremont, had now given Salisbury fresh cause for alarm: with a formidable new ally, he had nearly won control of central Yorkshire. Under this threat, the Nevilles' understanding with Richard of York was converted into a firm alliance.

* See p. 147.

X

The Duke of Exeter's Rebellion

After their great show of strength against the Nevilles in the autumn of 1453, the Percies thought it best to avoid the limelight for the next few months. With their enemies so favourably placed in the new political situation, Northumberland and his noble sons were naturally reluctant to leave their northern strongholds. Only Bishop William, secure in his order, went to attend the great council and parliament.[1] Egremont, for one, had more pressing business nearer home. He was still enlisting new followers. A motley collection they must have been! He was in York on 4 February, distributing liveries among men described as gentlemen, yeomen, a local fletcher and a drier of fish from Whitby. His objective at this time was to gain control of the city by winning over the artisans and attacking Salisbury's supporters. His henchman, Richard Bellingham, was sent into York on 6 May to beat up one of Salisbury's tenants.[2] Egremont was now planning a fresh outrage. The king's council appears to have had some inkling of new troubles and on 10 May it ordered the earl of Northumberland, his sons Lord Poynings and Ralph Percy, and their friend Lord Roos, to appear before it. This was the day Egremont had appointed for his supporters to muster: a large party of weavers, barbers and other tradesmen came from York to join him at Spofforth, and many others arrived from various parts of the county.[3]

Egremont was also joined by a new ally, Henry Holand, duke of Exeter. Holand's participation in the Yorkshire disturbances adds an element of mystery to an already confused picture. His territorial interests were far distant, he had no close ties of kinship with the Percies, and if he did share their hatred of the Nevilles, it was for an indirect reason. Both the Percies and Exeter had grievances against Lord Cromwell. Although the second earl of Northumberland had been restored in 1416, he did not recover possession of the former Percy inheritance easily. Among the once forfeited lands which eluded his valid claims were Wressell Castle and other property in Yorkshire and Lincolnshire, and these were now held by Cromwell through the king's grant.[4] Exeter had a dispute with Cromwell over conflicting titles to a number of manors in Bedfordshire, which they had submitted to arbitration in 1452. Far from being settled, their quarrel worsened to such an extent that on 9 March 1454 Cromwell petitioned in parliament that security should be taken from Exeter so that he should desist from attempts at violence.[5] Cromwell's fear of Exeter had undoubtedly prompted his marriage alliance with the Nevilles in 1453. Exeter thus had two grounds for disagreement with the Nevilles, their protection of Cromwell and the fact that Thomas Neville was now the husband of one of Cromwell's heirs to the disputed property. But, in the event, the forces mustered at Spofforth were not employed against the Nevilles.

Exeter and Egremont had one thing in common: each had a grandfather who had died in rebellion against Henry IV. Exeter's father, however, had fully retrieved the family's honour by a long and distinguished career in the French wars, and was for many years a member of the king's council. Apart from his estates, his son also inherited the offices of admiral of England and constable of the Tower of London. He had nothing to gain by treason and a great deal to lose. When Exeter's father died in 1447, Henry Holand, the only legitimate son, was seventeen years old and became the king's ward. The king granted the wardship to Richard of York who married Exeter to his daughter Anne, then (in 1447) a girl of eight. Possibly Exeter nourished feelings of resentment against his father-in-law and former guardian, but, again, this is not an obvious reason for his alliance with Egremont and the actions he took in his company. We might assume that their association was due to political reasons, but the record will show that it was not simply a case of opposition to York's protectorate inspired by loyalty to the house of Lancaster. Exeter's conduct raises serious doubts about his intelligence and stability, and it is tempting to presume that Egremont was exploiting the younger man's vain pretensions for purposes of his own.

The alliance had been sworn at Tuxford, near Doncaster, in January 1454, after which Exeter had returned to his home.[6] The council suspected his intentions and ordered him to attend it on 16 May. On that day, it received further news about him: Exeter had joined Egremont in the north and the two had assembled a large following, "to no good intent, as it is noised". Consequently it was decided that the protector, York, should go to disperse this gathering, with force if necessary. The council's assessment of the situation was extremely grave, for it could ill-afford the employment of York and a military force in the north at that time: Calais was under siege and the council was strenuously engaged in raising an expedition for its relief.[7] The conspirators were in York City on 14 May, calling on all and sundry to follow them. They seized the mayor and the recorder in the chapter house of the Minster and held them prisoners until they undertook not to offer any opposition to their captors' schemes.[8]

A massive concentration took place at Spofforth on 21 May: there were Percy tenants from all parts of Yorkshire and many more from Cockermouth; large numbers of tradesmen from York; a formidable contingent from Exeter's estates in Bedfordshire, including his bastard brothers Robert and William; and a band from Westmorland under the leadership of Henry Bellingham. According to the indictments, this gathering constituted an act of war against the king, for all were armed and banners were displayed. Exeter addressed the assembly. To his demand that he should assume the government of the kingdom it gave unanimous assent. He went on to claim the duchy of Lancaster for himself. He promised that he would particularly favour all Yorkshiremen who followed him, and that they would never have to pay taxes to the king or anyone else. Exeter then distributed a livery of white and red, the Lancastrian colours, saying "Take here the duke of Lancaster's livery". It was also alleged that Exeter and his friends sent a messenger to the king of Scots to urge him to wage war against King Henry, promising the Scottish king dominion over England.

This amazing story hardly commands immediate belief. It is reported in a number of indictments presented to a judicial commission at York a month later. We can accept as fact that the gathering took place – no jury would have fabricated anything on this scale – but Exeter's supposed actions are barely credible. The sheriff who had summoned the jurors to present these indictments was Sir John Savill, whose connections were with the duke of York and the earl of Salisbury; he would have made sure that the jurors were men who could be relied on to confirm the most unfavourable interpretation of Exeter's and Egremont's actions. They were not, however, a narrowly partisan jury, for they also made a number of charges against John and Thomas Neville. Moreover, it was not they who produced the account of the gathering at Spofforth; they only supplied the names of those present. The details of Exeter's speech were put to them, already written. One copy of the record is a document consisting of two membranes: the second, with the names of the accused, is in the style of writing usually practised by judges's clerks; but the first, relating what happened on 21 May, is in the "hand" of the privy seal office, the council's secretariat.[9] The charge, therefore, was presumably based on reports sent to the council, which drafted the form in which the indictment was to be made. It received more than one account, for this would explain the discrepancy in the narrative that the conspirators consented that first Exeter, and then the king of Scots, should rule England. The reference to Scotland was probably based on no more than an overheard suggestion that its king might be asked for assistance.

It is Exeter's supposed claim to the duchy of Lancaster that rouses our suspicions. He might easily have demanded greater influence in the government of the country, but he had no claim to immediate possession of the duchy: it was the king's patrimony beyond question.* Yet the council had reason to believe, five days before the Spofforth gathering, that Exeter had designs on Lancashire.[10] What is more, had the evidence been falsified by the Nevilles, it is strange that no attempt was made to implicate Northumberland, Poynings and Clifford. But, as we have already noted, Egremont did not direct his forces against the Nevilles, and the senior members of his family clearly had sufficient sense of responsibility to hold aloof from his wilder schemes. Finally, it must be borne in mind that Exeter and

---

* As Mr T. B. Pugh has kindly pointed out, Exeter's paternal grandmother was a daughter of John of Gaunt and Blanche of Lancaster. He would therefore have had a claim to the duchy (which was not incorporated with the crown estates) in the event of the deaths of Henry VI and Prince Edward, provided that neither had further issue. Gaunt had another daughter of the same marriage whose heir (King Alfonso V of Portugal) could then have claimed to share the duchy with Exeter.

Egremont remained out of favour even when York and his friends were no longer in power.

From Spofforth, Exeter, Egremont and their host advanced on York City. The mayor was ordered to deliver the keys to its gates and he dared not refuse.[11] Their movements can be followed a little further. Their first objective was to extend the area under their control and to raise yet more followers so that they would be able to withstand an army from the south. After an unsuccessful attempt to seize Hull, therefore, they moved to the west. Garter king of arms, bringing letters from the council to Exeter, arrived at Spofforth on 23 May, and a group of Percy tenants took him prisoner and robbed him of his horse and money. Egremont was at Skipton on the 28th, probably trying to enlist the Cliffords' followers.

The duke of York had now arrived in Yorkshire and one of Egremont's friends, Robert Mauleverer, tried to organise opposition against him. The main body of the rebels was then beyond Skipton. York sent reports to the council, which it received on 5 June, that Egremont was on his way to raise supporters in Cumberland and Westmorland. It had also heard that Exeter had sent seditious letters to Baron Greystoke and to the commons of Lancashire and Cheshire.[12] There were a number of risings in Exeter's favour in Lancashire, but the loyal local forces easily dispersed them. Hearing of a plot to seize Lancaster Castle, the council ordered Sir Thomas Harrington to hold it in strength. When Exeter entered the county, Thomas Stanley was sent to urge him to leave and take his complaints "of such injuries and wrongs as he felt him grieved" direct to the king, "whereupon he right sadly the premises considering, anon from thence gently departed".[13] Having failed in the west, and with York approaching from the east, Exeter abandoned his grandiose schemes and fled to sanctuary at Westminster.

The judicial proceedings against the participants in the recent disturbances were opened in York on 15 June, in the presence of the protector, the earl of Warwick, Baron Greystoke, two royal justices and the mayor, sitting as justices of oyer and terminer. They received indictments concerning offences committed since the beginning of 1453, for the commission issued in July 1453 had, not remarkably, been a dead letter. Three other commissioners arrived on 22 June, the earl of Shrewsbury and Lords Clifford and FitzHugh, the first two of whom added variety to the body's political flavour. Another session was held on the 26th, when the justices adjourned; these had been preliminaries only. York now returned to London. While the commission was sitting, Egremont remained out of reach, possibly at Cockermouth. About the middle of July, Exeter's friends in Lancashire held another gathering, this time at Wingates, near Bolton. They sent a message to Egremont, asking for his help, but they were easily dispersed before he could make any move.[14] It was probably news of this fresh disturbance which prompted York to risk the censures of the Church when, on 23 July, he had Exeter and his bastard brother Robert removed from sanctuary; Exeter was put in Salisbury's charge and sent to Pontefract Castle, while Robert was committed to Newgate prison.[15] Exeter was kept at Pontefract for nine months "with great heaviness and right chargeable costs".

After the king's recovery and York's dismissal from the protectorate, Exeter claimed that his imprisonment was due to "a sinister information made upon him by certain persons not well disposed". He was therefore brought to the king[16] but, presumably because he was unable to exculpate himself, confined in Wallingford Castle. Here he remained until he was brought to trial in parliament early in 1456, when he was apparently acquitted.[17] Later, in February 1459, he was committed to another prison, Berkhamsted Castle, where he spent two months before being released on giving bonds totalling more than £10,000, with the condition that he appeared before the council at Whitsun.[18] This protracted, if not continuous, detention does suggest that even Queen Margaret and her adherents had the deepest suspicions of Exeter's loyalty and that the reports of his behaviour in 1454 were generally believed. This distrust is also reflected in the absence of his name from the lists of "witnesses" to royal charters and from judicial commissions; unlike other important peers, he became a justice of the peace in only two counties, Devon in 1457 and Cornwall in 1458.* He did not become an adherent of the court until its final breach with York.

The earl of Northumberland had been charged before York and the other commissioners for his part in the Yorkshire disturbances in 1453. He applied to the king for the proceedings against him to be stayed until the following spring. When the council granted this petition on 23 July 1454, York was not present, nor was either of the Neville earls.[19] They had already set out for the north. Salisbury was

* His father had been a justice in nine counties.

in York on 1 August, and Duke Richard and Warwick, with Greystoke, FitzHugh and two professional judges, resumed their sessions on the 3rd, when the principal charge against Exeter was formally presented. This is the last day on which the commission is known to have sat. The indictments were sent to King's Bench, where they dragged on for many years: the proceedings against the earl of Northumberland came to an end in the Easter term of the first year of Edward IV, when it was reported that the earl was dead, as he had been for six years; the vicar of Ilkley was dismissed in 1462 on showing a pardon granted by Edward IV; the two bastards of Exeter were outlawed for not appearing on 25 February 1463; and a group of some fifty Percy tenants was still being summoned in 1468.[20] Many others, however, including most of the principals, escaped further prosecution by obtaining the letters of general pardon granted after the first battle of St. Albans which excused their recipients from having to stand trial for all rebellions, treasons, murders and many other kinds of offences committed before 9 July 1455. Among the first to receive this pardon were Exeter, Salisbury, Lord Clifford, Egremont and his brother Richard, in August, Henry and three other Bellinghams in September, and Greystoke and Sir John Salvin in October; even such lesser characters as Henry Kipping *alias* Tippyng *alias* Typplyng, yeoman *alias* gentleman, of Cockermouth and Spofforth, John Story, yeoman, of Hunmanby and Cockermouth, and many other Percy tenants thought it worth their while to pay 16s. 4d. to secure this immunity.[21]

Salisbury remained in the north throughout August and September 1454, touring his estates and stopping at Middleham, Barnard Castle and Sheriff Hutton. As chancellor, he had a great seal and some of the clerks of Chancery with him, so that he could continue his administrative duties during the vacation. On 22 September, he used the great seal to order the sheriff of Yorkshire to arrest people who were forming unlawful assemblies in the city and county of York, and a week later he appointed commissioners to call all Yorkshiremen to arms and lead them into Lancashire to suppress risings there.[22]

These measures suggest that Lord Egremont was once more on the move. His defiant career was now approaching its end. On 31 October, on a site already famous as the scene of the last great victory of Anglo-Saxon England, the younger Nevilles and Percies at last joined battle. The manor of Stamford Bridge was Neville property, lying abreast the Roman road from York to the east coast, and not far from the Percy manor of Pocklington. Egremont, with a force including two hundred men led by the bailiff of Pocklington, was presumably on his way westward when he encountered John and Thomas Neville. In the skirmish, the men from Pocklington fled, leaving Egremont to fall into the Nevilles' eager hands. They took him to their castle at Middleham, then before commissioners of oyer and terminer at York, where he was condemned to pay Salisbury damages of £11,200. It was a staggering sum. With no property of his own, and an income of barely £100 a year, Egremont could never hope to pay, nor, indeed, did he try. Salisbury doubtless realised this, but by taking a civil action against Egremont he made sure of his being kept under restraint as a debtor: there was little point in carrying him to King's Bench to answer the many charges of treason and felony already laid against him, for he merely had to produce his letters of general pardon to obtain dismissal. Egremont and his brother Richard Percy were taken to London and confined in Newgate.[23]

Like their fellow-conspirator Exeter, they remained in detention after the end of York's first protectorate. The court party also distrusted Egremont and was not prepared to assist him through any loophole in the law. He was kept in Newgate for two years and characteristically arranged his own release. A warder was bribed, arms smuggled in, and on the night of 13 November 1456, Egremont and his brother attacked the prison's keeper, freeing the other prisoners as they made their way out. While the latter took to the roof and fought off attempts for their recapture, the Percies made off on the horses which had been waiting for them.[24]

XI

The Sack of Elvaston

Derbyshire was another county where an outbreak of disorder demanded the attention of the council during York's first protectorate. Here the disturbances were on a smaller scale than in Yorkshire, for the participants were not magnates but landed gentry. It is conceivable that the dispute was political in origin, because one group was led by retainers of the duke of Buckingham and the second by a servant of York. There is no reason to believe, however, that the dukes were then on such bad terms that they were likely to prompt their followers to make attacks on each other and it is difficult to see what either peer had to gain from these localised operations. In any case, neither was mentioned in the subsequent judicial proceedings. It seems more probable that their retainers were acting on their own initiative and were taking advantage of the unsettled political situation to conclude a private dispute by their own enterprise. These disturbances in Derbyshire provide a forceful answer to those apologists of "bastard feudalism" who write of its stabilising properties. They are also instructive in the light they throw on the ramifications of the system. In the same way as the magnates recruited their retinues from the divided ranks of "county" society, so did their clients build up followings among the lesser squirearchy of their own neighbourhood.

Although Derby is only one hundred and twenty-five miles from London, the county could, in medieval times, be reckoned as one of the kingdom's more outlying shires. With its hills, the southern stump of the Pennines, rising to two thousand feet and intersected by glaciated valleys, Derbyshire still seems to belong more to the north than to midland England. In the middle ages, it was in the north for several administrative purposes, as the River Trent used to form a division for the operations of various crown officials; there were, for instance, two keepers of the king's forests, one for "south of Trent", the other for "north of Trent". In character as well the inhabitants appear to have been more unruly than their countrymen to the south. A sheriff making a claim for allowances in 1455 said that one cause of his being out of pocket was "riding with much people on his own costs in executing of his office because the people is wild".[1] The bare hills of the north and centre offered little prospect of an honest living and provided a refuge for men like Peter Venables who, in 1438, took to the wilds with "many misdoers being of his clothing" and lived by robbery, "like as it had been Robin Hood and his men".[2] The local gentry also seem to have been more turbulent than their southern counterparts. One of the earliest cases in Henry VI's reign of an outrageous crime committed by men of this class took place in Derbyshire.*

The predominant territorial power in southern Derbyshire was the duchy of Lancaster. The title of earl of Derby had been conferred on the earl of Lancaster's heir in 1337 and it was borne by Henry of Bolingbroke in the lifetime of his father, John of Gaunt. There was thus a strong local tradition of loyalty to the house of Lancaster which was transferred to the crown after Henry became king. With the duke of Lancaster on the throne, however, duchy tenants gradually lost the feeling of special attachment to their lord: he became less immediate a protector and to some appeared in the same light as he did to other tenants-in-chief of the crown throughout the realm.

In a district traditionally loyal to Lancaster, no family had a better record of service than the Blounts of Elvaston: Walter had followed John of Gaunt in all his campaigns and died fighting for Henry IV at Shrewsbury in 1403; his son John, a famous soldier and knight of the

---

* This was the murder by Thomas Foljambe and others of Henry Longford and William Bradshaw, and the mutilation of Sir Henry Pierpoint, in Chesterfield church, during a service, on 1 January 1434; in retaliation, apparently, for a murderous assault on Foljambe by Pierpoint on 14 September 1432. The indictments were heard by the duke of Bedford and other commissioners of oyer and terminer on 6 March 1434; they form the earliest special oyer and terminer file for the reign concerning felonies by gentry.[3]

EHL F

Garter, was killed at the siege of Rouen in 1418; and Thomas his brother and heir served under the Regent Bedford and became treasurer of Normandy. His son Walter, however, was to become one of Edward IV's most trusted lieutenants and so earn his elevation to the peerage as Lord Mountjoy in 1465. His father's military career helps to explain why the family transferred its allegiance, for a number of veterans of the French wars tended to support Richard of York. A further reason was the Blounts' feud with a neighbouring family. Thomas is not known to have been a retainer of York, but Walter entered his service and apparently became a member of his household no later that 1454.[4]

While the Blounts' breach with their feudal lord took an extreme form, their neighbours also preferred a more accessible patron than the ruler of the duchy of Lancaster. The other local families of similar rank, the class which provided the county's sheriffs, justices of the peace and members of parliament, were the Curzons of Kedleston, the Gresleys of Drakelow, the Longfords of Longford and the Vernons of Haddon. The Gresleys were closely associated with the Blounts, but the Curzons, Longfords and Vernons were retainers of Humphrey Stafford, duke of Buckingham.[5]

These were the two groups responsible for the outburst of violence in 1454. Its cause was a dispute of unknown origin between the Longfords and the Blounts. The first available indication that this quarrel was taking a violent turn dates from 1453. A party of Sir Nicholas Longford's servants came to Derby on 30 July when Thomas, a younger son of Sir Thomas Blount, was visiting the nunnery. At first these men waited outside for him in "le Nounegrove", but one, Ralph Twyford, became impatient and went into the convent grounds. As he came up to Blount, Twyford suddenly drew a long knife and attacked his quarry, inflicting serious wounds.[6] It is not likely that the Blounts refrained from retaliation, but – judicial records being what they are – only one side to the quarrel is known. The local situation certainly worsened sufficiently to reach the notice of the king's council. On 10 May 1454, royal letters were sent to Longford and Walter Blount requiring them to appear before the council immediately, and, to ensure compliance, the sheriffs of Derbyshire and Lancashire were directed to see that these letters were delivered.

The council soon learned what respect its letters, written in the king's name, received in Derbyshire, and how Longford treated "the bearer thereof strangely, whereof we marvel".[7] At the time the sheriff of Derbyshire received the writ for Longford, the latter was staying at his manor of Hough, in Lancashire. The sheriff sent a messenger to Hough, but Longford refused to accept the letter and his servants threatened to kill the messenger and so compelled him to leave. He came back the following day but prudently did not attempt to see Longford himself. Without dismounting, he put the letter on a bench by the door to the hall and told Longford's servants to tell their master about it. The messenger then rode off, but he had not gone far before he was overtaken by John Longford with a score of his father's servants, who set upon him with staves. They had brought the unwanted letter with them and tried to compel the bearer to eat it, a time-hallowed method of disposing of unwelcome royal writs. The wretched man said he would rather die than make a meal of some sixty square inches of parchment and a wax impression of the privy seal.* His tormentors then forced him to break and tear the letter, and spat on it themselves. He was taken back to Hough and set in the stocks, next conveyed in no little discomfort to John Warenne's house at Poynton, in Cheshire, to be imprisoned there, and eventually brought to Longford manor on 27 May.

For the last stage of his journey the sheriff's messenger had an escort of a hundred armed men. This large body was not formed to prevent his escape but as his captor's contribution to a larger concentration. Sir Nicholas Longford had called on all his friends to join him at Longford. The messenger saw Sir William Vernon of Haddon and his sons, and there were many other knights and esquires from the counties of Derby, Lancaster, Leicester, Stafford and Chester, who with their retainers formed an army estimated at a thousand strong. Longford had planned to bring his quarrel with Walter Blount to a violent conclusion. The next day, 28 May, this small army set out from Longford with banners flying and trumpets blowing and so came to Derby, where they sacked Blount's apartments in the house of the Black Friars and also the house of one of his servants. The sheriff of Derbyshire now tried to prevent further disorder by going to meet the rout in the market-place and reading to them his commission as a justice of the peace and a letter from the duke of York, the protector of the realm. To the sheriff's proclamation that they

---

* This would have been two and a half inches in diameter.

should keep the peace, Longford and his friends replied that no lord or sheriff or any other minister of the king would have their obedience or prevent them from carrying out their plans. As the sheriff, Sir John Gresley, was Walter Blount's cousin and ally, it is not remarkable that he could not command much respect as the king's officer, but by their disregard of his proclamation Longford and company could now be considered as rebels against the king.

The little army now continued its eastward march to Walter Blount's manor at Elvaston, four miles from Derby. He was not at home. His enemies therefore had to content themselves with doing as much damage as they could, battering the walls of various buildings, smashing doors and windows and breaking tables and benches into little pieces. They found three pieces of tapestry with Blount's arms hanging in the hall of the manor-house, and these were each cut into four pieces, to the observation that "for that said Walter Blount was gone to serve traitors, therefore his arms shall thus be quartered". Every room was ransacked: chests were forced open and court-rolls, deeds and other evidences taken out and destroyed; two dozen cushions decorated with the arms of Walter Blount and Sir John Byron (his father-in-law) were also each cut into four pieces; three hanging beds, one of silk, the others worsted, three featherbeds, four bolsters, and all the sheets, coverings and blankets, as well as napery and other soft furnishings, were likewise slashed with swords and daggers; and a pipe and a half of red wine and a barrel of "rumney"* were broken with cudgels. Taking a few weapons they found lying about, the gathering now retired and apparently dispersed.

Two days later the Blounts returned the visit. Walter, his brother Thomas – happily recovered from his wounds –, Nicholas Gresley, a son of the sheriff, and about a hundred more came to Longford's house on 30 May. Apart from forcing their way into the grounds, they are not credited with inflicting any worse damage than wounding four of Longford's servants. The king's council now ordered Nicholas Longford and Walter Blount to appear before it on 25 June and threatened penalties of £1,000 if they committed any further breaches of the peace, but a fresh summons was sent to Longford six days later, on 9 June, commanding his appearance on 24 October.[8] These disorders were also investigated in Derby itself on 1 July. The king's justices of oyer and terminer were then presented with formal

---

* A Greek wine.

indictments concerning these and other breaches of the peace. As York and Warwick were members of the commission, and Gresley the sheriff who chose the jurors, the Longfords were inevitably at a disadvantage. Nicholas Longford was also charged with a number of attacks on the property of Ralph Shirley, starting in 1450, and one of his servants, John Fowne, was named as a leading figure in a series of acts of trespass. The commissioners were unable to stay long in Derby and were directed by the council to release Longford and nearly one hundred others, most of them his adherents and servants, on bail until 18 September.[9] Eventually Longford was fined £193 for his misdeeds[10] and he probably had to pay much more in damages. He obtained royal letters of pardon on 20 August 1455. Sir Thomas Blount also received a general pardon later that year, and his son Thomas was likewise pardoned in February 1456.[11]

The Blount-Longford quarrel had led to the gravest disturbances in southern Derbyshire, but other feuds were being prosecuted at the same time. Sir John Gresley and Roger, brother of Sir William Vernon of Haddon, were called to appear before the king's council on 21 July 1455 as it had heard that they "have now late riotously assembled our people against our peace".[12] The dispute was referred to arbitration by the duke of Buckingham, whose award on 12 September decreed that the heads of the two families "shall be full friends and of friendly dealing, and pardon and lay apart either to [the] other all manner [of] grudgings and rancour of heart". There had been one death and many hard blows in the course of the quarrel, and a scale of compensation was laid down: £13 6s. 8d. for the murder, 13s. 4d. for a head wound, 6s. 8d. for lesser injuries, 40s. for a broken leg bone, and so on.[13] The award belongs more in spirit to the Anglo-Saxon tradition of the weregild than to a country which had known four centuries of law administered by a central judiciary. William Vernon and Gresley soon afterwards took the precaution of suing letters of general pardon.[14] Their feud, although not in itself particularly serious, is significant as an illustration of the way such disputes were dividing the society of a small area into well-defined camps: in an issue on a larger scale, the participants would join opposing sides, as the Vernons joined Sir Nicholas Longford in his attack on Elvaston and the Gresleys gave their assistance to the Blounts.

Another supporter of Longford whose name is rarely missing from the Derbyshire indictments of the 1450's was to be described in 1459 as one of the two dozen men who were "notoriously and universally throughout all this your realm famed and noised, known and reputed severally, for open robbers, ravishers, extortioners and oppressors".[15] This was John Cockayne of Ashbourne, a market town lying on the Roman road from Derby to Manchester as it enters Dovedale. The manor belonged to the duchy of Lancaster and within its bounds the family of Cockayne had held enough property to make its head the local squire, a position enhanced by a distinguished record of service in the duchy administration. Both John Cockayne's great-grand-father and grand-uncle – the second also a royal judge – had held the office of chief steward in north parts, and his father, Sir John, was described as a councillor of the duchy and his effigy in Ashbourne church shows him with the collar of double S worn by retainers of the house of Lancaster.[16] In contrast to his forbears, John the son was a lawless and dissolute ruffian. It is possible, however, to make him some allowance, for his father had so disposed of his property that for many years the son enjoyed only a small proportion of his inheritance. Sir John had arranged that all his lands in Warwickshire and Staffordshire should be held by his widow until her death, leaving John the son only the Ashbourne property. Sir John died in 1438, when John junior was some sixteen years of age, but his widow was still alive in 1466.[17]

John Cockayne's reputation had been made known to the second parliament of 1449, when two petitions were presented by men he had injured. Eighteen months earlier, he had been sued by Philip Okeover in the court of King's Bench for trespasses committed at Okeover, on the west bank of the Dove, in Staffordshire. According to Philip, Cockayne had from time to time hunted in the park at Okeover, without permission. Then in November 1449, when Philip was attending Lord Ferrers in parliament, Cockayne had sent nearly a hundred men to Okeover. They broke down the fences of the park and hunted until nightfall, killing all but five of the deer. They also went to the manor-house and "broke up the doors, bay windows and other windows of the said manor, with forms, trestles and tables dormant and burnt them there, and by the said fire roasted parcel of the said deer taken in the said park". A week before this, Cockayne himself had led a party thirty or forty strong to Blore in Staffordshire, where they burnt Ralph Basset's hay and pease and would have burnt his house as well had some neighbours not intervened. Basset and Philip Okeover both presented petitions against Cockayne in parliament; these were referred to King's Bench, where the damages of the two plaintiffs were each assessed at four hundred marks, a total of £523 6s. 8d. These two incidents were related, for Basset was Philip's father-in-law. The dispute continued, with Philip and Basset carrying the war into their enemy's camp, but it seems to have been concluded in 1462, when Cockayne renounced his claims to rights at Okeover.[18]

Cockayne's association with the Longford-Vernon party was indicated in the two petitions in 1449, which named Thurstan Vernon of Haddon as one of the leaders in both forays. In 1454, Cockayne took part in the raid on Elvaston and was one of those released on bail by the royal justices. A year later he escaped when Thomas Blount, seeking revenge, set an ambush for Roger Vernon, Nicholas Montgomery, Cockayne and their servants, on 2 July 1455.[19] Cockayne received letters of pardon in the following November, and again in 1458,[20] but his rake's progress was not held up by this implied ambition to be on the right side of the law. His local connections suggest that he was probably a "Lancastrian" partisan, and in December 1461 Edward IV appointed a commission to arrest Cockayne, who was said to be leading a band of marauders in Derbyshire. Two years later a second commission was ordered to apprehend Cockayne to make him appear in Chancery.[21] He was somehow able to make his peace with the authorities and resume residence at Ashbourne, but his name continued to be heard in the courts, in King's Bench in 1467 for giving livery to eight yeomen, and in Common Pleas in 1476, when his London tailor failed to recover a debt for £10.[22]

The last years of this bravado were suitably marked by indications of piety on his part and the coming of retribution. In 1485, he took part in the foundation of a chantry in Ashbourne church; among his co-founders in this conventional expression of religious sentiment were Richard Vernon, Nicholas Montgomery – another of Thomas Blount's intended victims in 1455 – and the sons of Cockayne's old enemy Philip Okeover.[23] Cockayne had eventually succeeded to all his father's estates, but by 1494 he was a ruined man. In order to discharge debts of £643 he made over all his lands to the father-in-law of his grandson and heir, with the exception of some property to support his wife and illegitimate daughter. He was allowed for his own use a weekly dole of 26s. 8d., to be paid at the door of Etwall church. He was then seventy-two years old and his paymaster could not have expected him to enjoy this pension for very long, but Cockayne lived for another ten years, until 1504.[24]

The Blount-Longford feud survived the judicial visitation of 1454. In April of the next year, a group of Longford's friends led by Henry Curzon killed Roland Blount in Derby.[25] The employment of Walter Blount as treasurer of Calais, under Warwick, probably helped to reduce the tension in his corner of Derbyshire. His importance under Edward IV, however, ensured his dominance there. The Longfords lost their patron when Buckingham was killed in 1460. They found another, first Edward's brother the duke of Clarence, later his chamberlain Lord Hastings. Following his new master, Sir Nicholas' heir, another Nicholas, was knighted by Edward after his victory at Tewkesbury in 1470.[26] Obviously it mattered little to men of Longford's class whether their "good lord" was a "Yorkist" or a "Lancastrian"; what did count was his ability to make his patronage effective in safeguarding their interests.

XII

The First Battle of St. Albans

If Henry's insanity had been a tragedy, his recovery was a national disaster. While he was incapacitated, England had known, for the first time since he fell under Suffolk's spell, the type of government most favoured by general contemporary opinion. "The complaint of the commons of Kent" had called for a council in which all the great peers of the realm had their place, and, Somerset excepted, this had been realised in 1453-4. But because a king, regardless of his competence, could not be refused the right to please himself in the choice of his advisers, the administration again fell into the hands of a narrow clique, and in consequence civil war, after being averted for four years, claimed its first victims.

Henry began to show signs of recovery on Christmas Day, 1454, and he was shortly afterwards able to resume his devotions and to learn that he had a son.[1] Since York's commission as protector was to expire when the king regained his sanity, the time had come for another reversal of political fortunes. The first step of the old court party, obviously, was to achieve the release of its leader, Somerset, and the queen may have assisted by securing Henry's assent. At a council held on 5 February 1455, Somerset was freed on bail, and a month later he was discharged from this restriction, the king declaring his trust in the duke's loyalty. As a considerable proportion of the lords present on both occasions, York included,[2] had been responsible for Somerset's committal, it must be presumed that their assent had been obtained by some compromise, and one chronicler, admittedly a hostile one, states that Somerset took an oath to take no more part in the government and never to come near the king.[3] Sworn or not, however, Somerset resumed his former position, and on 6 March he was restored to the captaincy of Calais, following the revocation of York's appointment.[4] Next, the senior offices of state were taken out of the hands of York's friends. Salisbury was replaced as chancellor by the new archbishop of Canterbury, Thomas Bourchier, on 7 March, and a week later the earl of Shrewsbury supplanted the earl of Worcester as treasurer. As for local administration, the restoration of Sir Thomas Tuddenham to the Norfolk bench on 28 March[5] threatened a return to the methods in vogue during Suffolk's ascendancy.

Salisbury's resignation is particularly significant. According to one chronicler, he resigned because he objected to the release from detention of the dukes of Somerset and Exeter and of the earl of Devon. This explanation is demonstrably mistaken[6] and a more convincing one is provided by the list of those present on the occasion. Three of the witnesses were related to York or Salisbury by marriage: the duke of Buckingham, whose wife was Salisbury's sister, and Buckingham's half-brothers, Archbishop Bourchier and Viscount Bourchier, who was married to York's sister. These men were not personal enemies of York and the Nevilles, but neither were they political allies, and the archbishop's appointment as Salisbury's successor as chancellor shows their readiness to serve the king.

The six other nobles who saw Salisbury resign were undoubtedly no friends of his and their presence makes it clear that his resignation was forced: these were Somerset, Wiltshire and Beaumont, the foremost members of the court group; and, most hostile of all, Northumberland, his son the bishop of Carlisle, and Lord Clifford.[7] After their long detachment from the political centre, the appearance of Northumberland and Clifford at this juncture was a development of the utmost gravity. It completed the fusion of two sets of enemies. Northumberland had realised that the advantage the Nevilles gained by their association with York had to be countered by his own alliance with Somerset. And with the Percies behind him, Somerset could begin to plan York's destruction. So much, at least, was feared by York and the Neville earls, who now precipitately withdrew from London, without even taking their leave of the king.[8]

Somerset had equally good cause to suspect the intentions of York and his friends. After six weeks' stalemate, he took the initiative by calling a great council to meet at Leicester on 21 May. Its declared purpose was to provide for the king's safety, which, as York and the Nevilles later said, "of common presumption implieth a mistrust to some persons".[9] It was not to be simply an assembly of peers, for writs were sent to every shire, naming representatives who were to attend. Their presence was presumably required to give the meeting a quasi-parliamentary character. Somerset was naturally reluctant to risk parliamentary elections, for the sheriffs had all been appointed during the protectorate and they could not therefore have been relied upon to prevent the return of members favourable to York. York's suspicions of the council's purpose would have been amply confirmed had he seen the list of hand-picked delegates. Norfolk was to be represented by Miles Stapleton and Thomas Tuddenham, Cumberland and the West Riding by the earl of Northumberland's retainers Henry Fenwick, John Pennington and William Plumpton, the last having as his colleague John Neville, brother of the earl of Westmorland and another ally of the Percies. No retainers of York and the Nevilles were included.[10] York remained with his allies and ignored royal commands to come to Leicester with a small following.

As the king with Somerset and others of the council began their journey to Leicester, York and the Nevilles came down from the north with a strength and at a speed which caught the royal party by surprise. On reaching St. Albans they learned that York's forces were only a few hours' march distant and outnumbered their own following, with probably three thousand men to their two thousand, and containing a higher proportion of seasoned troops, among them a strong contingent of "marchmen" led by Sir Robert Ogle, constable of the Bishopric of Durham,[11] who came, no doubt, with the blessing of Bishop Robert as his contribution to the family cause. The king's escort had the advantage of being in the shelter of the town and strengthened this position by erecting barriers across the streets. Not all the peers with the king could be considered as York's enemies, indeed one, Fauconberg, was Salisbury's brother; while others, like Buckingham, would have advised the king to negotiate with York. The first hours of daylight on 22 May saw York's army standing in the fields outside the town, while heralds passed from side to side. York and his friends protested their loyalty to the king, but they demanded that "such persons as they should accuse" should be surrendered to them so that justice could be done. When it became obvious that such terms would not be granted, York's troops tried to penetrate the barriers, but they were held off. Then Warwick, leading his men through the back gardens, broke the royal defences, and within less than an hour the town, and the king, were in York's hands.

The struggle scarcely deserves the name of battle. The number killed cannot be put at more than sixty, among them Somerset, Northumberland and Clifford. "And when the said Duke Edmund and the lords were slain, the battle was ceased."[12] Thus a contemporary discloses the true character of the first battle of St. Albans. It was murder, a settling of scores by the Nevilles against Northumberland and his ally Clifford, and – less certainly – by York against Somerset. In view of Warwick's own dispute with Somerset, it is possible that he was responsible for his death. York had had earlier opportunities for removing his enemy, but had attempted to proceed against him by judicial methods and seemingly still wished to do so on the morning of the battle. In contrast, Warwick's brutal record in later years shows a preference for immediate despatch.

Although York and the Nevilles had raised war against the king's standard, it is absurd to suggest that the logical conclusion to their victory would have been a change of dynasty.[13] So drastic a measure was out of the question. Not even the Nevilles would have supported York had he now laid claim to the throne, and there is no suggestion that he had this intention. Their purpose had been to remove their enemies from their positions of influence about the king, and they had achieved this in a more final manner than they had initially planned. And they had been able to do so only because, at that particular time, they had a more effective fighting force at their command than their opponents had. Extensive though their resources were, York, Warwick and Salisbury remained heavily outnumbered by the potential strength of the rest of the lords, and there were now fewer of their peers ready to support them than six months earlier. The duke of Norfolk had been at hand outside St. Albans and took an indirect part, through the employment of his herald, in the preliminary negotiations, but he did not join in the attack on the town and afterwards he abstained from close association with York. The earl of Devon, who had been with the royal party, joined the processional return to London, but he also absented himself from the subsequent political meetings. Lord Cromwell's recent alliance with the Nevilles was abruptly broken when Warwick, in his head-long way, accused him of being "the beginner of all that journey* at Saint Albans", although he had not been there, and spoke in such threatening terms that Cromwell rushed to the earl of Shrewsbury for protection.[14]

The victor's position was by no means secure. The king, no doubt, was virtually their prisoner, but they could not keep him in custody, nor could they conduct his government without the compliance of a significant portion of the lords. The first essential, both for their own security and for preventing the collapse of the administration, was to come to terms with those peers who, although not their enemies before the battle, had been alienated by their violence on that fatal day. The retention of Archbishop Bourchier as chancellor and the appointment of Viscount Bourchier as treasurer suggest that one of the terms on which Buckingham promised to "draw the line" with York was this guarantee that he and the Nevilles would not take over sole charge of the government. The earls of Pembroke and Worcester also returned to the council soon after the battle.† A parliament was called to meet on 9 July, and here York, Warwick and Salisbury published their explanation for the disaster, and the king, with the assent of lords and commons, declared that he believed them to be his faithful subjects. By this association of parliament with the king, York and the Nevilles had been provided with a more complete form of amnesty than letters of pardon granted on the king's authority alone. In order to prevent further recrimination, all blame was put on Somerset and two obscure minions. Then on 24 July, all the lords present took an oath to remain faithful to the king, a symbolic act which sought to restore their unity by stressing their common bond of allegiance.[16]

The death of Somerset had left many crown and duchy of Lancaster appointments vacant. York took the office of constable of England and obtained a grant of the royal castles of Carmarthen and Aberystwyth. The Nevilles did particularly well for themselves. Calais, which York had been unable to secure in 1454, was granted

* *I.e.* battle.
† Pembroke was at the council with York, Warwick and Salisbury on 4 June, and Buckingham and Worcester joined them on the 6th, when a petition by William Oldhall was granted.[15]

to Warwick, and this time its command was won by protracted and
costly negotiations with the garrison.[17] Salisbury and Warwick had
a new grant of the wardenship of the west march, which gave them
possession until 1475 at rates of payment nearly one-third higher
than before.[18] Following the death of Lord Cromwell, Salisbury
added the stewardship of the northern territories of the duchy of
Lancaster[19] to his other sources of authority in the north country.
His brother Lord Fauconberg shared another of Somerset's offices,
the constabulary of Windsor Castle, with John Bourchier, Lord
Berners.[20] Master George Neville achieved his bishopric, Exeter, at
the expense of John Hals, whom the pope had appointed on Somerset's recommendation; George was given possession of the see's
comfortable temporalities, although his consecration had to be
deferred for three years on account of his youth, a scandalous arrangement which enabled him "to collect revenues but not souls".[21]

Yet this successful exploitation of crown patronage was not
achieved by monopolising the sources of power. The draft of the
letter commending George Neville to the pope was signed by
fourteen prelates, by Buckingham as well as York, Warwick and
Salisbury, and by twelve other secular peers. Nor did York and his
friends intend the new regime to be regarded merely as an instrument
for advancing their own interests. The parliament called after St.
Albans had another purpose beside their rehabilitation. For the first
time the chancellor's declaration of the causes of summons are shown
at length on the parliament roll, in English, and five separate com-
mittees of lords and officials were set up to consider different items
of this programme – the reorganisation and supply of the king's
household, the payment of the garrisons of Calais and Berwick-upon-
Tweed, sea-keeping, the export of bullion, and pacification of
Wales.[22] No doubt most of the first short session was spent in reaching
agreement on the terms of the parliamentary amnesty, but from
the beginning York had reminded the commons of his reputation as
the champion of reform. In fact, before the prorogation on 31 July
new proposals for the resumption of crown grants and the appro-
priation of supplies to the household had been enacted and they were
soon being applied.[23] The way to the commons' hearts was through
their pockets. When they met again on 12 November they were
ready to show that York had regained their confidence.

XIII

The Fight at Clyst

Since the collapse of York's enterprise in 1452 and the subsequent disappearance of the earl of Devon from recorded view, William Bonville had been the supreme figure in south-west England. His stewardship of the duchy of Cornwall confirmed, he became keeper of Lydford Castle and the royal "forest" of Dartmoor in September 1452 and constable of Exeter Castle in the following April.[1] Numerous duties were assigned to him, the defence of the coast from invasion and against marauders at sea, the raising of loans for the crown, the investigation of reported disorders on land and acts of piracy. With him in these commissions there regularly appear a handful of other names – William Bourchier, Lord FitzWarin, Sir Philip Courtenay and Sir John Dynham, all friends of Bonville, and also Nicholas Radford, who had been his legal adviser for many years. To anticipate a later title, Bonville might well have been called the king's lieutenant in the west.

This local hegemony was sure to be challenged once Devon recovered his freedom of action. With York's first·protectorate, it became his turn to enjoy a place in the sun. Until the middle of April 1454, he was employed at Westminster as a member of the council.[2] His colleagues, however, doubted whether his acquittal had brought about a change of heart. Before his departure from the capital, they ordered him to keep the peace under a penalty of £1,000. He treated this injunction with his customary disregard and soon began a series of depredations against Bonville's tenants; while his sons brought

165

several hundred armed men into Exeter on 30 April to lie in wait for Bonville, thus preventing him from raising a government loan.[3] The council reminded Devon on 3 June of the penalty he was liable to incur,[4] but this deterrent was found to be inadequate and on 24 July the earl and a number of his friends had to make a new undertaking with bonds for £2,666 13s. 4d. Bonville had to give a similar assurance of good behaviour. This time the enemies refrained from hostilities and on 3 February 1455 they fulfilled the second condition of their undertaking, namely that they should appear in Chancery.[5]

Devon now appears to have veered towards the court, for he was with it at St. Albans and wounded in the fighting. Bonville is not known to have been there, but the employment of his poursuivant by the king's advisers[6] indicates that he could still be considered as a member of the court party. Devon rejoined York after the battle, but neither he nor Bonville is shown as a member of the council in the following weeks, and of the two only Bonville was present in parliament to take the oath to the king.[7] He had turned his enemy's position. So far he had survived Devon's hostility because he had the backing of the government. With the court party now broken and his particular champion Wiltshire in flight, Bonville found that his interests attracted him to the victors of St. Albans: they alone were in a position to defend him against any fresh violence by Devon. His entry into their ranks was doubtless made easy by his local ally, Lord FitzWarin, who was the brother of the chancellor and of Viscount Bourchier, the treasurer. Another link was provided by his wife's kinsmen by her first marriage, the Harringtons; they were clients of the earl of Salisbury. Bonville sealed his new loyalty with the marriage of his grandson and heir to one of Salisbury's daughters. Once more in favour with the government of the day, he obtained a grant of letters of pardon on 12 November 1455, and when, in the same month, a sheriff was appointed for Devonshire, he was able to procure the selection of one likely to favour him.[8]

Far from ensuring his security, however, Bonville's defection only provoked the earl of Devon to embark on greater extremes of violence. This time, Devon may well have argued, his enemy had been too clever by half: his new friends had too much on their hands already – war with Scotland, piracy on the seas, mutiny at Calais, disturbances in Wales, lawlessness throughout the realm, and, not least, the insecurity of their own position; they could not be expected to undertake police action in the south-west. Moreover, York's tenure of power was not assured; yet another swing of the pendulum might be anticipated at any time, and a new government would readily excuse any illegalities committed against one of its opponents. There could not be a more propitious moment to destroy his enemies, and in abandoning all restraint Devon had fresh in his mind the sight of York and the Nevilles settling their own quarrels at St. Albans. Why should he not follow their example?

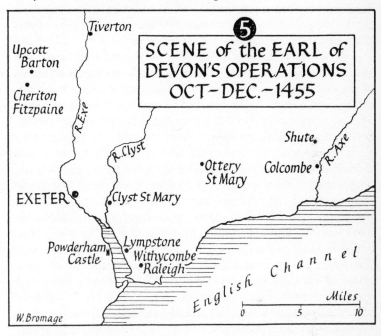

From the beginning of October 1455, Devon and his sons completely disrupted all ordered life in Exeter and the surrounding country. Their first move was to prevent the justices of the peace from holding their sessions in the city by an overwhelming show of force.[9] On the 22nd, Sir Thomas Courtenay assembled more than a hundred of his father's tenants and servants at Tiverton, the family seat thirteen miles north of Exeter: they were to take part in the most notorious private crime of the century, an outrage which is distinguished from most other violent deeds of this time by the fact that it was so obviously premeditated. A few miles from Tiverton, across the southern fringe of Exmoor, was the house of Nicholas Radford of Upcott. Radford, an old man now, was a lawyer of great distinction locally. He was an "apprentice of the law", that is, a barrister; he had not assumed the serjeant's coif, the equivalent of taking silk, for he had preferred to work in his native county, although he sometimes went to the courts at Westminster to represent his clients. There was always a valued place for such a man in county society, as legal adviser and as a trustee for property. In addition, Radford was often appointed to royal commissions in the south-west and he became a justice of the peace for Devonshire in 1437,[10] about the same time as he was appointed recorder of the city of Exeter. He was elected to parliament as a knight for the shire in 1435. Lord Bonville was one of Radford's oldest clients and his successful evasion of the earl's hostility probably owed much to his adviser's counsel.

Thomas Courtenay's party reached Upcott shortly before midnight on Thursday, 23 October.* They surrounded the buildings and set fire to the gates in the wall encircling the house. The tumult woke Radford and when he came to the window of his bedroom he saw a rabble of men lit by the flames from the gates. He called out to ask who was there and was there a gentleman among them. One of the yeomen replied, "Here is my lord, Thomas Courtenay, knight," and Courtenay said, "Radford, come down from your chamber and speak with me. I promise you on the faith and fealty by which I am bound to God, and as I am a gentleman and a faithful knight, that you will suffer no harm or bodily ill, or any damage to your property." Assured by this solemn promise, Radford came down and opened the main door. Courtenay entered, and his companions pressed after him into the hall. Radford was alarmed at their number, but Courtenay again reassured him and asked to be taken to his room. There Radford gave him food and drink, and afterwards they went into the hall and stood by "Le copborde", drinking Radford's wine.

As Courtenay held his host in conversation, his followers rifled the entire house, taking whole beds, napery, books, ornaments from

---

* There are three contemporary accounts of this murder: a petition to parliament by Radford's heirs; an indictment which closely follows the petition's narrative; and a letter written in London on 28 October 1455.[11] I have given translations of the conversation as reported in the (Latin) indictment so that this can be compared with the (printed) English version in the petition. The latter, it may be noted, is written in the hand of the privy seal office, suggesting official assistance in its drafting.

the chapel, and other household goods to a value put at a thousand marks, as well as £80 in cash;* the ruffians even toppled Radford's invalid wife out of her bed so they could take the sheets. When the loot had been removed, Courtenay said, "Hurry, Radford, for you must come with me to my lord, my father." Radford replied that he would gladly go and sent a servant for his horse. The servant returned to report that all the horses had been taken away, laden with the stolen goods. Radford turned to Courtenay and said bitterly, "Oh, Sir Thomas Courtenay, knight, you have broken your promise. I am old and feeble, and can hardly travel on foot, so I must beg of you to be allowed to ride." "Don't worry,† Radford," Courtenay returned. "You will soon ride well enough. Come with me." Then they left the house, and after they were a stone's throw distant, Courtenay had a few words with six of his men, set spur to his horse and hurried off, calling, "Farewell, Radford." The six men fell on Radford with swords and daggers and so killed him.

On the following Monday, the earl sent a party of his men back to Upcott, where Radford's body was lying in the chapel. They held a mock inquest, one of them acting as coroner and others, with assumed names, as jurors. They brought in a "verdict" of suicide. Radford's servants were then compelled to bear the body as if it were that of a heretic and, as they went, to sing a popular ballad known as the "Three men song". When they reached the churchyard of Cheriton Fitzpaine, the body was tipped from the coffin, stripped of its sheets, and pitched naked into a grave. The stones Radford had placed in the church in readiness for building his tomb were dropped on to his corpse, crushing it beyond recognition, so that no proper coroner could hold an inquest. The Courtenay servants, concluded the indictment, showed no more compassion than if they had been Jews or Saracens.

The murder of Nicholas Radford was the curtain-raiser for a series of military operations. Before the news was five days old in London, Devon and his sons, aided by Thomas Carrew of Ashwater, had collected an army of more than a thousand men at Tiverton, and on 3 November it advanced to Exeter. They entered without opposition and took charge of the gates as if they were the city's lawful garrison, questioning all who left and entered as to their destination

* £300 according to the petition.
† *Nulla cura.* "No force" in the petition.

or place of departure, and whose tenants or servants they were. Exeter was held in this manner until 23 December. Several members of Devon's army were later charged with breaking into houses and stealing property, but, considering the circumstances, the number of such incidents was small and there were no allegations of other crimes; the most serious offences were committed on the earl's direct orders. Thus he had the town houses of Bonville and FitzWarin ransacked. Master Henry Webber, the dean of Exeter, was arrested on 11 November and compelled to part with a gold cup and chain of the earl's, his pledges for a loan of £100 from the previous bishop. Webber was also robbed of money and a horse of his own, for which he had to make a deed of gift as the price of his release. The next day, a Sunday, a party of the earl's men removed Master John Morton from the choir of the cathedral as he was celebrating Mass; he was kept imprisoned until he redeemed himself by giving the earl £6 13s. 4d., a horse called a "hoby", and a bond for £40.

Nicholas Radford had entrusted a large part of his personal property to the cathedral clergy, and on 22 November the earl told the dean and Master Roger Keys, the treasurer, that if they did not surrender it to him he would instruct his men to break down the doors of the cathedral; in this eventuality, he said, he could not guarantee that his followers would distinguish between Radford's possessions and those of the cathedral. The dean and his colleague yielded under protest and a dozen of Devon's men went into the cathedral, from which they removed Radford's treasure, a most impressive collection of gold and silver plate valued at £600. Two days later, precious stones and more plate, said to be worth £70, were taken from a private house where Radford had left them. As these incidents took place three weeks after Devon's entry into Exeter, it is apparent that the seizure of Radford's goods was not a ruling motive, as has been supposed. We may, indeed, deduce that Devon resorted to plunder in order to pay his followers. Possibly he had not thought of keeping his army engaged for as long, but now, having failed to achieve his principal objectives quickly, he was preparing for a more protracted campaign.

Throughout the period of his occupation of Exeter, the earl from time to time sent parties to rob the houses of Bonville's supporters in the nearby countryside. For several weeks he conducted an intermittent siege of Powderham Castle, a strongly fortified mansion belonging to Sir Philip Courtenay. Courtenay earned Devon's enmity by his friendship with Bonville, but as he was the principal target for the earl's operations we must suspect a more compelling motive: this, presumably, was the fact that Devon must have felt that Powderham would have been his had a common ancestor not bequeathed it to the junior branch of the family.* Courtenay successfully withstood the first assault, on 3 November, but he called on Bonville for assistance. Bonville was then at Shute; before coming to Courtenay's aid, he sent a small party of his men to the earl's fortified house at Colcomb, which they robbed of all the movable goods, including fifty stones of wool, one hundred sheets, and vestments and wine. This was on 15 November, when the earl made a more serious attack on Powderham. His whole strength lay round the house all day, battering it with stones fired from serpentines. Bonville was now roused to help his beleaguered friend. As the earl held Exeter, he tried to reach Powderham by crossing the estuary of the Exe from Lympstone. Devon had anticipated this manoeuvre and lay in wait with a detachment said to be 500 strong. When Bonville reached Lympstone on 19 November, the earl drove him back, killing two members of the relieving force.

Bonville retired to recruit more supporters, and Devon had no doubt that another attempt would be made to relieve Powderham. He called the mayor and councillors of the city to meet him on 22 November: Bonville, he said, was approaching with "a great multitude of people" and might enter while Devon was away from Exeter; if this happened, Devon would return to drive him out and the citizens could not hope to be immune from the fighting. The earl pressed this argument as he wanted the mayor and councillors to forbid Bonville entry, but they gallantly refused, saying that as this was the king's city it was not in their power to refuse to open their gates to any lord. Devon then left to make another attempt to batter down the walls of Powderham with his cannon, while the citizens "came to the mayor in good array (*i.e.* armed) and walked with him and did the mayor's commandment in keeping of the peace". Powderham continued to hold out and Devon returned to Exeter. He remained until 15 December, when he "departed out of the city

---

* Powderham is now the seat of the earl of Devon. He is a direct descendant of Sir Philip Courtenay, for whose heirs the title was revived in 1831 after being dormant for nearly three centuries.

with his people into the field by Clyst and there bickered and fought
with the Lord Bonville and his people, and put them to flight, and
so returned again that night into the city". This is the fullest contemporary account we have of the fight at Clyst. There are no figures
of casualties, but when Clyst Heath was first cut by the plough in
1800, bones of many slain were uncovered.* The mayor tactfully
presented the victorious earl with six pipes of red wine and arranged
for the city to be illuminated that night.[12] Devon followed up his
advantage by sending about 500 men under Thomas Carrew in
pursuit; on the 17th, they pillaged Bonville's house at Shute without
encountering any resistance and secured a great booty of household
furnishings, foodstuff and cattle.

So far, Bonville and his friends had been left to provide for their
own safety. The disturbances in Devonshire were the subject of
anxious discussion at Westminster; news of fresh outrages arrived
within a few days of their occurrence, circulated rapidly and gained
proportion in the telling: the size of Devon's army was inflated to
800 horse and 4,000 foot. These exaggerated reports were used as a
lever by the duke of York's friends in the house of commons when
parliament reassembled on 12 November. The situation in the south-
west demanded direct intervention by the crown, but the king was
indisposed and incapable of taking action.† Led by York's councillor
William Burley, the commons pressed the lords to appoint a protector
of the realm "to whom the people of this land may have recourse
to sue to for remedy of their injuries". After several days' discussion,
the lords admitted the need for making this appointment and named
York as protector. After a conventional show of reluctance, York
accepted his nomination and the king gave his assent on 19 November.[14]

Having acquired the authority of protector, York showed no great
haste in using his powers where they were most needed. The earl of
Devon was at last dismissed from the commission of the peace on

---

* Some of these remains will belong to the casualties in the fight on the same
field in 1549.

† The king was unable to come to parliament and York was empowered to
act in his place. Professor Lander has demonstrated that none of the available
contemporary evidence shows that Henry was again insane, as has hitherto been
presumed.[13] On the other hand, the organisation of the king's council strongly
resembled that during Henry's insanity in 1453-4, which in its turn was modelled
on the council of his minority.

3 December, and two days later royal letters were sent to a group of peers and knights in the south-west, including the earl of Wiltshire, Bonville, FitzWarin, Philip Courtenay and John Dynham, ordering them to stand in readiness to assist York when he came to suppress the "riotous and ungodly demeanings" of "the great people the which rob and spoil daily, as it is said", the king's true subjects in Devonshire. York was still on the point of departure on 16 December, when the citizens of Exeter were instructed to give no assistance to Devon and his sons if they persisted "in their forwardness and misrule".[15] Not until Bonville came hot from Clyst did York set out. Hearing, no doubt, of the protector's approach, Devon's ardour deserted him, and he came to meet York at Shaftesbury, where he was arrested and sent a prisoner to the Tower of London.[16]

The earl did not remain in custody for very long. It had been proposed to bring him to trial at Westminster but this design was "countermanded" by 9 February 1456.[17] York's ascendancy was waning and on 25 February he was relieved of his commission as protector. If, as we have suggested, Devon had counted on such a political reversal to relieve him of the legal penalties of his military exploits, the event fully justified this expectation. Again at liberty, he returned to Devonshire, and soon there were fresh gatherings of armed retainers. The government issued a proclamation on 29 March to order the disbanding of assemblies in Devonshire and Somerset.[18]

The earl continued to dominate the Exe Valley with his overwhelming might. A large party, numbered, as usual, at 500, was sent under his son John to prevent those coming to the sessions of the peace from entering Exeter. For a week it lay outside the city, and on 8 April it entered and filled the High Street. Lord FitzWarin and Philip Courtenay had come as justices of the peace and to publish the recent proclamation, but Devon's men forced them to leave without carrying out their commission. There were no further incidents of this nature before the arrival in the city on 6 August of the commissioners of oyer and terminer appointed to investigate the recent disturbances; Bonville's sometime patron, the earl of Wiltshire, headed the commission, and another member was Sir John Fortescue, the chief justice, who was attended "with right a great fellowship".[19] The proceedings followed the usual pattern. Parliament had asked that both Devon and Bonville, as being equally to blame, should be imprisoned until a commission of oyer and terminer had visited the south-west, and that the sheriff of Devonshire, who was thought to favour Bonville, should be suspended from his functions in this connection; this petition was refused.[20] Consequently this sheriff was able to produce a grand jury dominated by Bonville's supporters, led by Walter Ralegh, himself a victim of Devon's plundering bands, and including John Bonville and John Ralegh. They inevitably presented a very black list of offences by the earl and his followers, but all they found against Bonville was the raid on Colcomb; the jury stressed that when he attempted to relieve Powderham on 19 November he was acting in his capacity as justice of the peace, as if his sole intention had been to read a riot act to Devon's fifteen hundred ruffians.

The royal government was obviously unimpressed by the file of indictments against Devon, for it restored him to the commission of the peace for Devonshire on 12 September, and in the following year he and his sons Thomas and Henry were pardoned all charges against them, including the murder of Nicholas Radford.[21] Bonville remained a magistrate but after 1456 he was no longer a regular nominee to other local judicial commissions; this semi-retirement, however, may have been due to his advanced age. There is no evidence of further strife between him and the Courtenays of Tiverton in the last four years of Henry VI's reign. His enemy, the earl, died at Abingdon in January, 1458, and there were some who professed to believe that the queen had poisoned him.[22] He was only forty-four years old, but his family had a poor medical history: the fifteenth-century earls of Devon were short-lived and several sons died without heirs. The new earl, Radford's murderer, was an active supporter of the queen. Bonville again trimmed his sails to the new wind and avoided being involved in the proscription of the "Yorkists" in 1459. For a time, he was associated with the earl in commissions to resist the "Yorkists" and to seize their lands, but after their victory at Northampton he once more gave York his support, as did his fellow-victims of Devon in 1455, Lord FitzWarin, Philip Courtenay, Roger Dynham and Walter Ralegh.[23] The last embers of the west country feud were finally extinguished in the general carnage. Both Bonville's son and grandson were killed with York at Wakefield and he fell himself at St. Albans on 17 February 1461; he had escorted the king to the field and stayed with him after Warwick had been routed, but despite the king's promise that he would be spared, the queen and the earl of Devon had him executed as a traitor. Six weeks later, Devon himself received no more mercy when he was captured after Edward IV's victory at Towton.

XIV

The King's Peace and the Queen's War

The first battle of St. Albans cast a shadow over the last years of the reign: there "was evermore a grouch and wrath had by the heirs of them that were so slain".[1] Hall's story of "Butcher" Clifford killing York's young son, Rutland, at Wakefield may be apocryphal, but his supposed words reflect the temper of the times: "By God's blood, thy father slew mine, and so will I do thee and all thy kin."[2] Henry's reign had seen violent feuds caused by less serious matters than murder. No one could have expected Beaufort, Clifford and Percy to forgive and forget, least of all York and Neville. The legacy of St. Albans was a political scene dominated by the fear that sooner or later the blood-feud would be renewed. Whenever they came together, the lords were attended by retinues numbered in several hundreds. Yet the nobility as a whole was not divided into two armed camps busily preparing for the next round of hostilities. There certainly was no great demand for armour in London.*

Before the end of York's second protectorate, it was being reported that there was a sharp division of opinion in the royal court on future relations with him. Henry seemingly wished to make a formal appointment of York as his chief councillor and lieutenant, with less powers than he had held as protector. In contrast, Queen Margaret –

* Robert Smart, "a poor soldier" returned from France, "fortuned him to be at the table" with Thomas Webber, a London brewer. Smart lost thirty five shillings, and having no money gave his armour in payment. Then he found himself in prison on a plea of debt, for Webber said "that because there is no war, that he cannot well sell the said cuirass". This was in 1456.[3]

176

"a great and strong laboured woman" – was making tireless efforts to gain power for herself.[4] King and queen persisted in their opposing policies. Nothing definite came of Henry's supposed proposal, but he obviously bore York no malice and he treated him with marks of favour. The queen was more hard-headed. She regarded York as a danger to the crown. She need not have suspected that he nourished designs to supplant Henry and rob her son of his royal inheritance. What she had good cause to fear was that York's aim was to possess the reality of power, that he would deprive the king of his personal right to govern, and that he would employ its patronage and financial resources for his own ends. Twice already had the crown's authority fallen into his grasp, and the result had been the disarray of Margaret's closest companions, attempts to regulate the household and its revenues, and the loss of the means to reward her friends and servants. She was determined to prevent a third protectorate, prepared to go to any lengths to ensure that her son should not succeed to the shadow of a throne. Being French, she inevitably had an exalted conception of the nature of royal authority. As Henry was clearly neither able nor willing to defend the rights of his crown, this meant that she had to take a direct part, to enlist supporters and advance them to key positions in the administration. Naturally, she found ready champions among the enemies of York and the Nevilles. And thus civil war became inevitable.

At first, the king's well-meaning purpose seemed to prevail. He came into parliament on 25 February 1456 and relieved York of his commission as protector. This was not an assertion of authority, for, as the terms of York's patent required, he was dismissed with the assent of both lords and commons.[5] Their agreement was probably given on the understanding that the ministry established after St. Albans would not be replaced. Certainly there was no immediate change. The Bourchiers remained in office, and until the second week of March, after which there is a break in the relevant record sources, York and the Nevilles were attending the council, and Salisbury is otherwise shown to have been there in June.[6] Provision was made for paying the arrears of York's wages as protector, and on 12 May he was given a profitable lease of royal mines in Devon and Cornwall.[7] In July he visited Henry at Windsor and wrote on his behalf to rebuke the king of Scots for his recent violations of the Border. Then York went north, and sent King James II another contemptuous letter from

Durham. York's approach persuaded James to give up his hostile plans.* This employment suggests that Henry had charged York to be his lieutenant in fulfilling the king's duty to defend the country. The duke was quite ready to accept these burdensome marks of royal confidence. His conduct was less correct when his direct interests were concerned. Thus he gave the queen the opportunity she had wanted to gain control of the organs of government.

While York was engaged against the Scots, the officers and tenants of his estates in the southern marches of Wales were employed on another kind of military exercise. For years South Wales had been in a state not far short of anarchy. A number of great magnates had territorial interests here. Apart from York, these were Buckingham, Warwick and Norfolk. The king also had his principality of South Wales (Cardiganshire and Carmarthenshire) and his duchy of Lancaster estates in Monmouthshire. Somerset had gained an influential hold by securing grants of strategic offices, the constabularies of Carmarthen and Aberystwyth, the stewardship of Kidwelly, and both positions in Monmouth. It was not so much the lords who were to be blamed for the disturbances as their local officers. Of these the most outstanding offenders were Griffith ap Nicholas, Somerset's deputy at Carmarthen, and Sir William Herbert of Raglan, who was York's principal lieutenant in this area. Both attempted to dominate the districts surrounding their commands. The activities of Griffith and his sons produced a reign of terror in the southern counties of the principality, and in 1452 royal officers were afraid to arrest them. The king's council ordered Somerset to dismiss Griffith, but although he signed the warrant he did not obey it. Herbert's operations were equally dangerous to the peace. In 1453 he was accused of making "great assemblies and routs of people".

The rapid political fluctuations at this time worked against a restoration of order in Wales. While Somerset and two of his colleagues could order Herbert to keep the peace and appear before the council, it was a very different matter in the following year, when Somerset was in the Tower. Then it was Griffith's turn to be cited, but he imprisoned the bearer of the king's letters in Carmarthen Castle, telling him that as he was a servant of York "he should fare

* James had on 28 June written to the French king stating that he had promised to help York to gain the English crown to which, James understood, York had a clear right. York's actions indicate that he had rebuffed James' offer.[8]

much the worse". Another opportunity to bring Griffith to account
came after the battle of St. Albans. He was again called before the
council,[9] but now York and his friends were able to take more far-
reaching measures. The death of Somerset enabled them to alter the
balance of power in South Wales in their own favour by taking over
his former offices: Warwick became steward and constable of
Monmouth, Edward Bourchier steward of Kidwelly, and York
constable of Carmarthen and Aberystwyth.[10] The parliamentary
programme in July 1455 included an article "to ordain and purvey
for restful and sad rule in Wales, and to set apart such riots and
disobediences as have been there before this time used". No such
general provision appears in the acts of this parliament. As was usual
when questions of law and order were involved, the matter was
dealt with in a partisan spirit. The only act of this parliament concerning Wales was directed against Griffith ap Nicholas. A petitioner*
urged York to take possession of Carmarthen and Aberystwyth and
expel Griffith and his ruffianly garrisons. Parliament decreed that if
he was still in either castle without York's licence on 1 March following, he was to be attainted of high treason.[11]

York had still not gained control of these two castles at the end of
his protectorate. In June 1456, it was reported that Edmund Tudor,
earl of Richmond, the king's half-brother, was at war in Wales.[12]
It is probable that the queen had instructed him to take charge of the
royalist interests in South Wales. Without receiving an official grant
replacing York's, Richmond took possession of Carmarthen Castle.
York could have sought redress for this injury by legal means, by a
petition to the king, but there was little chance of this passing the
council. Instead, Sir William Herbert tried to settle the matter by
direct action. On 10 August, he and Sir Walter Devereux† raised a
force estimated to number two thousand men from York's lands in
Herefordshire and Radnor and led them to Carmarthen, laid seige
to the castle and took it, making Richmond their prisoner. They
also seized Aberystwyth Castle. The records of the principality were
removed from Carmarthen Castle and with them the royal seal for
South Wales; this Herbert and Devereux used to seal a commission
appointing them to hold a judicial session, when they released a
number of alleged outlaws and men accused of various crimes.[13]

* Griffith ap David ap Thomas, esquire.
† See his earlier exploits in Appendix V.

Herbert's seizure of Carmarthen provoked an immediate reaction from the court. Within a week, when the news would have arrived, the king was on his way from Windsor to Kenilworth.[14] Here he would have rejoined the queen, who had been spending the summer in the midlands.[15] Now she was able to influence him and develop her plans to take control. Herbert's exploits had strengthened her hand. No doubt he could justify them on the grounds that he was taking possession of the castles for their lawful custodian, but he had taken the law into his own hands and his assembly of an army and its march across Wales could be interpreted as an act of raising war against the king. Moreover, this operation was only the latest in a series of recent actions whereby Herbert and his associates had flouted the crown's authority, including the virtual occupation of the city of Hereford.* Margaret intended to use this opportunity to defeat his challenge to her policy of consolidating the royal position in South Wales. A strong case could be made against him as a lawbreaker, and the lords, called to a great council at Coventry at the end of September, could not refuse to support measures for bringing him to justice. Both Herbert and Devereux had obeyed a summons to appear before the king there. Devereux was confined in Windsor Castle and the great council advised the king to put Herbert in the Tower of London.[17]

Margaret could take further advantage from the situation. Behind Herbert was York. Presumably Herbert had only been carrying out his master's instructions. Certainly York was accused at the council of committing some unspecified offences and Buckingham and other lords urged Henry to rebuke the duke and impress on him the fact that it was only through the exercise of the king's grace that no proceedings would be taken against him.† The queen would have

---

* He had seized control of the city on 15 March, arrested the mayor, emptied the prisons, and overawed a session of Herefordshire justices of the peace so that six burgesses were condemned and straightway hanged for their supposed part in the murder of his kinsman, Walter Vaughan, two days earlier. For a year afterwards, the citizens complained, they lived in constant fear of Herbert and his villainous Welsh followers, to the complete disruption of their normal lives.

Herbert was at Cowbridge, Glamorgan, on 12 April 1456, where he attacked and robbed a servant of the earl of Wiltshire. His brother Thomas was said to have gathered eighty men at Ross-on-Wye on 20 June with the intention of riding to Kenilworth to kill the king.[16]

† Although the account of the great council at Coventry quoted here is not

preferred more rigorous measures, but Buckingham had thwarted her.[18] This gave her a strong argument to put to Henry: if Buckingham could not be relied upon to support her against York, no more could his half-brothers the chancellor and treasurer. More dependable men had to be put in their places. The Bourchier brothers were dismissed and Bishop Wainfleet of Winchester and the earl of Shrewsbury were appointed. The privy seal had already changed hands on 24 September, when it was entrusted to Laurence Booth, Margaret's own chancellor. With this key appointment, her hold on the administrative machinery was made secure. Like Suffolk with Moleyns, she had grasped the mainspring of all government action, the office whose warrants controlled all branches of the administration.

The new government showed its mettle in its measures to restore order in the Welsh marches. Herbert had escaped from Coventry, made for Wales and began to enlist men in order to resist.★ He was proclaimed a rebel and a reward of five hundred marks was offered for his capture.[19] The court prepared to take military action against him. In January 1457, the master of the ordnance came to Kenilworth with twenty-six "new guns called serpentines, for the field", twelve hundred pounds of sulphur, two hundred and ninety-four pounds of gunpowder, eighteen hundred pounds of saltpetre, a culverin, a ball of iron and a ball of lead. He had also constructed three "great serpentines" which could be carried anywhere and were, he claimed, sufficiently powerful "to subdue any castle or place that would rebel".[20] Buckingham, Shrewsbury, Wiltshire and a number of other peers were in attendance and presumably provided the king with an army.

At the end of March the court moved on to Hereford and spent the whole of April there.[21] No resistance was offered and most of Herbert's associates appeared before a commission of oyer and terminer on 28 April. Herbert was still at large, but on a promise that his life and goods would be spared, he came to the king at Leicester, submitted and received a pardon.[22] Some of his friends

dated, its relevance to Herbert's operations is inescapable. This council also passed an ordinance requiring lords to seek redress of injuries by legal means and not "by way of fact" (*i.e.* by force). This is precisely what Herbert had just done on York's behalf.

★ He allegedly came to Abergavenny on 25 October 1456 and gave orders that the men of that lordship and of Usk, Caerleon, Glamorgan and Llandaff should assemble under arms.

received less tender treatment. Sir Walter Devereux, his son and eleven other esquires were taken to London for trial in King's Bench. The judges were prepared to release them on bail until a jury could be produced, but the council ordered them to be kept in prison; they were acquitted on 3 February 1458.[23]

The different treatment given to the leaders of York's followers was intended to divide them. The court's purpose was to detach Herbert and in the short run it was successful.[24] In the task of building up a party, Margaret had two nuclei in the surviving members of the old court group and in the families of the victims of St. Albans. The new treasurer, Shrewsbury, was a great source of strength, being a magnate in the same class as York, Buckingham, Salisbury and Warwick. This was also an important qualification in a treasurer to such a poverty-stricken king: on several occasions he had to advance money from his own coffers to pay royal creditors.[25] His loyalty was probably strengthened by rivalry with York in Ireland, where he was a great landowner. So too was Wiltshire, who had now inherited his father's earldom of Ormond. Shrewsbury's marriage to Wiltshire's sister had presumably been arranged with a view to uniting the Irish interests of their houses. Wiltshire was retained as a salaried member of the king's council from 1456; in 1458 he replaced Shrewsbury as treasurer. Two other peers were paid as councillors, Lord Beauchamp, the steward of the household, and Lord Grey of Ruthin.* The pardons granted in 1457 to the earl of Devon and his heir for their excesses in 1455 indicate that they had earned the queen's favour.

Of the second group of the queen's supporters, Somerset's heir was a violent young man who had to be restrained from attacking the Nevilles. He became a regular attendant at court, although his behaviour was not calculated to add to its quiet.† The new earl of Northumberland came to Coventry on 28 February 1457 and was received at court with marked favour. He sealed a new contract as warden of Berwick and the east march which gave him possession of the office for ten years, a longer term than in any of his previous

* Wiltshire and Beauchamp were paid from Easter 1456, Grey from 28 October following.[26]

† On 11 October 1456 there nearly was a riot in Coventry after "a great affray" between his servants and the town watch in which two or three of the latter were killed. Somerset was given £100 for unspecified services to the king in October 1457.[27]

indentures.[28] His brother Sir Ralph Percy was appointed constable of Dunstanburgh Castle, Northumberland, and his retainer Henry Bellingham was made receiver of Kendal, doubtless at the earl's request. He may also have inspired the simultaneous appointment of Humphrey Neville as constable of Richmond Castle.[29] Considering the earl of Salisbury's interests in the same area, Humphrey's installation in this fortress was presumably arranged in order to challenge his local influence. As a member of the senior branch of the Neville family, he would have little love for the man who had secured a large share of the hereditary estates of the earl of Westmorland. His appointment appears to be a deliberate attempt to reopen an old wound.

A far more serious blow was suffered by Salisbury when his brother the bishop of Durham died later that year. His control over the Bishopric was now broken. The queen lost no time in advancing Laurence Booth to the see, and he preferred the senior to the junior branch of the Nevilles as his principal secular support. Thomas Neville of Brancepeth replaced Lord Fauconberg as steward, the chief officer in the temporal government of the county palatine, and John, Westmorland's brother, became the leading member of the Durham judiciary.[30] As the childless Westmorland was an invalid, John was the effective head of the family; he was raised to the peerage in 1459.

One outstanding figure whose role is difficult to assess was the duke of Buckingham. When his half-brothers were dismissed in 1456, it was reported that he "taketh [it] right strangely". At the same time, although he would not condone York's recent conduct, he had saved him from the queen's hostile designs.[31] Buckingham had been a regular member of the council since the end of Suffolk's ascendancy, his wife was Prince Edward's godmother, and he was one of the peers who stood as sureties for Somerset on his release in February 1455. For all this, he could not be considered as a fervent member of the court party to the same extent as Wiltshire, for instance. He was, no doubt, too much the "overmighty subject" ever to lose his identity in a faction. Nor does he appear to have had any private cause for ill-feeling against York and the Nevilles.* His wife was Salisbury's sister and although a connection of this kind, made when the parties were children, carried little weight, it helped him to maintain close rela-

---

* Mr C. A. J. Armstrong has shown that Buckingham's eldest son was not a casualty of the first battle of St. Albans, as has often been said.[32]

tions with the Nevilles. On 9 May 1458 he stood bail for his brother-in-law Fauconberg to appear in Chancery.[33]

Buckingham is distinguished from all his contemporary peers by the integrity of his character. In a list of notable casualties since 1447, drawn up in the reign of Henry VII, only Humphrey of Gloucester and the duke of Buckingham are called "good". He was killed at Northampton. Although he was not on the list of York's "mortal and extreme enemies", he stood by the king to the very last, acting as his spokesman, anxious to shield him from a personal encounter with the ferocious Warwick.[34] This was the same part as he had taken in the exchanges before the first battle of St. Albans, and as there, presumably because his championship of the king's authority would allow no compromise, he was unable to prevent bloodshed. Loyalty to Henry was Buckingham's ruling principle. It was a personal devotion; it did not lead to his supporting Queen Margaret. Henry's great desire was to restore peace among his lords, whereas the queen was preparing for war. The king had lost real control of the administration to his wife. He never had been the effective ruler and now, it seems, he was further enfeebled by his injury at St. Albans.* But with Buckingham acting as his self-appointed guardian, Henry was able to keep up the impartial forms of constitutional government. Great councils were called periodically without any attempt to exclude York, and up to 28 July 1459 his name was regularly recorded as a "witness" to royal charters.[36]

In the autumn of 1457, a real danger of French invasion made the problem of reconciling the lords a matter of urgent necessity. Commissions of array required private enemies to work together in defending the country against its external foes, and Warwick was appointed to "keep the sea" since the lord admiral, Exeter, showed little capacity for this duty.[37] The French danger did not materialise but it had helped to produce an atmosphere which encouraged Henry to attempt to restore harmony. Although Warwick, Salisbury and York had been officially exonerated, they had not made their peace with the families of their slain opponents. A great council was called to London in November, but it was poorly attended and consequently adjourned to January 1458. The lords gradually arrived with their

---

* In a conversation alleged to have taken place in August 1457, it was said of Henry that "he sleepeth to much thereto [*i.e.* since] he was hurt at Saint Albans".[35]

now habitual large retinues. York and the Nevilles were slightly outnumbered by the fifteen hundred men led by Northumberland, Egremont and Clifford, and even more when the ducal hotheads, Somerset and Exeter, brought a further eight hundred; but their lodgings were in the city while their enemies were outside Temple Bar, and the mayor kept five thousand men under arms to prevent a disturbance. The king delivered a homily, seemingly decked with scriptural and classical allusions, and having thus exhorted the lords to settle their differences in a peaceable manner, retired to Berkhamsted to await the result.

After nearly a month, the parties were brought to agree to conditions by the mediation of the chancellor and Archbishop Bourchier, and on 24 March the king returned to deliver the award. Its terms were mainly financial. York, Warwick and Salisbury were to establish a chantry at St. Albans, where masses would be celebrated for the souls of the slain, and to give compensation to their families. York and Warwick were to renounce crown debts amounting to £4,000, so that five thousand marks could be assigned to Somerset's widow and heir, and one thousand to John Clifford. The Percies were to be satisfied by Salisbury, his wife and younger sons giving up their claim to the damages awarded against Egremont in 1454. Egremont was himself bound over to keep the peace for the next ten years. As a further precaution, the king later that year gave him a life grant of Wressell Castle, Yorkshire, on his promise to go abroad on pilgrimage. It had been a cheap settlement as far as York and the Nevilles were concerned, for all they had to do was to give up bad debts. The empty reconciliation was solemnised by a procession to St. Paul's Cathedral.[38]

A year later both parties were preparing for war. The immediate reason for the final breakdown is not easy to establish. It may be that the court was alarmed by the reports it received on the negotiations which Warwick was conducting with the duke of Burgundy on York's behalf in the summer of 1458 and concluded that York's desire for a Burgundian marriage for one of his sons could only mean that he was bent on a forcible seizure of power. Yet nothing was said about this diplomacy when the court listed his misdeeds for presentation to parliament. Warwick's naval operations in the Channel, consoling though they were to the nation's pride, included wanton acts of piracy against neutral shipping and gravely embarrassed the government's relations with friendly powers. These activities may have prompted the court to deprive Warwick of his captaincy of Calais[39] in November, but its principal motive was to have this base and its garrison under the command of a custodian loyal to its domestic policies. Recent administrative changes indicate that the queen was preparing to take a stronger line. Lord Stanley, whose fidelity may reasonably have been suspect, was replaced as king's chamberlain by Sir Richard Tunstall.* Wiltshire took over from Shrewsbury as treasurer of the Exchequer, and Sir Thomas Tuddenham became treasurer of the household. He began to draw directly on the revenues collected by the sheriffs, many of them now household officers, which had previously been paid into the Exchequer.† This policy of tapping the county revenues at source made certain that the court would have funds at its immediate disposal. Since, for reasons of security, it was tending to spend a considerable part of each year in the midlands, it would not need to send to London for money, an obvious advantage in the event of civil war.

The war cannot be said to have begun at any particular moment, but a vulgar brawl in November 1458 might be considered as the point of no return. When Warwick was attending the council in London, one of his servants quarrelled with a menial of the royal household. The guard then set on Warwick and his retinue, and he had to fight his way to his barge and so make his escape. The queen blamed Warwick for the incident and demanded his arrest, but he withdrew to Calais. In the prevailing atmosphere of suspicion and ill-feeling, he naturally concluded that this had been a deliberate attempt to murder him.[42] There could be no further hope for reconciliation, and this made it impossible for the government to rule the country. In April 1459, the court sent out letters requiring men like John Paston to attend the king at Leicester on 10 May, bringing with them as many followers as they could raise and enough money to pay their expenses for two months.[43] On 7 May, three thousand bows were ordered for the royal armoury in a warrant opening with

---

* Stanley had been appointed during York's second protectorate. About this time his heir married a daughter of Salisbury. In 1459 the son refused to serve against Salisbury and congratulated him after his victory at Blore Heath.[40]

† The Exchequer's subordination to the household was ensured by the appointment of the treasurer of the chamber as Wiltshire's deputy. This suggests that the revival of the "chamber system" under Edward IV had begun in the last years of Henry VI.[41]

the words "considering the enemies on every side approaching upon us, as well upon the sea as on land".[44] Yet the first military action did not take place until 23 September. The queen, recruiting in Cheshire, learnt that Salisbury was on his way from Yorkshire to join York and Warwick at Ludlow. She sent a force to arrest him but he fought his way through at Blore Heath.[45] When the main royal army reached Ludlow on 12 October, however, York's concentration broke up and its leaders fled to their bases overseas, the duke to Ireland and the Nevilles to Calais, taking with them York's son and heir, Edward, earl of March. The desertion of Warwick's soldiers from Calais was one reason for this collapse, another the failure of Herbert to bring reinforcements from Wales.

The signs are that the court had taken the initiative. In its tendentious account of York's treasonable actions, he and the Nevilles were said to have planned to pounce upon the king at Kenilworth, but as the royal army had been in the field before Salisbury reached Ludlow, this is barely credible. Yet they had confronted the king's army at Ludford and opened fire with their artillery before the rout. Moreover, they had rejected an offer of pardon. The court could thus make a case against them. A parliament was called to meet at Coventry on 20 November, the sheriffs being given the names of those who were to be returned. It passed an act of attainder against York and his chief adherents, condemning them as traitors, extinguishing their titles and confiscating their offices and estates.[46] The forms of law were observed in full, but the presence on the drafting committee of Tuddenham's crony John Heydon[47] betrays the partisan spirit in which it was framed: inconvenient facts were suppressed, like the answer York and his friends made to the offer of pardon. They had urged the king to ignore their enemies, who hoped for their destruction in order to appropriate their lands and offices.[48] This is precisely what did happen. Before the end of the year, numerous grants of offices and of pensions from the forfeited estates had been made to those who had rallied to the court.[49] Pamphlets were distributed to justify the proscription,[50] but it is possible that these extreme measures won sympathy for the victims. In contemporary opinion, the inheritance was sacrosanct, and its violation, even by judicial process, was considered an outrage to one of the pillars of society. Others might fear that the greed of Margaret's followers had not yet been satisfied.[51]

Eight months later all was changed. At the end of June 1460,

Warwick, Salisbury and Edward of March had crossed from Calais, and within two weeks had passed through London and on 10 July encountered a depleted royal army outside Northampton. As at St. Albans, several hours were spent in an unavailing effort to bring the king's party to discuss terms. Warwick's forces then attacked, under orders to kill only lords, knights and esquires. Thanks to the treachery of Lord Grey of Ruthin, Warwick had an easy victory. Henry was taken unharmed, Buckingham, Shrewsbury, Beaumont and Egremont were killed outside his tent. The victors treated Henry with respectful consideration. They had made it clear on their arrival in the country that they intended no disloyalty to his person.[52] This declaration was not insincere. Proof of this comes from a report on the capture of Lord Rivers in the previous January. On being taken to Calais, Rivers was furiously rated by Salisbury "that he should be so rude to call him and these other lords traitors, for they shall be found the king's true liege men". Warwick and March "rated him in like wise".[53] Their purpose was to gain control of the government and recover their confiscated estates. With the king their prisoner, they now had these objectives within their grasp.

York however had now set his sights on the crown. He did not return from Ireland until two months after the battle of Northampton. As he neared London, his march assumed the character of a royal progress, with the arms of England displayed. He arrived on 10 October, three days after the opening of parliament, and entering its chamber in Westminster Palace advanced on the vacant throne and laid his hand upon it. "All the lords were sore dismayed."[54] Not even the Nevilles had been expecting this claim to the crown, still less were they ready to allow it.[55] York's enemies, naturally enough, were not present, but a number of peers who had attended the "parliament of devils" at Coventry, sometime associates like Norfolk, Bourchier and Bonville, had come over to the victorious party. At Coventry, however, they had repledged their loyalty to Henry[56] and they were not prepared to commit perjury now. York subsequently put forward a formal claim based on his descent from Edward III through Lionel of Clarence and the Mortimers, a stronger title, he stated, than that of Lancaster. Henry asked the lords to answer for him, and after the justices had refused to help, saying the matter was beyond their competence, the lords stated their reasons for rejecting York's claim. These he answered with such overwhelming arguments that the peers were obliged to admit his title.

A good case could have been made for Lancaster if Henry IV had based his claim on direct male inheritance from Edward III, but he had preferred to trace his title through his mother's line to Edmund Crouchback, son of Henry III; his pretence that Crouchback and not Edward I was Henry III's elder son was, as York said, an obvious lie designed to mask his usurpation. No weight could be attached to enactments in parliament since, as Henry IV was not legitimately king, his parliaments could not be lawful. The same reason invalidated any oaths made to Henry IV and his heirs. Nevertheless, the lords remained unwilling to deprive Henry, and the remarkable arrangement was made whereby this admittedly unlawful king was to keep the throne for the rest of his life so that the lords' consciences should remain clear; while York was persuaded to let his right to the crown remain in suspense until Henry died. As the lords were well aware that York was the senior by ten years, it would appear that they had completely frustrated his aspirations; although at a later stage in the parliamentary discussions the suggestion was made that Henry might choose to abdicate.[57] But it was York who died first: before the year was out, he had been killed in a foolhardy attack on vastly superior forces at Wakefield. According to tradition, his severed head was decked with a paper crown and placed over one of the gates of York City, so that all might mock the outcome of his kingly pretensions.

CONCLUSION

The New King

The rejection of York's claim to immediate possession of the throne makes it clear that his allies had not fought for the cause of Yorkist legitimacy. Four months later, on 3 March 1461, a small group of these same lords agreed that his son Edward, earl of March, should become king. Before Towton was fought, a number of other peers had accepted him. The Nevilles, the Bourchiers, Norfolk and about a dozen more lords had had a change of heart.[1] Nothing could make them accept Richard of York as their king in the previous October. Why were they now ready to put his son on the throne? They could put forward a legalistic justification. Although York's title to the crown had been proved and admitted in parliament, he had made a compact with Henry, allowing him to remain king. Henry could be said to have broken this compact by conspiring to destroy Richard. Thus York's temporary renunciation was no longer binding. There was no need to arrange a formal deposition of Henry VI, as in law he was not king at all. Since York was dead, Edward his heir had been the lawful king from the day of his death.

This argument was produced in parliament in November 1461. Actually, Edward IV dated his reign from 4 March, two months after York was killed. But obviously other reasons were urged at that first Yorkist council. One explanation favoured by historians is that Warwick put his young cousin on the throne in the belief that Edward would be amenable to his control. Perhaps this thought did enter Warwick's mind, but more immediate considerations beset

190

the "Kingmaker" and his colleagues. The fact was that they had no choice. For their own self-preservation they had to crown their own candidate. Since the second battle of St. Albans on 17 February, Henry was no longer in their charge, but in the north with Margaret, Somerset, Northumberland, Devon and her other champions. A final trial of strength had yet to come. If the Yorkist lords were defeated, they could expect no mercy. The murder of Salisbury after his capture at Wakefield, the execution of Bonville, despite Henry's promise of safety, after the second battle of St. Albans, were sufficient warnings of this. But even if they were completely successful and captured Henry, Margaret and their son, this would be no permanent guarantee of their future immunity.

York and his friends had been able to secure influential places in the government three times in the last six years, once because of Henry's complete and unconcealable incapacity, twice through their having the virtual custody of his person as a result of military victory. Their first two periods in power had ended when Henry reclaimed his indisputable monarchical right to govern, and on both occasions the sequel had been the dismissal of York and his associates from the council and the reinstatement of their personal enemies. Supposing Henry was retaken in 1461, after three failures the Yorkists could not hope to keep him in subjection for the rest of his life – he was only forty years old – nor his son after him. In 1453, they had taken the precaution of imprisoning Somerset, the man with most influence over Henry and their chief enemy. But now, Somerset's place had been taken by Margaret, and Warwick and his colleagues may well have decided that it would be a simpler matter to depose a king than to neutralise so redoubtable a queen.

The fundamental reason for the recognition of Edward IV was the nature of medieval government. The Yorkist lords were as conservative as their enemies. They could not bring themselves to contemplate any constitution other than that to which they had been accustomed. The king was under the law, but he had an absolute right to choose his own ministers and advisers. There was no convention which obliged him to accept and retain officers against his will. This could only be done by force, by exposing the country to the perils of civil war, a dangerous undertaking where the penalties for failure were execution and confiscation; and in the whole course of England's history to that time no baronial group which had forced its will on the king and left him on the throne had been able to prevent him from recovering control. But with the corruption of the legal system in Henry VI's reign, and the growing scale and intensity of private feuds, the composition of the king's council had become a matter of vital importance to the lords involved in these disputes. No doubt there were economic motives behind a lord's ambition for a place in the council; few denied themselves some pickings when the opportunity came. Far more pressing, however, was the desire to deny power to his personal enemies, to prevent them from using the crown's authority to his own discomfiture: the jurisdiction of the council was heavily loaded in the favour of its members and their dependants, and they could appoint congenial commissioners of oyer and terminer, select sheriffs whose choice of juries would guarantee the verdicts they required. The undisturbed possession of their lawful estates, immunity from vexatious suits, freedom to prosecute claims to property without hostile interference from the royal court, official protection from violence, these were the benefits to be gained by a place on the king's council, both by the lords themselves and their retainers; the rapid fluctuations of political fortunes between 1453 and 1456 had repercussions on the local administration of the law throughout England and Wales.

Henry through his simplicity remained outside the party struggle. York and his allies looked upon him as merely the pawn of the court party, as he was their own when they were in power. They could accuse Somerset of misgovernment, others could be blamed after his death. It was not for the sake of some convention that Henry remained free from criticism: he was blameless. But the queen, by enlisting the enemies of York and the Nevilles, compromised her husband's crown. She pledged it to a baronial faction, and the logical course for the opposing group was to set up its own king. York, possibly, had realised this in 1460. The only sure way to stop the political pendulum and to keep power was to take the crown himself. As the leader of a powerful faction, made up of lords who had joined him because of their disputes with individual members of the court group, he stood at the head of an agglomeration of maintenance with links in all parts of the country; he was, one might say, a "bastard feudal king". Like the kings of feudal times, however, he was only "first among equals"; he had no absolute right to command. But arrogant and impetuous, he put forward his claim to the English crown without first making sure of the consent of his chief adherents. They saw no need to replace Henry: they had nothing against him, he was in their charge and they had control of his government; their surviving enemies had not yet given proof of their might. Their conversion came when they lost their royal prisoner. It was fortunate that they had a candidate with a defensible hereditary title to the throne.

Edward was accepted as king because a baronial faction wished to retain its hold on the organs of government. In 1470, Henry VI was restored for the identical reason. In the previous year, Warwick had made a forcible bid to retrieve his waning influence in Edward's government. A well-organised rising caught Edward by surprise and he became the earl's prisoner. Warwick then tried to carry on the government but found that he could not keep Edward under restraint. Once at liberty, Edward soon resumed control, Warwick fled abroad and his estates were confiscated. Now he was an impoverished exile. The only way to regain power, and his lands, was by making his peace with Queen Margaret and undertaking to restore Henry. Edward was again caught off his guard and had to leave the country, while Henry was brought out of the Tower and put back on the throne. The pattern of events in 1469-70 was remarkably similar to that in the later 1450's: there were the same initial attempt to rule through physical control of the king, the same failure, the same remedy. Warwick was a kingmaker by necessity. The amazing *volte-face* which made him the ally of Margaret and his other old enemies was the last resort of a ruined man. It was an extremely hazardous gamble, for even if Henry's restoration had been permanent, Warwick would have been hard pressed to maintain his supremacy once Margaret and her adherents had returned to the royal court. In 1470, Warwick took on the role of kingmaker for the same personal motives and in the same desperate spirit as he had done in 1461; the repeat performance emphasises how little his acceptance of Edward IV owed to the merits of Yorkist legitimacy.

The Neville-Percy feud was the chief single factor which turned political rivalry into civil war. Richard of York could not have renewed his challenge to Somerset without the Neville alliance. The first battle of St. Albans was the immediate outcome of the harnessing of this private quarrel to the central issue between the two royal dukes. The feud continued as a secondary theme in the following years. The third earl of Northumberland gave his support to Queen Margaret through his desire to avenge his father's death. This he did at Wakefield. After the battle, the earl of Salisbury was taken to Pontefract Castle and beheaded on the following day (31 December 1460). He was not, seemingly, executed on the orders of the Lancastrian commander, Somerset, but as an act of private vengeance. His widow, at least, thought she knew who was responsible. After Edward's accession, she made a formal appeal of murder against nine obscure men as principals, and listed a total of thirty-nine others as accessories; the majority were retainers and tenants of the earl of Northumberland.* The countess was taking a private means of redress for what was, in fact, a private injury. Northumberland's name was presumably omitted from her list because he too was then dead.

Two heads of the house of Percy had now fallen in battle against York, thus establishing, it might seem, a notable record of devotion to Lancaster. But again, the events of 1469-71 provide a second outstanding illustration of the fickleness of baronial loyalties to royal dynasties. When Warwick fled overseas, Edward brought Northumberland's son out of the Tower, restored his lands and title, and made him warden of the east march, an application in reverse of the Lancastrian policy of guarding the north by setting Neville against Percy. When Henry was restored, Northumberland was confirmed in his estates but the wardenship was given to Warwick's brother, Lord Montagu, the previous occupant.³ On Edward's return from exile, he landed at Ravenspur, as Henry IV had done, and made his way through Percy territory; had Northumberland wished to stop him, it would have required no great effort, for Edward's following was small. The earl, however, "sat still"; indeed, Edward is said to have exhibited letters from Northumberland advising him to return by this route. Although he did not join Edward, Northumberland did deter Montagu from proceeding against him,⁴ and so Edward

* The knights she named were Richard Tunstall, Ralph Percy, William Plumpton, George Darell, Gervais Clifton, John Courtenay, John Pudsay, Roger Clifford, Henry Bellingham, William Everingham, Thomas Metham and Richard Aldborough. Altogether thirty-eight of the forty-eight were Yorkshiremen, including seven of the principals.
Plumpton was also accused by Robert Percy (possibly a retainer of Salisbury and obviously not a close connection of Northumberland) to have "laboured to have his head stricken off" following his (Percy's) capture at Wakefield.²

was able to go through to the Midlands, gather an army and regain the kingdom. Northumberland had remained true to the only policy his family had consistently pursued, the establishment of its own dominance in the Border country; to this the Nevilles were a more serious threat than any king in England. So far as the fourth earl was concerned, Henry VI was a Neville king, and he was not prepared to defend his throne if by so doing he upheld Warwick's supremacy and enabled Montagu to remain in the wardenship which was a traditional part of the Percy empire. Northumberland was certainly not a convert to the Yorkist cause, for although he answered Richard III's call to oppose Henry Tudor, he came to Bosworth merely to await the result.

If the two most important combatant families showed so little consistency in their attachments, we cannot expect to find much evidence of loyalty to either royal house among the general mass of the population who took no active part in the civil wars. There are no indications that any of Henry VI's humbler subjects regretted his deprivation.* Only at the highest level was there any notable break in the continuity of central or local administration in 1461. The civil service held fast to its tradition of indifference to political change; the judiciary, the two chief justices excepted, remained unmoved; and the commissions of the peace disclose that only a small proportion of each county's leading gentry had irretrievably committed themselves to the losing cause. Even among the nobility there were some who had spent their lives in personal service to Henry yet made no attempt to defend him and became councillors under his successor.[6]

Henry was not a king to inspire devotion, indeed he fell far short of his people's expectations of what a king should be. His personal failings were more apparent than ever before in his last years on the throne. His intentions were excellent, there is no doubt of his grieved concern about the divisions among the lords, but he did not speak to them as their sovereign, commanding them on their obedience to desist from conduct destructive of his people, but as a humble preacher, seeking to convince them of the error of their ways. Again, when York challenged his crown, he left it to the lords to decide whether they preferred him to his rival. And finally, in accepting their ultimate conclusion, he consented to the disinheritance of his

---

* No one appears to have been accused in Edward's first three years, at least, of expressing any sympathy for Henry VI.[5]

own son. By this act of renunciation, he gave up his last claims on his subjects' loyalty.*

It cannot be presumed, either, that the ordinary subject rejoiced in the triumph of Edward IV except in so far as it promised an end to the period of conflict. The cold reception given to him by the Yorkshire townsmen and country folk in 1471 revealed their indifference. There are, however, some indications that his accession was welcomed in southern England. The tumultuous assent of the inhabitants of London on 4 March 1461 was, no doubt, stimulated by the fiery oratory of popular preachers like Friar Brackley, and still more by fresh memories of their bombardment by the Lancastrian garrison of the Tower and by the alarming reports of the savage behaviour of the "northern men" so recently at their gates; although it is possible that more substantial citizens may have hoped for an improvement in economic conditions on the strength of Warwick's naval operations in 1458 and Duke Richard's record of support for financial reform. In 1460, the people of Kent had given a friendly reception to the Yorkist lords coming from Calais, and some were in Edward's army at Towton.

Some curious testimony comes from the west country. There were a number of popular risings here early in 1462. In two districts, the Portsmouth area and western Dorset, the rioters had a common refrain which began with a statement that it was to them that Edward owed his crown.[7] Absurd though this claim is, it is important if it reflects a widely held opinion, and it does at least suggest that peasants in Wessex had initially shown some enthusiasm for their new king. Somerset provides a pointer in the same direction. In May 1462, a mason of Wells assembled an enormous crowd from this and adjacent counties, for the alleged purpose of sacking Glastonbury, by spreading reports that the abbot was a traitor and scheming to send a great sum of money to Henry VI.† Supporting evidence of popular support for Edward in this part of the country is found in his charter for Bristol, granted in 1462 as a reward for the good service of the mayor and commons. Similar expressions of his appreciation for services rendered appear in other royal charters granted in the same

---

* As Shakespeare realised (*King Henry VI, Part III*, Act I, sc. i).

† About twenty thousand people were said to have gathered, an exceptionally large estimate for an indictment. The mason, John Stowell, was fined ten marks.[8]

year to Norwich, Colchester, Stamford, Ludlow and Rochester.[9]

In all these places the local history of recent years offers an explanation for their inhabitants' prompt acceptance of the new dynasty. Stamford and Ludlow had been possessions of Richard of York and were involved in his attempted coup in 1452. In Norwich, there had been some signs of support for him in 1450 and there can be little doubt that the citizens' resentment of the treatment they had suffered during Suffolk's ascendancy* lay behind their readiness to disavow Henry VI. People of both Rochester and Colchester had taken part in the revolt associated with the name of Jack Cade. There had been a persistent current of hostility to Henry's government in Kent, for which the malpractices of its local representatives were primarily responsible, and it is probable that in Hampshire and Dorset also the commons' attitude to York in 1461 was conditioned by the grievances which had produced the risings in 1450 and 1451 and by memories of how order had been restored. The earl of Devon had been able to win recruits in Somerset in 1451 by professing his concern for the common weal; this suggests that the kind of appeal by which Richard of York attempted to gain popular backing against the court received a sympathetic hearing in this part of the country.

Thus there had been discontent with Lancastrian government in all those districts where Edward's seizure of the throne apparently won a popular welcome. The new dynasty's humbler supporters were as much moved by their private interests in accepting him as were the magnates who fought on his behalf. This is made clear in the words of the Wessex peasants in 1462:

> We commons have brought King Edward to his prosperity in the realm of England, and if he will not [be] ruled after us as we will have him, as able we were to make him king, as able we be to depose him and put him down and bring him there as we found him.[10]

These self-styled kingmakers spoke for all their fellow-countrymen who had preferred York to Lancaster.

When Edward II and Richard II were deposed, accusations of misgovernment were made against them in parliament to show that they were unworthy of their crowns. No such process was made against Henry VI. He was removed on the grounds that he was not the

* See Appendix III.

lawful king, because his hereditary title was weaker than that of Richard and Edward of York. Henry's reign was depicted as a period of national calamity, of disaster abroad, of crime, riot and poverty at home; but these ills were allegedly the consequences of Henry IV's usurpation, not of his grandson's incompetence. Yet the lawless state of English society, and the inability of Henry VI's government to provide a remedy, were in themselves adequate reasons for his deposition. It was the primary duty of a medieval king to defend his people and administer justice among them. As Henry could not fulfil these responsibilities, he forfeited his right to the loyalty of his subjects. As Hobbes wrote: "The obligation of subjects to the sovereign is understood to last as long, and no longer, than the power lasteth by which he is able to protect them."[11]

APPENDIX I

The Molecatcher's Tale

It is unwise to call any record unique, but no other word is more appropriate for describing the statement made by Robert Goodgroom when he turned "king's evidence". The contemporary legal expression was that a felon became the king's approver when he made a formal statement before coroners implicating others besides himself in certain offences. Goodgroom, however, was not content to accuse other people of committing felonies: he charged his victims with conspiring to commit treason. Consequently, when the appeal failed, he had to suffer the penalties for treason, instead of being hanged as a felon. This is remarkable enough, but what gives this record its unique flavour is its wealth of circumstantial detail. Goodgroom had the skill of a Titus Oates in preparing accusations so fully and plausibly that they almost have the ring of truth. The appeal is also distinguished from other appeals in that it is in English. Although the jury decided that it was a pack of lies, Goodgroom's narrative deserves a place in any anthology of the earliest English short stories.

A man became an approver only after he had been brought to trial for offences he was supposed to have committed and presumably because he had no hope of being acquitted. Goodgroom was indicted before the justices of the peace for Kent at Canterbury on 20 May 1439. He was charged as Robert Goodgroom, *alias* Robert Green, currier, of London, *alias* Robert Bewer, "moletaker", of Ospringe, in Kent, *alias* Robert Goodgroom, labourer, of the same.* The charges may be translated in these words:

* Proper names modernised.

"On Monday, 13 April 1439, he came to Stalisfield, Kent, and with force and arms, *viz.* with swords, staffs and knives, broke into and entered the parish church, stealing from it two silver chalices (worth £6 13s. 4d.) and one corporas with a case (5s. od.), the property of the parishioners.

"On the night of Wednesday, 1 April 1439, he likewise broke into the church of St. Nicholas, Romney, and took a silver and gilt 'paxebrede' (33s. 4d.), a belt decorated with silver and silver gilt (6s. 8d.) and two corporal cloths (2s. od.), the property of the parishioners.

"On the same night, he also broke into the church of St. Laurence, Romney, and took a chalice (50s. od.), the property of the parishioners."

On being charged, Goodgroom pleaded not guilty. A jury was ordered to be called for 20 July, at Rochester, and he was left in the sheriff's custody. The jurors did not come then, nor to Canterbury on 22 September, when a third order was issued for 11 January 1440. Goodgroom then asked for a coroner to be assigned "for various matters concerning the king". The justices asked if he confessed to the charges against him, and he admitted his guilt, again asking for a coroner. As required, he took an oath that he would not charge anyone of treasons or felonies unless they were guilty, and that his appeal was true. He thus became the king's approver. Three days were then assigned for him to make his appeal and two coroners were appointed to take it down.[1]

The coroners were ordered by a writ from King's Bench, dated 6 February 1440, to send a copy of the appeal into that court. There it was enrolled, in the following words:*

> It is to have in mind that I, Robert Goodgroom of Ospringe in the county of Kent, molecatcher, otherwise called Robert Green late of London, currier, approver of our lord the king before Robert East and Hamo Beale, coroners of our said lord the king in the said county, that is to wit at Maidstone [on 12 January 1440], acknowledge† that:

* In this copy of the document, the spelling of words, including proper names, has been modernised, as have the punctuation and dates. With money, marks have been converted into pounds, shillings and pence. Readers who are interested may compare this text with a more strictly rendered one printed elsewhere.[2]　　　　　　　　　　　　　　　† *I.e.* admit.

About [10 October 1438], I the said Robert Good-groom, came to the manor of Graveney where Thomas Burgess, esquire,* dwells, and there coming inward met with one Richard Croft of the parish of Graveney of the said county of Kent, yeoman,* dwelling with the said Thomas Burgess.

The which Richard said to me, the said Robert Good-groom, "Robert, thou art welcome, for I must hear of thee thy craft for to take moles."

And I, the said Robert Goodgroom, said to the said Richard, "I shall you the said craft teach gladly if you would it learn."

Then the said Richard bade me go into the garden of the said manor and spy for moles, if any were therein. And as I was walking alone into the said garden ward, I came by a house in the said manor [which] is called a cheese house, and there then I see a great smoke in the same house, and so went forth to the said house and found the door of the same house fast shut. Wherefore I went to the window of the said house, being on the north side, and with a dagger the said window opened, and so looking into the said house saw a little fire under a distillatory made of earth. And there I saw lying on a cheese vat in the said house an arm and a hand of a dead man.

Wherefore I turned again and met the said Richard and asked of him what house the said cheese house was. The which Richard answered and said it was a cheese house.

And then said I, "So me seemeth, for I looked in and there I saw a dead man's arm lying on a cheese vat."

The which said Richard said to me, the said Robert Goodgroom, "Ah, Robert, sawest thou that? I pray thee keep counsel and hold thy peace, for and thou knewest as much as I do what a man might do with such an arm, thou wouldest use the same craft." And further-more the said Richard said to me, "Thou hast a craft the which I know no man can [do] but thou, and if thou

* Noted as being detained in the Marshalsea prison.

wilt teach me thy craft, I shall tell thee what strength
that arm hath and what power it hath, if thou wilt assure
me that thou wilt teach me thy craft of taking of moles."

Whereupon assurance was made between us. And then
the said Richard said to me, "Take when thou wouldst
the arm of a dead man that hath lain in the earth nine
days and nine nights, and put in the dead hand a burning
candle, and go to a place where thou wilt, and though
there be therein a hundred people, they that sleep shall
sleep, and they that wake [shall] not move whatever thou
do. And also, Robert," said the said Richard "seeing
thou are assured I shall teach thee a craft the which shall
avail thee in a week £40."

And then said I again, "I got not so much with my
craft in all my life. What is your craft? I pray you tell
me."

And the said Richard told me, "Thou shalt take five
manner [of] herbs, the names of which I have written
in a book, and the flesh of a dead man that hath lain in
the earth nine days and nine nights, and grind the herbs
and the flesh together as small as mortress.* And then take
and put it in a pot of earth and stop it well with wax,
and set it down in the earth and let it stand there and
congeal [for] forty days and forty nights. And then at the
end of forty days and forty nights, take it up and put it
in a distillatory, and distill it to water and put it in pots,
for thou mayest with three drops thereof slay both man
and beast, for it is the worst poison in the world."

And then I asked of the said Richard, "Have you any
of this standing in the earth?"

The said Richard said, "Nay, but I wot where [there]
is."

Then I said to the said Richard, "I pray you tell me
where it is."

And then said the said Richard, "Go to the place of
John Sinclair of Faversham in the county of Kent, gentleman,† and if thou mayest come into the garden, go into
the north part of the said garden into the corner, and

---

* *I.e.* pottage.   † Noted as being in the Marshalsea.

there shall you find a pot standing in the earth with the same matter."

And so then I went to the place of the said John Sinclair, to Faversham in the said county, that is to wit [on 12 October 1438*], from the said manor of Graveney. And so I came and knocked on the inner gate.

And then came the butler to the said John Sinclair, and asked, "Who is there?"

And then answered I and said, "I am here, Robert Goodgroom, molecatcher."

And then said the butler, "Welcome. Come near and drink."

And so he had me into the buttery and [we] drank. And then I asked leave of the butler to go into the garden and seek after moles, and the said butler bade me go in God's name.

And then I went into the garden of the said John Sinclair, into the north part, and did there test the ground with my mole staff, and there found a pot of earth containing three pottles lapped all about in yellow wax, covered above with a linen cloth, the which wax contained in thickness half an inch. And then I took away all the earth about the pot and took my knife and cut up a hole of the wax upon the pot's mouth, and there did come out of the said pot a foul smoke and a great stink. And then I looked into the pot and it was within as black as pitch. And therefore I covered the pot again with the linen cloth and the earth.

And in the meantime came the said John Sinclair, his wife and his man, from the church of Faversham through a meadow into the said garden by a postern gate. And he seeing me, the said Robert Goodgroom, about the said pot, came to me with a baselard drawn, called a wood-knife, and his man with a dagger drawn, and said to me, "What makest thou here, thief? Thou shalt be dead."

And there they took me and led me out of the said garden into the stable beside the outer gate of the said John Sinclair, and said that I should be dead but† I

---

* A Sunday.   † *I.e.* unless.

would swear upon a book that I should never discover★ of the pot which I had seen.

Then I answered and said, "Sir, how should I discover this matter? I wot not what it meaneth."

And then said the said John Sinclair, "Thus, for I know well [that] thou nor no man of Kent nor of Essex could not have found that pot without† thou hadst been taught thereto by some of my counsel. And therefore seeing thou art so far of my counsel, thou shalt swear upon a book or else be dead."

The said John Sinclair sent for a book and made me to swear. And when I was sworn, I asked the said John Sinclair of what matter I should keep counsel.

And the same John said to me, "Now thou art sworn I shall tell thee. Lo, Robert, thou knowest well the great wars of France is great hindering to this realm, and also the dear years of corn,‡ and also by the taking of corn by the king and other certain lords, the which is to the said realm and commons great destruction." Wherefore, the said John Sinclair said that he and those that be of his counsel and of his assent would make a remedy therefore, [so] that there should not be so many lords in this land as there be, not to have the rule of this land as they have had herebefore.

Then asked I how many lords there were that should be destroyed, and of§ what manner, and "Who is of your counsel and assent?"

Then said the same John Sinclair, "Forasmuch as thou art sworn to me before and knowest somewhat of my counsel, I shall tell thee all. There is one of the city of York whose name is John Liverton dwelling in the city of York at an inn called "The Hart and the Swan", yeoman, and another whose name is called John of Stanegate of Lowestoft in the county of Suffolk, merchant. The third is the said Richard Croft of Graveney beforesaid, yeoman. They‖ and I, the said John Sinclair

---

★ *I.e.* make known. † *I.e.* unless.

‡ Other sources confirm that there was a scarcity of wheat in Kent at this time.[3] § *I.e.* by. ‖ MS. *that they.*

of Faversham in the county of Kent, gentleman, that is to wit, that we together [on 13 October 1438] accorded and imagined how and in what wise we should destroy the lords abovesaid."

Then asked I, "Sir, what lords be those?"

The said John Sinclair said, "The king is one, Humfrey, duke of Gloucester, another, the duke of Norfolk the third."

Then I asked how this purpose should be brought about.

Then said the said John Sinclair, "Thus, with the pot that thou foundest in my garden and with other craft, for we be accorded at Christmas come twelvemonth after [13 October] abovesaid this purpose shall be done and brought about."

Whereupon I took my leave and went my way to London and occupied me with my craft, that is to wit taking of moles, until [6 January 1439].

And then I, the said Robert [on 8 January], hired a horse of one Pain, brewer, dwelling in Finke's Lane at "The Cock on the Hoop", paying for the said horse every day four pence. And so I rode forth into the north country ward and came to the city of York [on Tuesday 27 January following], and rode to the said inn of the said John Liverton and there I was lodged from the said Tuesday noon till Saturday then next following at noon, within the which time I and the said John Liverton fell in communication and [he] asked me of what country I was. I said I was of Kent. He asked me what tidings [there were] out of that country.

"Sir", I said, "I can* none but good, save [that] one John Sinclair of Faversham greets you well and would wit if you would keep your promise that you have made or not, and whether you have put your water in proof or not."

The which John Liverton said to me, "For his love thou art welcome, and that the water is good thou shalt see it proved."

And so I and the said John Liverton went into a loft

* *I.e.* know.

chamber beside the hostelry door, and a black dog went with us. And the said John Liverton took out a little pot of his right sleeve, fast closed with a little peg, and there called the dog to him and dropped three drops of that water upon the dog's back, and the said dog fell down dead and his four feet upward.

"Lo", he said, "here is a good proof."

And I said unto the said John Liverton, "Sir, is there any more men in this country that can this craft?"

The said John Liverton said, "Nay, save one John of Stanegate of Lowestoft in the county of Suffolk, merchant, which is accorded to meet with us at the time assigned."

Whereupon I having this in knowledge took my leave and departed and came to London.

And so the said [12 January 1440], at Maidstone, I the said Robert, approver of our said lord the king before the said coroners, acknowledge myself to be the king's traitor, forasmuch as I had knowledge of the treasons of the said John Sinclair, John Liverton, John of Stanegate and Richard Croft against our sovereign lord the king, Harry the Sixth, Humfrey, duke of Gloucester, and the duke of Norfolk, falsely and traitorously imagined, [and] have kept and concealed [them] from the said king and his council and his ministers unto this day of my knowledge. Whereupon I, the said Robert, approver of our said lord the king, appeal the said John Sinclair [*etc., naming all four again in full*], of that they falsely and traitorously at Faversham on the said [13 October 1438] imagined and conspired the death of our said sovereign lord the king and the said dukes, for to have poisoned them with the said poison, as it is above rehearsed, within the time of Christmas [1439], where and in what place our said sovereign lord the king and the dukes abovesaid were in England; the which said treasons I, the said Robert, approver of our said lord the king, will prove upon the said John Sinclair, John Liverton, John of Stanegate and Richard Croft in what[ever] wise our sovereign lord the king will ordain.

Also I, the said Robert, . . . acknowledge and appeal John Dandelion of the parish of St. Johns within the Isle of Thanet in the shire of Kent, gentleman, that he [on 28 April 1438] at the aforesaid parish of St. Johns unto a place called the shore in the aforesaid isle, sixty quarters of wheat and eighty quarters of barley with his carts by night time from the dwelling place of the said John Dandelion carried, and the said wheat and barley to divers enemies of our said lord the king's of the part of Flanders, whose names be to me, the said approver, unknown at the time being, in a ship of our aforesaid enemies there being, then delivered falsely and traitorously, in sustentation and fortifying of our said enemies of the part of Flanders abovesaid. Whereupon also I, the said Robert, approver, the 28th day of April abovesaid was present in the house of the said John Dandelion in the parish of St. Johns abovesaid, and knowing the said treason in the said form to be done, the counsel of the said John Dandelion from the said 28th day of April unto this time falsely and traitorously have kept and concealed.

Also I, the said Robert, . . . acknowledge and appeal the said John Sinclair of Faversham in the county of Kent, gentleman, and Thomas Wolf of Stalisfield in the same county of Kent, husbandman, of that they [on 11 March 1439] at Faversham in an inn called "The Ship" accorded and falsely and feloniously conspired how and in what wise they might slay and destroy Edward Guildford, that time being sheriff of Kent beforesaid.* And there the said John Sinclair took and sold to the said Thomas Wolf half a pint of the said poison, taking therefore [£2 13s. 4d.] in hand, and so that the said Thomas should go and poison the said sheriff, for because that he had impeached to our said sovereign lord the king certain friends of the said Thomas Wolf of the rising last in Kent, and [they] therefore were put to death.†

---

* He was sheriff then, and survived the "conspiracy" by ten years.

† Five men of Tenterden, Kent, were executed as traitors at Maidstone on 13 June 1438, after trial on charges of heresy and rebellion.⁴

Also I, the said Robert, . . . acknowledge and appeal Thomas Burgess of Graveney in the county of Kent, gentleman, and Anne his wife, sometime the wife of John Martin, justice of our lord the king, and the said Richard Croft of Graveney in the said county, yeoman, and John Sinclair of Faversham in the same county, gentleman, otherwise called John Gerard, of that they [on 22 May 1436] at Graveney in the shire of Kent, falsely and feloniously with the same water and poison abovenamed poisoned the said John Martin,* the which should have lived till this day, as the said Thomas Wolf told me, the said Robert, approver, [on 15 April 1439] at Stalisfield in the house of the said Thomas, as the said Thomas Wolf told there to me, the said Robert, and that the said John Sinclair told him so.

Upon which matter we, the said coroners, asked of the said Robert, approver, if he were privy, consenting or deed-doer to the poisoning of the said John Martin. The which Robert said "Nay", he had never other knowledge of that matter save by the telling of the said Thomas Wolf, the which Thomas said [that] all the country knew well it was so.

Also I, the said Robert, the king's approver, acknowledge before the said coroners . . . that where I, the said Robert, was imprisoned in the stocks at Stalisfield, and there being so in prison, that it to wit [on 13 April 1439†], the said John Sinclair by the said butler, his man, sent to me that if I would ask [for] a coroner and acknowledge felony, and for to foreswear the king's land, I should have for my labour twenty shillings and ever after of him good mastership where that ever he met me, forasmuch as I, the said Robert, knew the counsel of the said John Sinclair in the matters abovesaid.

All these matters that I, the said Robert, have acknowledged to you coroners I require you, as you would

* John Martin, a justice of Common Pleas, died on 24 October 1436. He was not an old man. His widow died in 1458 and was buried with him in Graveney church. Thomas Burgess, her second husband, died in 1452 and had his own memorial in the same church.[5]

† This was the day he robbed Stalisfield church.

answer to our sovereign lord the king, that you write them in my mother tongue, for I understand neither Latin nor French, and also that you have written all my matters of my appeals as I have told you word by word and in none otherwise.

The record concludes with the formal account of the proceedings in King's Bench, summarised as follows:

On 9 February 1440, Goodgroom, who had been committed to the Marshalsea, appeared before the judges and said that he intended to maintain his appeal. Burgess, Croft, Sinclair, Dandelion and Wolf surrendered themselves to the Marshalsea. Being brought into court, they pleaded not guilty. On an order being made that a jury should be called for 10 April, they were released on bail. On this day, the sheriff gave the names of the jurors he had called and he was told to produce them three weeks later. The five accused were again given bail. Goodgroom was asked if he wished to maintain the appeal against Dandelion, Agnes Burgess and Stanegate. He said he did, but the court ruled that the appeal against the first two was insufficient in law and they were discharged. Stanegate pleaded not guilty, a jury was called for 27 April, and he was released on bail. The sheriff again failed to produce the jurors and he was told they must be brought on 4 May. This day all the persons required came to court. Burgess, Croft, Sinclair and Wolf were found not guilty, as was Stanegate, who was tried separately; all were discharged. His appeal having failed, Goodgroom was sentenced to be dragged from the Marshalsea in Southwark through the city of London to Tyburn, and then hanged, drawn and quartered, his remains to be exhibited in suitable places. The sentence was carried out immediately.[6]

APPENDIX II

Crime and Pardon

The prerogative of mercy was an undisputed attribute of the English crown and, except in the great franchises of Durham, Chester and Lancaster, it was exercised by the king alone. Being personal to the monarch, it fell into abeyance when he was not officially acting as the head of his government. There was an exception to this rule relating to one kind of homicide. In 1390, parliament attempted to restrict the excessive liberality with which pardons were being issued. A statute recognised two kinds of homicide: that committed in self-defence or by misadventure, and "murders done in await, assault, or malice prepense". Pardons for the first kind could be obtained from Chancery as a matter of course, that is, without requiring the king's personal authorisation; but the statute made almost impossible conditions for the second type of offender to obtain the king's grace.[1] During Henry VI's minority, a total of only fifteen pardons for homicide issued from Chancery: all these crimes had been committed in self-defence or by misadventure, as Chancery was informed by certificates from the justices.[2] Only one other pardon was granted to a felon in these fourteen years, to a woman condemned to death for theft as the result of a malicious indictment; this she obtained by a petition in parliament.[3]

After the end of the minority, the number of letters of pardons for crimes issued under the great seal rapidly increased. There still were some pardons for homicides in self-defence which Chancery issued without any royal warrant, but the great majority of pardons were

obtained by the submission of petitions to the king. Some of these
were made in general terms, pardoning the recipients all or certain
kinds of felonies committed before stated dates. One such pardon
was granted to John Bolton in 1444. In the parliament of the following year, the commons petitioned that he should be brought to trial
despite this pardon; the king, they said, had been ignorant of Bolton's
offences when it was granted. He had been accused of brutally
murdering a woman after an unsuccessful attempt at rape, and had
subsequently turned approver. The commons wanted him to suffer
the penalties for high treason if he was found guilty. In reply, the
king refused to send Bolton for trial but decreed that he should be
imprisoned for life.[4]

Other letters specify the crimes of which those pardoned had been
accused. Thus on 15 December 1437, seven Devonshire men were
pardoned for an exceptionally horrible crime – the blinding, mutilation and eventual murder of a clerk; they had been formally indicted
before justices of the peace, but the letters of pardon mention no
mitigating circumstances to explain why the king should have exercised mercy in this case. A tailor of Southampton, accused of murder
by a coroner's jury, likewise obtained a pardon without any statement of reasons for leniency. The rector of Ewhurst, Surrey, had
been indicted for the rape of a married woman in three different
courts and was once fined for this offence. The king was informed,
however, that he had been falsely accused and he was therefore
pardoned.[5]

An increasing proportion of pardons state that their recipients had
been maliciously charged and were guiltless. There could be no more
devastating indictment of the legal system itself. Accepting that these
plaintiffs for the king's mercy had been falsely accused, it was a
deplorable state of affairs that the king – or rather his ministers – had
to take over the function of the courts to establish their innocence.
But the assertions that these indictments were malicious came from
the petitions submitted to the king. No doubt some may have been
true: malicious indictments were common enough at this time, but
so common, we may suspect, that plaintiffs for the king's mercy
found it good policy to protest that they were the victims of such
malpractice.

The number of royal pardons in general terms or for specified
offences totalled between twenty and thirty in each year after 1437,

although there were over forty in the regnal year 1441-2.* Not all the offences described were homicides, although they were the most common. For example, in the regnal year 1444-5, five men received pardons in general terms, and there were fifteen cases of homicide, five of theft, and single instances of rape, harbouring murderers, concealing knowledge of treason, illegally exporting bullion, and unspecified felony.

All these people had been indicted, one alleged murderer twice, before coroners and justices of the peace. The man indicted for rape "is guiltless, as he says". Two accused of murder were "guiltless, as is said". Seven other indictments were said to be malicious, and two of the homicides had supposedly been committed in self-defence, though there were no judicial certificates to confirm this. Two of the pardons are more detailed than the rest. One man struck an officer of the king's household on the head with a staff, so killing him; there is no suggestion of self-defence or provocation. A yeoman of Shacker-stone, Leicestershire, at the instigation of a neighbour, lay in wait for his victim, came upon him from behind, and split his skull with "a twohandbill". Again, no extenuating circumstances were put forward.[7] This appears to be the very kind of crime which the statute of 1390 aimed to put beyond the king's power to pardon.

The pardons considered so far might be described as "special pardons", in that they were granted to individuals who had made direct application to the king, and were obtained by the exercise of his grace in the case of each separate petition. In contrast, the king periodically announced the grant of a general pardon, and theoretically, all who wished could then, within a limited term, come to Chancery to obtain copies made out in their names upon payment of the requisite fee for sealing (16s. 4d.). By the terms of a letter of general pardon, the king pardoned the nominee all acts of treason, felony, trespass, contempt, evasion or abuse of the law committed before a certain date, together with any resulting sentences of out-lawry, confiscation or fine. In addition, he was excused a great range of possible offences against the king's feudal, statutory and admini-strative rights, such as marrying the widow of a tenant-in-chief or selling or buying land without his licence, or having failed to pay debts to the crown. Some of the clauses such as breaches of the

* Perhaps the number should be higher, as not all letters of pardon were enrolled.[6]

statutes of provisors could only be of benefit to the clergy. The first time a general pardon had been granted was in 1377, to mark Edward III's golden jubilee, and there had been a number more in the three following reigns. There had of course not been one in the minority of Henry VI.

The first general pardon of his reign was granted at the request of the commons in parliament on 27 March 1437, a concession which signified that the king had come of age.[8] The next was also announced in parliament, in 1446.[9] Its successors were all issued in the hope of bringing about a general pacification following recent disturbances, and except in 1455 there was no parliament in being at the time: one followed York's attempted coup in 1452;[10] another came after the first battle of St. Albans;[11] another was announced in January 1458, before, but obviously connected with, the "reconciliation" of the victors of that battle and their victims' families;[12] and the sixth of the reign, in January 1460, followed the proscription of the "Yorkists".[13]

As a general pardon covered so many categories of offences, it is obvious that not all of those who purchased a copy would have been doing so in order to evade the penalties of criminal activities. Abbot Wheathampstead, for one, bought letters of general pardon for his abbey of St. Albans in 1452 "for greater security" and in 1458 to avoid the legal consequences of thieves escaping from his gaol.[14] General pardons were obtained by prelates, temporal peers, religious and civic corporations, groups of trustees and executors; for these grantees the clauses relating to crime were of least interest. Their aim was to avoid inconvenience and pecuniary loss should the officers of the royal bureaucracy investigate their business transactions. Thus a group of trustees covered themselves by buying a pardon, and they produced it when Exchequer officials confiscated land which they had granted without the king's licence.[15] When a general pardon was available, it was quicker and much cheaper to obtain one than to apply for a licence to buy or sell land, submit to an official enquiry into its value, and pay a fine relative to this valuation, fees for royal warrants and letters patent, and douceurs to the various officials concerned. Hundreds of recipients of these pardons,* however, were of comparatively humble status, few of them likely to be involved in dealings in land held of the crown, and for them the purchase of

* For numbers of general pardons, see table on p. 216 below.

letters from Chancery would have been an unaccustomed undertaking, hardly to have been made except for some pressing cause.
These people were most likely to have been interested in the clauses
relating to crimes which they may have committed or of which, at
least, they feared they might be indicted.

The minimum number of recipients of general pardons who had
been accused of crimes can be assessed. The letters stipulated that
anyone pardoned who had already been indicted had to answer in the
royal law courts in case any individual they might have injured
wished to object. The rolls of King's Bench show considerable
numbers of people answering to indictments and then producing
their general pardons and being dismissed. In the two years following
the announcement of the pardon in 1446, a total of 172 persons have
been noticed as appearing in King's Bench and producing copies of it.
Of these, twenty-four answered to indictments for murder, among
them a case of petty treason where a servant had murdered his master
by giving him arsenic; he was aided by his victim's wife, who subsequently became his own. Robbery with violence, cattle-stealing
and other kinds of theft accounted for fifty appearances. There were
eight cases of breaking in, five with rape of the householder's wife.
Four men were charged with abducting an heiress in Devonshire, and
five others with rape, one of them a vicar accused of committing the
offence during confession. There were twenty-six cases of personal
assault, violent entry and seizure of landed property, poaching and
trespass; one of treasonable speech; two of riot; and two of coining.
Twelve people answered for sheltering felons. The remaining cases
were mainly concerned with matters like failure to appear in court
or to produce accused persons.[16] As the number of general pardons
granted in 1446-7 was 3,319, it would therefore appear that only a
very small proportion were taken by people with criminal records;
although it is possible that more answered in other courts or did not
trouble to appear.

Although a general pardon was nominally available to all comers,
there is reason to believe that obstacles were put in the way of some
possible applicants. York's supporters in 1452 were certainly not able
to obtain pardons easily.* In the same year, the chancellor was asked
not to allow Roger Church, a notorious Norfolk character, to have
a "pardon of the common grace", and if he did apply he was not

* See p. 101 above.

successful.[17] Two Yorkshiremen had sued in Chancery for this pardon but were unable to pay for it.[18] Moreover, all people with charges against them had to give security for good behaviour before Chancery supplied them with letters of pardon, and habitual criminals might have found this an insuperable obstacle.

The general pardon was to some extent an admission of the failure of the legal system to bring accused people to trial. The pardon of 1437 was applicable to all offences committed before 2 September 1430. One of its recipients was a woman who had killed her husband in bed. This was done in 1425, not in the remote north or west, but at Kingston-on-Thames. She had been discovered and charged, but had made her escape and was outlawed.[19] Yet, although theoretically banished from all society, unable to own property, and beyond the protection of the law, she had survived for twelve years. This was ten years less than John Scotland had lived in outlawry while contriving to ply his trade in London.[20] The pardon of 1446 permitted criminal records to be cleared to 9 April of that year. Some of those who benefited had been indicted several years before this. One was Agnes Fish, who had stolen wool in 1426.[21] Not only had she been able to live as an outlaw in London, but she had not thought it worth her while to obtain a pardon in 1437. Another pardoned in 1446 was a Sussex labourer who had been an outlaw since he hanged his wife in 1431.[22] Despite these clear indications that the sanction of outlawry could prove to be quite ineffective, the fact remains that these people did eventually wish to be free to live as normal subjects under the law. We may wonder, however, how many outlawed persons decided that there was nothing to be gained in seeking the king's pardon.

In these circumstances, the readiness of the king to grant pardons appears less damaging to the preservation of law and order: its administration was already ineffective. The crown, it could be said, was cutting its losses by permitting people who might in any case have escaped the penalty of their crimes to resume ordinary lives. There was always the hope that they would reform, like the sheep-stealer who told Henry, with tears and sighs, of his horror at all his misdeeds.[23] But, at the worst, the crown did profit financially from the fees paid in Chancery for its letters of pardon. For all this, some of the crimes which Henry pardoned were atrocious, and by admitting their perpetrators to his grace he not only appeared to condone them but openly admitted the powerlessness of his government. A weak administration cannot afford to confess its weakness. If it could not make an attempt to punish the most notorious crimes, there was little hope of curbing its subjects' propensity for violence. The law inevitably fell into contempt when the crown persistently denied justice the escort of "her sharp sergeant Rigour".[24]

Total numbers of general pardons issued		
Year of grant	Letters issued	Reference (*Accounts of the Hanaper of Chancery*)
1437	1,866	Exchequer L.T.R.: Foreign Accounts, no. 71, rot.E.
1446	3,319	*ibid.*, 81, rot.A, L.
1452	2,430	*ibid.*, 86, rot.C; 87, rot.C.
1455	2,057	*ibid.*, 89, rot.G; 90, rot.C.
1458	2,434	*ibid.*, 92, rot.C; 93, rot.C.
1460	342	*ibid.*, 94, rot.C.

APPENDIX III

The Norwich Riots

The history of the city of Norwich during the reign of Henry VI is marked by a series of disturbances which had no contemporary urban parallel for intensity and persistence elsewhere in the country. There were riots at the elections of mayors in 1433 and 1437, and in 1443 there was a dangerous rising directed against the cathedral priory. In consequence, the crown twice suspended the city's constitution and took over its government. There were two basic reasons for this strife, both common in the medieval history of English boroughs. One was competition between the wealthy merchants and the lesser craftsmen for control of the city's government. In 1414, the latter, after much agitation, had been admitted to a place in this local government, when they were permitted to nominate the candidates for the mayoralty and to elect sixty representatives to form, with the original governing body of the mayor and twenty-four aldermen, a common council as the legislative assembly. Under the leadership of Thomas Wetherby, the heirs of the former oligarchs attempted to regain exclusive control, the first known incident in their campaign being the attempt to manipulate the mayoral election in 1433 which led to the riot. The wealthier citizens were not united, for a second group of aldermen, headed by Robert Toppes, led the opposition to Wetherby's faction. The second cause of disorder was friction with the cathedral chapter over jurisdictional boundaries. Henry IV's charter of 1404 gave the city the status of a county without defining its limits, and the mayor and his officers attempted to exercise their legal powers within the convent's enclave inside the city. The bad relations with the priory were probably worsened by anti-clerical sentiments. The friars, notoriously hostile to the well-established and prosperous monastic orders, were popular, and the recent burning of two heretics suggests that subversive doctrines had been circulating in the city. Opposing economic interests may have lain beneath both constitutional issues, but the available records offer little direct evidence about this.

Despite the inherently local origins of the disturbances, the popular party – as we might call Wetherby's opponents – blamed the duke of Suffolk's councillors for their ensuing tribulations. On 1 November 1450, the crown appointed a commission of oyer and terminer to hear charges of trespass, oppression, maintenance and other abuses of the law in Norwich. The indictments presented by the juries of the city's four wards were devoted to the activities of Sir Thomas Tuddenham, John Heydon, John Ulveston and John Bellay. As at the recent session of similar commissioners in the county,[1] the juries all began their accusations with a general charge, namely that these four men, with the prior of Norwich's steward, had made a league for the purpose of corrupting justice for their own profit. The jurors of each ward offered a different date for the formation of this alleged conspiracy – 20 October and 20 December 1434, 10 and 20 October 1436; this suggests lack of collusion. Many examples of extortion were cited: one, for instance, was that in 1441 the citizens gave Tuddenham £80 when he promised to persuade Suffolk to be their "good lord"; but ten days later, he "urged and made him their hard, unfavourable and unloving lord". Two of the charges had no bearing on the citizens' affairs. One repeated the accusation made against Suffolk in the last parliament that he had conspired with the duke of Orleans to wage war against the king. The Norwich jurors went on to say that subsequently, on 20 April 1450, John Heydon, a member of Suffolk's secret council and knowing him to be an adherent of the French king, urged various people in Norwich to support the latter against Henry VI. Another allegation was that Tuddenham and his fellows counselled Suffolk to put the duke of Gloucester to death.[2] The introduction of these charges was doubtless inspired by a wish to put Tuddenham and company on trial for their lives.

The events of the years 1433–50 are heavily documented[3] but nearly all the evidence is of a partisan nature. The indictments presented to a commission of oyer and terminer in 1443[4] differ so much in content from the records of the similar commission in 1450 that it is hard to believe that both describe events in the same place at the same time. A third account of these incidents was written by a citizen in 1482 and this, like the 1450 indictments, shows the popular party as the innocent victims of an unscrupulous conspiracy.[5] The facts remain, however, that there was serious friction between two groups of citizens, and that the popular party transferred the full weight of its animosity from Wetherby's group to Tuddenham and his associates. The reason for this development was that most prevalent of fifteenth-century ills – maintenance. Tuddenham, or rather, his master Suffolk, took Wetherby's part in his dispute with his fellow citizens. Had Suffolk been alive – but innocuous – in 1450, he would have been the main target of their attack, but, of course, it was only because he was dead that proceedings could be taken against his minions.

Suffolk's patronage of Wetherby dates from about 1435, when he, Tuddenham and Heydon were admitted to the gild of St. George, to which Wetherby and his civic associates belonged. As Wetherby himself was a landowner, his connection with the earl and Tuddenham is the more comprehensible than if he had been a mere burgess.[6] After their setback in 1433, Wetherby's party regained ground when Robert Chaplain was elected mayor in 1436. Chaplain tried to have Wetherby restored to the aldermanship of which he had been deprived in 1434.[7] He was unable to contrive this, but Wetherby did become one of the city's justices of the peace. John Hawk, one of his associates in the election plot in 1433, despite his subsequent disqualification from holding office, was appointed the city's under-sheriff, and John Heydon became its recorder. This recovery of influence suggests why, in 1450, the city jurors alleged that the plot to destroy their liberties was made about this time.

The popular party did not have cause to suspect Suffolk's attitude towards them before 1437. On 21 March he persuaded the city's governing body to accept his arbitration, and he then decreed that Wetherby should be restored as an alderman and that his accomplices in 1433 should regain the freedom of the city though not their former offices. Wetherby's enemies now followed his example of enlisting a champion. They prevailed upon Humphrey of Gloucester to forward a petition to the king's council against Wetherby, who was in consequence cited to appear before it. At the same time, the council was informed – allegedly by Wetherby – that the citizens were making compacts against the next election of a mayor. Two commissioners were therefore sent to supervise the election; the choice of the bishop of Carlisle for this mission would seem to be somewhat peculiar were it not for his personal connection with the earl of Suffolk.[8] The bishop and his colleague were unable to keep order. A crowd said to be two thousand strong gathered in the market place on the day of the election (1 May), and with them were Toppes and eight other aldermen and "the most part of the gild called the Bacherye". When Wetherby with some two hundred "well ruled commoners" tried to approach the Guildhall, they were "beaten and evilly treated". Such, at least, was the account given by Wetherby, Chaplain and two other city magistrates; their report was not a formal judicial record, for they claimed that when they called a jury it was afraid to say anything about the disturbance.[9]

The king's council now suspended the civic government, appointed a warden, and temporarily banished Toppes and his eight colleagues to Bristol and elsewhere.[10] Within a few months, however, on the grounds of economy, the council replaced its warden by a mayor of its own choice. It appointed John Cambridge, one of Toppes' chief supporters, who may even have been the popular candidate for the mayoralty. The council, in fact, had modified its opinion of the situation in Norwich, and seems to have realised that Wetherby was by no means free from blame for the uproar. He was provided with employment outside the city, as a collector of customs at Great Yarmouth. Toppes, on the other hand, was appointed to the crown's commission of the peace for Norwich.[11] The citizens were again being governed by their own leaders, but these were now officially the king's agents and removable at his will; this limitation served as a safeguard for their good behaviour. In December 1439, the citizens successfully called on the king to cast "an eye of pity" upon them and restore their privileges.[12] In the following May, Toppes was elected mayor and Wetherby was put in prison on a plea of trespass in the city court.[13]

The next wave of disturbances arose from disputes with the cathedral priory. According to a London chronicler, the trouble was caused by the prior, who sought to impose "new customs and bond-ships" on the commoners of the city.* Official records, on the other hand, indicate only the offences of the citizens. After the recovery of their liberties, the mayor and his officers attempted to exercise jurisdiction in those parts of the city which were the priory's property and exempt, it claimed, from their authority: the city sheriffs arrested defendants in civil actions and the city coroners held inquests in this supposed enclave. Another action treated as an invasion by the corporation was the survey made by the mayor and others of the city walls, when in the course of their perambulation they passed through the prior's fee. The city officers also carried out arrests and inquests on corpses in the adjacent countryside.

The prior began legal proceedings early in 1441, when he obtained a copy of an inquisition taken in 1426 which told against the city,[15] but both sides had already made contact with influential allies. The alleged association of the prior's steward with Tuddenham and company, and charges against the latter of "maintaining" the prior's suits, indicates where the chapter sought a champion. The citizens hoped to refresh the kindly interest of the duke of Gloucester, but his influence was not enough to prevent the prior of Norwich from obtaining preferential treatment in the council. A commission was appointed in July 1441 to enquire into all kinds of offences committed in the city; its leaders were the bishop of Norwich, the duke of Norfolk and the earl of Suffolk, who were all predisposed to favour the prior rather than the citizens. The bishop was equally involved in the matter of disputed jurisdiction and the duke had lately joined the earl as a champion of Thomas Wetherby. The crown's partiality had indeed already been revealed in the previous May, when both bishop and prior were given the privilege of executing royal writs in their estates in the city.[16]

The commission sat at Thetford on 31 July. Of those appointed, only two professional justices and Sir Thomas Tuddenham were present. With a county jury, they opened their record with a statement upholding the strict limitation of the city boundaries as shown

* In 1443, a group of men were accused of going from Norwich on 20 January to enlist support against the prior of Norwich in King's Lynn and elsewhere in Norfolk; they said that he wanted to levy 4d. from every carucate of land in the county, 4d. for every baptism and 2s. from every married woman, to take tolls on all foodstuffs carried into the city, and to have 20d. from everyone in Norwich with a latrine overhanging the river and 3d. from every woman washing woollen cloth on its banks.[14]

in the inquisition of which the prior had recently obtained a copy; and from this, it inevitably followed that the citizens' actions outside these bounds were described as illegal.[17] The citizen's view of the sessions at Thetford was given in 1450: ignoring the fact that Tuddenham was a member of the commission, they said that he, with Heydon and others, upheld the prior's cause before the justices with the result that the city lost £800.[18] The points in dispute were then settled by Suffolk's arbitration, apparently in the prior's favour, since the citizens refused to accept the award.* They were simultaneously engaged in lawsuits with the abbey of St. Benet's and the priory of Wendling, and both actions seemed to be going against them. Suffolk was again involved, apparently using his influence to the city's disadvantage.

These repeated setbacks to the citizens' ambitions eventually brought about the extraordinary outburst in January 1443. The indictments against the citizens allege that on the 22nd William Hempstead, the mayor, the two sheriffs, eight aldermen including Robert Toppes, with his wife, and sixty-eight others, "who then had the rule of the city", planned a rising to intimidate the bishop and the priors of Norwich and St. Benet's into abandoning their lawsuits. This was, presumably, a formal meeting of the city assembly, and it seems remarkable that these responsible people should have organised a violent demonstration: their memories would have been very short had they not remembered how the crown had reacted to the last disturbance in the city. The indictments, however, are not consistent in naming the mayor and his senior colleagues as participants in the various stages of the rioting. We are tempted to conclude that the assembly on 22 January expressed itself strongly on the city's setbacks but that the rising itself was spontaneous.

The day of the outbreak was a major feast of the Church, the Conversion of St. Paul (25 January). It was a holiday and an occasion for processions. In view of the current feeling of being menaced by powerful enemies, the citizens would have entered into these festivities with greater enthusiasm and unanimity than usual, to show their solidarity and give proof that they were not to be intimidated. The indictments describe part of the procession: John Gladman rode as

---

* The prior therefore asked the king for a special assize. Suffolk was one of the three councillors present when this petition was granted on 1 December 1442.[19]

its king, with three men before him bearing a crown, sceptre and sword, and behind twenty-four others carrying bows and arrows, wearing crowns on their sleeves, "as if they were yeomen of the crown". It was suggested that this savoured of treason. The account of 1482 puts the procession in a completely different light, describing it as an entertainment such as was commonly given in most towns on Shrove Tuesday. This account hardly squares with the fact that Shrove Tuesday was six weeks distant on the day of the procession, but at least it connects the event with a religious festival, a circumstance which the hostile indictment conveniently overlooked.

The account of 1482 also relates that on 25 January 1443 Thomas Wetherby and the legal advisers of the abbot of St. Benet's came to Norwich and tried to persuade the mayor and assembly to seal a bond for £100; this was to ensure the observation of an award by the earl of Suffolk that the city's mills, which interfered with the abbey's water supply, should be destroyed. As we have observed, the citizens were on holiday and in an excitable mood; a large gathering formed outside the Guildhall as this business was being discussed. At the alleged instigation of two aldermen, Robert Toppes and William Ashwell, a group of tradesmen led by Thomas Snarler, a cutler, forced its way into the building and removed the chest holding the common seal, thus preventing the sealing of the bond.

Next day, the prior of Norwich supplied the final provocation when, on his orders, two men were arrested in the city on a plea of debt and taken to his prison. Tumult now broke out. With the appropriately named Snarler again to the fore, a great crowd made for the gate to the priory precinct. This was closed in their faces, but they managed to batter their way to the prior's prison in Tombland and freed the two men. The main gate to the convent withstood the assault and all the citizens' battering could achieve was to break off a small piece of iron. A trench was dug, as for a mine, and guns were put in position. Now we can perceive how hastily and in what amateurish a fashion this attack had been conceived, for the citizens found themselves unable to use their artillery. Fortunately for them, on the following Tuesday (29 January), two country gentlemen and a clergyman came to pacify the rioters, and one of them was known for a soldier in the French wars. He was taken a prisoner to the Guildhall, threatened with defenestration, and thus persuaded to direct the bombardment. The monks then surrendered. Far from

carrying out their supposed threats to sack the cathedral and slaughter
its custodians, the citizens were content to remove a sealed writing of
1424 by which the mayor of the day admitted the priory's exemption
from his jurisdiction.

For a week the citizens defied the duke of Norfolk, whom the
king's council had instructed to take charge of the city. When he was
eventually admitted, Toppes and seven other ringleaders were
arrested and sent to the Tower of London.[20] Sir John Clifton, a local
landowner who was also a member of the gild of St. George, was
appointed the king's governor, and under his administration the
unpopular awards made by Suffolk before the rising were carried out.
Wetherby's influence at this time is revealed by the appointment of
John Hawk as common clerk. When a judicial commission came to
enquire into the riots, on 4 March, Wetherby was responsible for
instructing the city's attorney, who speedily abandoned the defence
and threw the city on the king's mercy. The judges declared that
Norwich's franchises were forfeit and imposed a collective fine of
£2,000; this was subsequently reduced to 1,000 marks. Charges were
heard against individual rioters and they were condemned to pay
fines totalling £1,504 17s. 4d.[21] The city remained in the king's hands
for more than four years. In the Michaelmas term of 1447 the
citizens were permitted to apply to King's Bench for the formal
conclusion of the proceedings, and on 12 November judgment was
given that the city's liberties were to be restored as the collective
fine had been paid.[22]

These events explain the citizens' bitter hatred of Suffolk and his
henchmen. The events leading up to the outburst of 1443 – the
restoration of Wetherby and the unfavourable settlement of the
disputes with their conventual neighbours – were due to him: he
may have been acting fairly, according to his lights, but this was not
the point. Then the treatment of the citizens after the riots further
embittered their resentment. Their account in 1450 of the judicial
sessions in 1443 is obviously tendentious. They claimed that Tuddenham, Heydon and company were wholly responsible for the instigation of these proceedings, and that they blackmailed Toppes and others
with threats to indict them for high treason, so that they could be
put to death, and thus extorted payments from individuals as well
as a fine of 1,000 marks from the citizens generally, which fear, not
guilt, compelled them to give to Suffolk for the king; as a result of

this intimidation, the city lost £20,000 altogether and many people had fled from it. Far-fetched though these allegations might appear, there are at least grounds for believing that the proceedings in 1443 were scarcely conducted with impartiality. The city jury was heavily packed with Wetherby's supporters: it included William Grey, his candidate for the mayoralty in 1433, and Hawk and three others who had been disfranchised for their part in this affair.[23] It would have been remarkable if Tuddenham and his colleagues had not been in Norwich at the time, and in view of their record for extortion in the county it is hardly likely that their sole object was to ensure that justice was done.

The citizens' hopes of vengeance in 1450 were soon dashed: Tuddenham and Heydon were too well entrenched in the favour of the king's court to be caught in any judicial snare. But the citizens' reaction to their oppression did not rest here. Some, at least, went on to express their dissatisfaction with the government which protected their enemies. In 1450, there was an outburst against the bishop, Walter Lyhart, on account of his association with the king's court.[24] A local gentleman was reported to have attempted to organise a rising in Norwich in favour of Richard of York in the autumn of that year, saying that on his return from Ireland he would take the crown, and a number of residents were accused of taking part in a riot on 16 July 1451, when they schemed to follow the example of Jack Cade and kill some of the county notables, whom they called "traitors". These incidents came to light when a judicial commission visited the county in 1452.[25] It is curious that no one thought fit to mention the first at the sessions in 1450: we might suspect that this silence reveals sympathy with the offender's opinion. A brief glimpse further forward tells us more. A contingent of one hundred and twenty fought on Edward IV's side at Towton,[26] and on 12 February 1462, when granting the city a charter, Edward referred to its good conduct, the expenses it had borne and the services it had freely given against his enemies.[27]

APPENDIX IV

The Imprisonment of the Duke of Norfolk

The information about Norfolk's first detention appears in a warrant dated 28 April 1447, for payment of the expenses of Thomas Montgomery, marshal of the king's hall. *After* attending the duke in Kenilworth Castle and the Tower of London, Montgomery had attended Sir John Astley and then escorted the duchess of Gloucester from Leeds Castle to London.[1] The duchess was brought from Leeds for her trial in July 1441, and again *en route* for Chester early in 1442.[2] Astley took part in a tournament held before the king on 30 January 1442.[3] Presumably, therefore, Norfolk's detention was before the end of 1441, and it is most likely to have been in 1440. On 2 July of that year he made a bond in the enormous sum of 10,000 marks to stay in the king's household. This was probably the occasion of his release from the Tower. He promised in the bond to do no harm to John Heydon.[4]

Sir Robert Wingfield was ordered to surrender to the Tower on 3 September 1440 and released on 18 June following.[5] The reason for his detention may have been his part in the duke's quarrel with Heydon. Certainly neither was detained because they were pitted against each other. This dispute came later. They were still on good terms on 1 November 1440.[6] Wingfield had served the duke's father as steward, and received from him the manor of Hoo, Suffolk, and a life grant of the office of chief steward from the son.

Norfolk wanted to regain possession of Hoo, and this appears to have caused the quarrel. His methods of argument were exceptional.

He brought a force of men, with cannon and other siege engines, battered Wingfield's house at Letheringham, forced an entry, ransacked the building and removed valuables amounting to nearly £5,000, according to his victim's valuation. On 26 November 1443, Norfolk was bound in £2,000 to keep the peace towards Wingfield and to appear before the council on 26 April 1444. The dispute was then put to arbitration, and in the award made on 4 May, Norfolk was ordered to pay Wingfield 3,500 marks (£2,333 6s. 8d.) in compensation for the assault and plunder of Letheringham manor and to give him other revenues in exchange for Hoo.[7]

Wingfield was an equally unruly character. He was ordered by royal signet letters not to go within seven miles of the duke, but he disregarded this command. In January 1448 a special commission heard a long list of his misdeeds. More than a score had been committed in the previous fortnight: he had instigated murderous assaults, broken into houses to take goods and into parks to poach game; he had maintained evildoers and rescued two, one of them his son, from prison; he had intimidated jurors, and the clerk of the peace; he had offered 500 marks for the head of one of Norfolk's retainers.[8] Wingfield had been bound over to keep the peace in 1447, and as a result of his exploits he was called to King's Bench to say why he should not forfeit his bond. He appeared on 9 February 1448 and pleaded not guilty. A day was appointed for his trial, but five days later he received the king's pardon for all his offences and forfeited securities.[9] This favour he presumably owed to the queen or Suffolk; Wingfield had been in her service from the time she left France[10] (in 1445), but Suffolk had probably recommended him.

The proceedings against Wingfield were doubtless prompted by Norfolk. The appointment on 1 September following of the judicial commission to deal with the case of the duke's attack on Letheringham was obviously initiated by Wingfield, since a fee was paid in Chancery for its issue.[11] This belated resort to legal process was probably made in retaliation for his own prosecution and also as a means of putting pressure on Norfolk to carry out the undertakings he had made in 1444. It was presumably on account of Wingfield's formal complaint that Norfolk was committed to the Tower on 28 August (1448); he was released six days later.[12]

APPENDIX V

The Civic Disputes in Hereford

The commission of oyer and terminer which visited Hereford in August 1452 received a large number of indictments[1] which had no direct bearing on its primary purpose, which was to try those involved in the duke of York's attempt to overthrow the government. This was usual enough, because commissions of this kind which had been appointed at the instance of the crown were given general powers to receive and judge a wide range of offences committed within a certain district.* In this case, various types of felony as well as treason were among the commission's terms of reference. Most of the indictments at Hereford concerned cattle-rustling and horse-stealing, often by Welshmen, but a number reveal discord among the inhabitants of the city. The substantial burgesses who formed the jury for the city found in the visit of the commission an excellent opportunity to strike back at their local enemies. The ringleader of their opponents appears to have been one John Weobley, who is described either as a yeoman or as a tailor. The earliest crime imputed to him was that he had incited a man to commit murder in 1446. The other references to Weobley, however, show him as acting in association with a number of fellow-citizens.

The earliest instance of collective action by this group was on 21

---

* Commissions of oyer and terminer were also appointed, at a price ranging from 6s. 8d. to 40s., on application by individuals who wished to have particular alleged offences against themselves tried locally by special judicial commissions; they may have been able to nominate some if not all of their members. For an example of a "private" commission see p. 227 above.

October 1448. Richard Green, the mayor, and a number of citizens had met in St. Peter's church for the purpose of electing a new mayor when a party of about thirty men forced their way in, brandishing weapons, and threatened violence if an election was held without their consent. It is probable that the intruders outnumbered the electors, for only four men beside the mayor were named as being thus menaced. Whether this pressure was successful does not emerge, but in the following year one of the threatened electors, John Welford, became mayor. In March 1450, he had occasion to arrest one of Weobley's friends, but other members of this group forcibly released the captive. The indictment continues: "they called on all Welshmen in the city to stand with them against the mayor and citizens, and so the Welsh rose in their aid. And thus a division was made between the English and the Welsh, as in a land at war, and each side took the part of his country against the other." It would be a mistake to accept "Welsh" too literally: the word was probably applied by the longer established citizens of Hereford to all living to the west of its walls and particularly to those who had settled in the city. The names of members of the "Welsh" faction given in the indictments are mostly English. As comparative newcomers to Hereford, however, they were outsiders in the eyes of the older residents, who excluded them from taking part in the city's government. A further round in this conflict took place at the end of Welford's mayoralty when the electors assembled, as before, on the Monday after St. Luke (19 October 1450). This time two hundred men were said to have invaded the Tolsey (Guildhall) and threatened not to let any citizen leave until the mayor they wanted had been appointed. Again we do not know the effect of this intrusion, but four days later, when burgesses were chosen to represent the city in parliament, John Weobley was one of those appointed; neither of the two members sent to the last three parliaments was re-elected. This was the parliament where the commons were so well-disposed towards the duke of York.

So far the conflict had been confined to the city. It took a new turn on 4 January 1452. On that day Sir Walter Devereux of Weobley gave his livery to a total number of thirty-two Hereford men; apart from four yeomen and one "gentleman", all were tradesmen – shoemakers, butchers, tailors, bakers, weavers, fletchers and a wax-maker, a saddler, a glover and a smith. John Weobley was one of the yeomen and it may be supposed that he had suggested that his party should seek the protection of the lord of the manor where he had probably been born. He had another link with Devereux, for the latter was also a member of parliament in 1450. A month later, the members of this faction made a compact to assist each other, that the quarrel of one, for good or ill, should be the quarrel of all. Finally, on 28 February, they planned a demonstration in favour of the duke of York, which took place on 3 March. Although the conspirators were formally charged with plotting to wage war against the king and with assembling under arms, this seems to have been as far as their treason went: they remained in Hereford, presumably holding the gates in York's name until news of the fiasco at Dartford came to evaporate their ardour.

Sir Walter Devereux undoubtedly instigated the rising in Hereford. He was York's leading adherent in Herefordshire, holding from the duke his manor of Weobley and the office of constable of Wigmore Castle. His patronage of the discontented party in Hereford was certainly not prompted by mere affection for democratic government but by a desire to further his master's interests. Hereford was the natural centre for gathering the warlike tenants of York's various marcher lordships, where they would be ideally placed both for blocking the main route from South Wales and for mounting an advance over the Severn into the Thames valley. The civic divisions in Hereford offered the opportunity to win friends in the city who might, at need, open the gates to York's military forces.

APPENDIX VI

The Warwick Inheritance

Reasons for the quarrel of Richard Neville, earl of Warwick, with Edmund Beaufort, duke of Somerset, can be traced in a number of records concerning the estates once held by Neville's father-in-law, Richard Beauchamp, earl of Warwick (1382-1439). A tantalisingly brief notice by John Rous, the Warwick family annalist, might appear to suggest that Neville was involved in serious difficulties on account of his wife's inheritance. He reports of Anne Beauchamp that "She was married to Sir Richard Nevile, son and heir to Sir Richard Earl of Salisbury, for whose sake he had much trouble".[1]

Richard Beauchamp had married twice. His first wife was Elizabeth, daughter and heir of Thomas, Lord Berkeley (1353-1417). Under an entail to heirs male, certain parts of Berkeley's property passed to his nephew James, but most descended to Elizabeth. James long strove to enlarge his territories by violence and litigation against Elizabeth and her heirs, but without success. After her death in 1422, Beauchamp held her estates "by courtesy of England". On his death, this Berkeley property was partitioned among the three daughters of the marriage: Margaret, the second wife of John Talbot, later earl of Shrewsbury; Eleanor, wife of Edmund Beaufort; and Elizabeth, wife of George Neville, Lord Latimer.[2]

Beauchamp married again in 1423. His second wife was the sister and heir of Richard Despenser (1396-1414), and the issue of this marriage were Henry and Anne, Richard Neville's wife. Henry succeeded to his father's earldom of Warwick and was later, in 1445,

231

TABLE

WARWICK AND

Thomas Beauchamp,
earl of Warwick
(1314-69)

Thomas Beauchamp,
earl of Warwick
(c. 1339-1401)

Elizabeth Berkeley *m.* (i) Richard Beauchamp,
(c. 1386-1422)   earl of Warwick
                      (1382-1439)

Margaret *m.* John
Talbot (first)
earl of Shrewsbury
(as his second wife)

Eleanor *m.* Edmund
Beaufort, duke of
Somerset

Elizabeth *m.* George
Neville, Lord Latimer

III

ABERGAVENNY

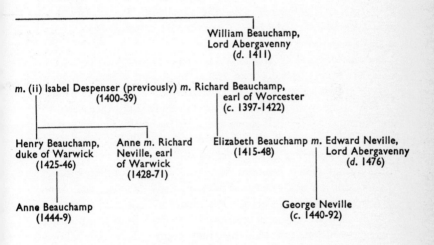

William Beauchamp,
Lord Abergavenny
(d. 1411)

m. (ii) Isabel Despenser (previously) m. Richard Beauchamp,
(1400-39)   earl of Worcester
(c. 1397-1422)

Henry Beauchamp,   Anne m. Richard   Elizabeth Beauchamp m. Edward Neville,
duke of Warwick   Neville, earl   (1415-48)   Lord Abergavenny
(1425-46)   of Warwick   (d. 1476)
                   (1428-71)

Anne Beauchamp   George Neville
(1444-9)   (c. 1440-92)

created duke of Warwick. His mother also died in 1439 and he inherited her estates. In 1344, the descent of the lands of the earldom had been restricted to the male heirs of the sons of the then earl, Thomas Beauchamp,[3] but when Duke Henry died in 1446 this entail had apparently become a dead letter through the extinction of other male lines descending from Earl Thomas. Henry was succeeded by his only child, Anne, who died, aged five, on 3 January 1449.

In the earldom of Warwick, Anne's heir was her aunt Anne Neville since she was Duke Henry's only sister in the whole blood. His three half-sisters, the issue of his father's first marriage, were barred from any claim at common law by the long established doctrine of the exclusion of the half-blood. The principle underlying this doctrine was that the heir should be the heir of the person last having seisin: "possession by the brother makes the sister heir". The doctrine had been accepted in England by A.D. 1200 and it was still accepted in the fifteenth century.[4]

The title of Anne Neville appears to have been clear enough, but royal letters on the subject of Anne Beauchamp's estates suggest that the crown's recognition of Anne Neville's title was not whole-hearted. Some royal grants affirm her sole right, but others seem to favour claims by her half-sisters and their husbands. The earliest of these letters certainly implied that the rights of all four women to share the Beauchamp estates were equal. This was a licence dated 12 July 1449 which describes Margaret, countess of Shrewsbury, Eleanor, duchess of Somerset, Elizabeth, Lady Latimer, and Anne Neville as the heirs of Richard Beauchamp; it authorised them to enter into possession of all lands held by Anne Beauchamp at her death and which descended to these four women. On 23 July following, however, the king granted the title of earl of Warwick to Richard and Anne Neville, stating that she was Duke Henry's heir.[5]

In October of the same year, inquisitions *post mortem* were somewhat tardily taken in respect of Anne Beauchamp's estates and here again, in the lands of the earldom, the county juries affirmed that Richard Neville and his wife were Anne's heirs.[6] On 2 March 1450, a fresh grant of the title of earl of Warwick was made to them, this time adding a remainder in favour of Margaret, countess of Shrewsbury. The Nevilles were so far childless[7] and this remainder was a reasonable provision since Margaret was the oldest of the three daughters of Richard Beauchamp's first marriage and in the event of Anne Neville dying without issue these women would have been her heirs general.

One of the appurtenances of the earldom was an office of chamberlain of the Exchequer which was hereditary to the earls. Once more, Anne Neville was recognised as Henry's heir when she and her husband were given royal confirmation of their possession of this office on 6 December 1450.[8] The half-sisters and their husbands immediately protested. In a petition to the king they claimed that Warwick, acting on his own authority, had taken over the chamberlainship on 7 December and expelled its temporary incumbent; by this action he had endangered their hereditary rights. In consequence, on 24 January 1451, the king committed the office to temporary custodians until the Exchequer court could determine the claims to its possession.[9] A further indication that the half-sisters were still pressing claims to share the earldom's estates and that the crown was not unsympathetic came later that year. Duke Henry's widow had died on 28 December 1450 and on 10 June they were licensed, together with their husbands and Richard and Anne Neville, to enter the lands which the duchess had held in dower; although this time it was recognised that the Nevilles had the sole right to an undefined part of the property which would have descended to Anne Beauchamp had she still been alive.[10]

There is more than one possible explanation for these royal licences. Some of the lands may have been subject to entails which so regulated their descent that the doctrine of the exclusion of the half-blood could not be applied. Again, Earl Richard Beauchamp or Duke Henry might have granted certain remainders to the three older women; although if this were so it is peculiar that the customary processes involving royal licences and other enrolments in Chancery were not observed. It is hard to believe that an outright attempt was made to deny the application of the doctrine of the exclusion of the half-blood to the Beauchamp lands. Yet a suspicion that this was the case is not entirely unreasonable. The prevailing spirit of contempt for the law, the readiness to pursue claims, however slender, and to back them with all the means at the contestants' command, lend some colour to this supposition. And the means at the disposal of one or the half-sisters' husbands, namely Somerset, were formidable indeed.

Like Suffolk before him, Somerset had ready access to the instruments of royal authority, and he could have employed them to

advance his wife's suit. Even so, had this been his intention, there is
no evidence that he had any success. The records of inquisitions *post
mortem* taken in the year of his death do not show that he then held
any of the Warwick property.[11] Moreover, if Somerset had tried to
dismember Warwick's lands and win a share of them by the abuse
of royal favour, it is extraordinary that no contemporary notice of
the matter survives – the scandal would have been tremendous. The
only part of the Beauchamp inheritance for which there is clear
evidence of his interest is the chamberlainship of the Exchequer. Here
the king had been prevailed upon to ignore his own confirmation
of Neville's title to possession and the issue was reopened for determination by the Exchequer court. In fact, this court was seemingly
unable to come to a decision for three years. Obviously it was not
inclined to proceed to judgment as long as Somerset had the king's
favour. It was no longer under any restraint from that quarter at the
close of 1453, when Somerset was in the Tower and Warwick an
influential member of the king's council. Now the Exchequer gave
judgment in the earl's favour and he was restored to possession on
15 February 1454.[12]

This challenge by the half-sisters and their husbands to Neville's
assumption of an appurtenance of the earldom suggests that they
may well have also contested his wife's sole right to its landed
property. The licences of 1449 and 1451 could be taken as indications
that they were so doing; the interval of nine months between Anne
Beauchamp's death and the taking of inquisitions *post mortem* was
unusually long. It is arguable that Somerset was responsible. A third
licence might seem to support this theory. On 12 December 1461,
Edward IV authorised Warwick and his wife, as Duke Henry's heir,
to enter all the lands held by Anne Beauchamp as her grandfather's
heir and a moiety of the lands which had belonged to her mother.[13]
This does suggest that the Nevilles were not in possession of all the
lands they claimed as the countess's inheritance. Yet the licence could
have been no more than a safeguard, to exonerate Warwick for his
entry into properties since the reversal of his attainder (November
1459) in the previous year. There are sufficient other possible explanations, however, to deter further speculation and, in the present state
of our knowledge, to forbid the admission of this record as evidence to support a theory that an attempt was made to partition
the Beauchamp estates ten years earlier. It might be best to leave

this question open: there are grounds for suspicion, but no more.

Another part of Richard Beauchamp's estates were the castle and lordship of Abergavenny. Richard's uncle, William Beauchamp, had married the subsequent heiress to this and other properties. In 1396, he had entailed Abergavenny on the male issue of himself and his wife; if this male issue should fail, the lordship was to pass to his brother Thomas, earl of Warwick, and his male heirs. William's son Richard, earl of Worcester, had died without male issue. His daughter Elizabeth married Edward Neville and he became Lord Abergavenny; but, on account of the entail, the castle and lordship from which he took his title were taken by Richard Beauchamp, earl of Warwick and subsequently passed to his son, Duke. Henry. Anne Beauchamp had next succeeded despite the entail restricting the inheritance to male heirs. In 1449, after her death, Edward, Lord Abergavenny petitioned the king for possession of the property, claiming that he and his wife had been wrongfully disseised by Richard Beauchamp, earl of Warwick, and his two immediate successors; Edward seemingly made no reference to the entail in his petition. His request for a licence to enter was granted, but the king's letters had no effect. Neville of Warwick took and kept possession of Abergavenny.[14] There do not appear to have been any serious repercussions: Edward was the earl of Salisbury's brother and thus Warwick's uncle and presumably the family bonds were strong enough to prevent a serious breach.

The problem of the ownership of Abergavenny was not an easy one to determine. Warwick and Edward Neville could both claim that their wives were residuary heirs, and three generations of Beauchamps of Warwick had been the last to hold seisin. But the affair is a significant reminder of the impotence of the crown to dispose of property in the face of determined opposition. Warwick, clearly, was prepared to ignore royal letters patent which threatened his interests. It must be emphasised, however, that the letters granted to Edward Neville were a licence to enter; they imply that the recipient had a right to possession and that the king had recognised this right. But a licence did not by itself confer a legal title: if the recipient's claim could not be sustained in law, his licence was worthless. It obviously was without value in this instance. Might not the same have been the case with the licences granted to Anne Neville's half-sisters in 1449 and 1451?

Warwick and his wife acquired other estates as her share of her mother's Despenser inheritance. On Anne Beauchamp's death, the lands in which she had succeeded Duke Henry as Isabel Despenser's heir devolved on the latter's heirs. The descent of the estates was governed by an entail and they were divided as Isabel's nearest heirs were her two daughters. She had married twice. Her first husband was Richard Beauchamp, earl of Worcester, who died in 1422; their sole issue, as we have already noticed, was Elizabeth Neville, Lady Abergavenny. Elizabeth died in 1449 and her heir was her son George Neville. Warwick's wife was the second daughter and heir.

The lands to which they now succeeded were not the whole of Isabel Despenser's inheritance. She had been the heir of her brother Richard Despenser, who died in 1414 without issue. He did leave a widow, herself yet another Neville, Eleanor, who next married Henry Percy, second earl of Northumberland. Henry V made a formal grant of dower to her in 1415 but it was not until 1447 that she was able to receive this third part of her first husband's lands.[15] Here is another example of royal letters and feudal convention being successfully disregarded by a powerful and influential magnate. Richard Beauchamp of Worcester and Richard and Henry Beauchamp of Warwick all enjoyed full possession of the Despenser property and it was only when the last was succeeded by a child that Eleanor obtained her dower.

There are no known reasons for suspecting that any challenge was made to Anne Neville's title to a moiety of the unencumbered portion of the Despenser lands. The king, by letters patent dated 12 July 1449, granted the custody of this moiety to her and Warwick for as long as they should remain in the king's hands;[16] this would have been until they were of full age, when they would have livery. But before the Nevilles could secure possession of this portion of the Despenser lands, the property as a whole had to be valued and then partitioned between them and the heir to the other moiety. Operations of this kind were normally supervised by royal officers with the assistance of local juries. Any co-heir would naturally take close interest in the business and try to make sure that he received no less than his fair share. When the Despenser lands were divided, however, the co-heir with Anne Neville was a boy of thirteen. Who was to protect his interests? His father was still alive but the wardship of his lands belonged to the crown. The king did not exercise this custody directly in George's case but farmed it out. The disposal of the custody was thus a matter of considerable importance when the Despenser property was partitioned.

The first to have charge of George Neville's moiety was Lord Tiptoft (later earl of Worcester), by a grant dated 10 June 1449. In 1450 Tiptoft surrendered his royal letters granting the custody and on 22 May the king gave Warwick charge of all the lands in which Anne Beauchamp was seised in fee tail at the time of her death as long as their keeping belonged to the king. The royal letter making this concession related only to the Despenser estates: it stated that these were entailed and were thereby to descend to George and Anne Neville. Since Anne Neville's portion had already been granted to her and Warwick, the lands now committed to him were George's inheritance. A fresh committal was made to Warwick on 26 March 1452, when the lands in question were described as a moiety of the lands held by Anne Beauchamp in fee tail then in the king's hands, and the committal was to last as long as their keeping pertained to the crown. Again, the lands here referred to could only have been George Neville's share of the Despenser property and Warwick's tenure of them was thus to last until the boy came of age and received livery out of the king's hands. Yet on 15 June 1453 Somerset was granted the custody of the very same property, although this time it was described as the lands once held by Anne Beauchamp and in the king's hands on account of George's minority. There was no indication that Warwick had surrendered his custody, although the recent act of resumption may have been deemed to have cancelled it.[17]

This committal of George Neville's lands to Somerset was not the cause of Warwick's breach with the royal court. There are signs that this had occurred in the summer of 1452. But it was seemingly the reason for Warwick's relations with Somerset deteriorating to the point of open conflict. Glamorgan was part of the Despenser territory and it was from here that there came reports of military preparations. The king's council ordered the two peers to come before it on 21 July, and it is therefore probable that the trouble had begun immediately after Somerset's grant of custody on 15 June. This dispute was not about the ownership of land but about the farm for the custody of the lordships of Glamorgan and Morgannoc.[18] The property in question, therefore, was not Anne Neville's moiety of the Despenser estates, to which she had a clear and recognised title in fee tail, but to the moiety of George Neville nominally in the king's hands but actually held at farm.* Warwick, we may presume, firmly opposed Somerset's efforts to take over the custody of George Neville's lands: he was threatened with losing a source of profit, and Somerset's occupation of one of the Despenser moieties might have embarrassed Warwick and his wife as possessors of the other moiety. Hitherto he had been comfortably placed; with the whole estate in his charge, he could certainly have made sure that his share would not comprise less than half the value of the whole. Perhaps Somerset claimed that Warwick had taken more than his just share[20] and tried to gain more for George in order to increase his own temporary profit as keeper.

The outcome of the council's proceedings in this dispute is not known. King Henry became insane soon after they were begun and, as in the case of the chamberlainship of the Exchequer, political circumstances turned in Warwick's favour. There is no formal record of a further committal of George's lands, even after Somerset had been killed at St. Albans. Presumably Warwick continued to hold the custody on the strength of the king's grant of 26 March 1452, and York and his fellow councillors naturally did nothing about it. Warwick was certainly occupying the lordships of Glamorgan and Morgannoc when he was attainted in 1459.[21]

The evidence we have reviewed is incomplete and some of the individual records do not appear to be mutually compatible or are so imprecise in themselves as to allow excessive scope for speculation. Further research may permit a more satisfactory account of these proceedings. We may however make a few general observations on the available evidence. In the first place, the elements of confusion in the circumstances of Richard Beauchamp's vast estate were in themselves likely to afford potent reasons for disagreement. He had held lands in his own right and in those of his two wives. Were these lands ever distributed to the satisfaction of his various heirs? At his death, the deeds concerning his properties were in France.[22] Were they returned, and if so into whose hands did they pass? Separate entails

---

* Most of the revenues assigned to Eleanor, countess of Northumberland, as the widow of Richard Despenser, were drawn from Glamorgan.[19] She is not mentioned in the council's letter, however, and Warwick and Somerset could hardly have had cause to quarrel for the custody of her rents.

governed some of the estates. Through the failure of the direct male line of the Beauchamps of Warwick these conveyances raised further problems. Then the ambiguous attitude of the crown, its seemingly conflicting grants and licences, aggravated the complexities. And to these factors we must add what is known of the characters of the two chief persons concerned, Somerset's reputation for greed[23] and Warwick's hasty and suspicious nature, his readiness to make accusations and follow them with violent action.[24] We may, on balance, decide that there is no case for believing that Somerset schemed to have the Beauchamp estates partitioned, but Warwick may well have suspected that he did. As the Exchequer court continued to put off hearing his claim to the chamberlainship, his suspicions would have hardened. His appointment to a commission of oyer and terminer on 6 July 1452[25] indicates that he had not then quarrelled with Somerset, but the break took place in the next two or three months. Somerset's intrusion into Glamorgan as the keeper of George Neville's lands was the final provocation. The conclusion came when Warwick opened the attack at the first battle of St. Albans.

SOURCES

The most comprehensive survey of recent research on this period is E. F. Jacob, *The Fifteenth Century* (Oxford, 1961). J. H. Ramsay, *Lancaster and York* (Oxford, 1892), remains the fullest narrative account. J. R. Lander, *The Wars of the Roses* (1965), provides a collection of extracts from contemporary literary and documentary sources. The standard work on literary material is C. L. Kingsford, *English Historical Literature in the Fifteenth Century* (Oxford, 1913). For the Public Records, see the *Guide to the Contents of the Public Record Office* (H.M.S.O., 1963), Vol. I.

Biographical details given in this book, unless other sources have been cited, have been taken from *The Complete Peerage*, by G.E.C. (1910–59); *The Handbook of British Chronology*, ed. F. M. Powicke and E. B. Fryde (Royal Historical Society, 1961), for officers of state; and J. C. Wedgwood, *History of Parliament* (1936–8), Vol. II (Register of Members of the House of Commons).

All the manuscript sources quoted below are Public Records, unless a statement to the contrary is given.

The following abbreviations have been employed:

(i) for Public Records, using the Office's references

C.1 – Early Chancery Proceedings, Series I.
C.53 – Chancery, Charter Rolls.
C.67 – Chancery, Supplementary Patent Rolls. (Those cited are better known as Pardon Rolls.)
C.81 – Chancery, Warrants for the Great Seal, Series I.
C.139 – Chancery, Inquisitions *post mortem*, Henry VI.
E.28 – Exchequer of Receipt, Council and Privy Seal. (These are records of the Privy Seal Office.)
E.101 – Exchequer K.R., Various Accounts.
E.404 – Exchequer of Receipt, Warrants for Issues.
KB.9 – King's Bench, Ancient Indictments.
KB.27 – King's Bench, *Coram rege* Rolls.

[The number of the roll will follow C.53, C.67 and KB.27. For the remainder, the first number following will be that of the file or box, and the second that of the piece. As the pieces in E.28 are not numbered, dates will be given if they do not appear in the text; the files are arranged chronologically.]

(ii) for works in print

BIHR. – *Bulletin of the Institute of Historical Research.*
BJRL. – *Bulletin of the John Rylands Library*, Manchester.
CCR. – *Calendar of Close Rolls* (Public Record Office, 1892–1963).

CPR.   – *Calendar of Patent Rolls* (Public Record Office, 1891–).

EHR.   – *English Historical Review*.

PL.   – *The Paston Letters*, ed. J. Gairdner (1910).

PPC.   – *Proceedings and Ordinances of the Privy Council of England*, ed. N. H. Nicolas (Record Commission, 1834–7).

Rot. Parl. – *Rotuli Parliamentorum* (1783).

SD.   – *Select Documents of English Constitutional History, 1307-1485*, ed. S. B. Chrimes and A. L. Brown (1961).

TRHS.   – *Transactions of the Royal Historical Society*.

Introduction

1   *Rot. Parl.* V, pp. 463-4.

2   E. Hall, *Chronicle* (1809), pp. 245-8.

3   *King Richard II*, Act IV, Sc. i, lines 137-8, 146-7. See also E. M. W. Tillyard, *Shakespeare's History Plays* (1959), pp. 40-54.

4   *A Relation of the Island of England*, ed. C. A. Sneyd (Camden Society, Original Series, no. XXXVII, 1847), p. 46.

5   C. L. Kingsford, *Prejudice and Promise in Fifteenth-Century England* (Oxford, 1925), pp. 76-7; K. B. McFarlane, "England: the Lancastrian Kings", *Cambridge Medieval History*, Vol. VIII (Cambridge, 1936), p. 411.

    More recently Mr McFarlane has suggested that the civil war was reluctantly undertaken by the lords in order "to rescue the kingdom from the consequences of Henry VI's inanity". I find it impossible to believe that the "Yorkists" were prompted by such high-minded motives, and it cannot be said that the peerage acted with unanimity. Nor, as will appear at some length, do I agree with Mr McFarlane's contention that the preceding private warfare of various magnates was not the seedbed of the Wars of the Roses, or that they had little influence on the alignment of parties. ("The Wars of the Roses", *Proceedings of the British Academy*, Vol. L, for 1964 (1965), pp. 97, 105-6). I regret that this valuable and illuminating article did not appear until the final stages of the preparations of this book.

6   S. B. Chrimes, *Lancastrians, Yorkists and Henry VII* (1964), p. xii.

7   *King Henry VI, Part I*, Act II, Sc. iv; *King Richard III*, Act V, Sc. v, line 19.

8   *CPR. 1446-52*, pp. 187, 189, 201; *CCR. 1454-61*, pp. 197-8; and see p. 53 below.

9   *PPC.* V, pp. 35-9, 57-8, 192; *CPR. 1436-41*, pp. 246-7, 282-3.

10 C. L. Kingsford, "The First Version of Hardyng's Chronicle", *EHR.* XXVII (1912), p. 749.

11 Kingsford, *Prejudice and Promise*, p. 49; A. H. Thompson, *The English Clergy and their Organization in the Later Middle Ages* (Oxford, 1947), p. 55.

12 KB.9/49; 288, no. 58.

13 *Concilia Magnæ Britanniæ et Hiberniæ*, ed. D. Wilkins (1737), Vol. III, pp. 539-540; see also *Rot. Parl.* V, pp. 152-3.

14 KB.9/228-99. Almost every file has three or four cases.

15 First, apparently, by C. Plummer, in his edition of Sir John Fortescue, *The Governance of England* (Oxford, 1885), p. 15.

16 For recent work on this subject, see N. B. Lewis, "The Organization of Indentured Retinues in Fourteenth-Century England", *TRHS.* 4th series, Vol. XXVII (1944), pp. 29-39; K. B. McFarlane, "Bastard Feudalism", *BIHR.* XX (1943-5), pp. 161-80; G. A. Holmes, *The Estates of the Higher Nobility in Fourteenth-Century England* (Cambridge, 1957), pp. 58-84; W. H.

Dunham, *Lord Hastings' Indentured Retainers, 1461-1483* (New Haven, Connecticut, 1955), pp. 7-14.

17 J. Fortescue, *De Laudibus Legum Anglie*, ed. S. B. Chrimes (Cambridge, 1949), pp. 25-33, 38-9, 66-71.

18 M. M. Postan, "Some Economic Evidence of Declining Population in the Later Middle Ages", *Economic History Review*, Second Series, Vol. II (1949-1950), pp. 226, 233; J. E. Thorold Rogers, *Six Centuries of Work and Wages* (1886), pp. 327, 539.

19 H. L. Gray, "Incomes from Land in England in 1436", *EHR.* XLIX (1934), pp. 630-9.

20 H. M. Cam, *Law-Finders and Law-Makers in Medieval England* (1963), p. 52.

21 K. B. McFarlane, "England and the Hundred Years War", *Past and Present*, no. 22 (1962), pp. 3-13.

22 E. Power and M. M. Postan (ed.), *Studies in English Trade in the Fifteenth Century* (1933), pp. 1-38.

23 Postan, *loc. cit.*, pp. 221-46.

24 Rogers, *op. cit.*, p. 326.

25 C. D. Ross, *The Estates and Finances of Richard Beauchamp, Earl of Warwick* (Dugdale Society Occasional Papers, no. 12, Oxford, 1956), pp. 14-18.

26 T. B. Pugh, *The Marcher Lordships of South Wales, 1415-1536* (Board of Celtic Studies, Cardiff, 1963), pp. 178-9.

27 J. M. W. Bean, *The Estates of the Percy Family, 1416-1537* (Oxford, 1958), pp. 83-4.

28 *Rot. Parl.* V, pp. 14-16, 269-71.

29 M. M. Postan, "The Fifteenth Century", *Econ. Hist. Review* IX (1939), p. 166.

30 Bean, *op. cit.*, pp. 94, 103-8.

31 K. B. McFarlane, "The English Nobility in the Later Middle Ages", Comité International des Sciences Historiques, XIIᵉ Congrès International, *Rapports* (Vienna, 1965), Vol. I, pp. 337-45.

32 Gray, *loc. cit.*, pp. 614-18. T. B. Pugh and C. D. Ross, in "The English Baronage and the Income Tax of 1436", *BIHR.* XXVI (1953), demonstrate that these figures are too low, but here they are used for comparative purposes.

33 *The Chronicle of John Hardyng*, ed. H. Ellis (1812), p. 388.

34 *PPC.* IV, pp. 112-13; Ross, *op. cit.*, pp. 15-16; Bean, *op. cit.*, p. 94.

35 *Rot. Parl.* IV, pp. 329-30, 352-3, 344, 421-2; *CPR. 1429-36*, pp. 370-413.

Chapter I

1 *CPR. 1429-36*, p. 589.

2 C.81/703-4, 1367; Privy Seal Office, Warrants, Series I, file 5; E.28/58.

3 *PPC.* IV, pp. 287-9.

4 *PPC.* III, pp. 296-300.

5 *PL.* I, no. 18.

6 J. Blacman, *Henry the Sixth*, ed. and translated by M. R. James (Cambridge, 1919).

7 *Chronicle of John Hardyng*, p. 410.

8 KB.27/742, Rex 7.

9 KB.9/245, no. 46; *The Brut*, ed. F. W. D. Brie (Early English Text Society, 1905, 1908), Vol. II, p. 485; C.81/1370, nos. 13-14. The terms of the warrant do not all appear in the pardon as printed in *CPR. 1441-6*, p. 278. The preacher's name is confirmed in the household account, E.101/409, no. 11,

fo.33v. For Carver's detention, see *Excerpta Historica*, ed. S. Bentley (1831), p. 390.

10 KB.9/260, no. 40a.

11 KB.9/262, nos. 2, 78.

12 KB.9/122, no. 28; printed by R. F. Hunnisett in *Sussex Notes and Queries*, Vol. XIV (Lewes, 1954-7), p. 119.

13 Privy Seal Warrants, files 5-20.

14 *CPR.1446-52*, p. 68; *The Brut* II, p. 513.

15 *PPC*. V, pp. 88-9.

16 E.28/58-88; C.81/1424-85.

17 *PPC*. IV, p. 110; C.53/187, m. 39.

18 *PPC*. V, p. 71, and VI, pp. 312-15; *SD*. pp. 274-6.

19 S. B. Chrimes, *Introduction to the Administrative History of Medieval England* (Blackwell, Oxford, 1952), pp. 248-9.

20 J. F. Baldwin, *The King's Council in England during the Middle Ages* (Oxford, 1913), pp. 184-92.

21 KB.9/260, no. 40a.

22 *CPR.1446-52*, p. 63; C.53/190, m. 29. The last reference is dated 15 July 1449 but it may be presumed that he remained in office until his death in 1450.

23. T. Gascoigne, *Loci e Libro Veritatum*, ed. J. E. T. Rogers (Oxford, 1881), p. 191; cited in *Cambridge Medieval History* VIII, p. 400. Gascoigne might here be quoting from the allegations of the rebels in 1450.

24 Gascoigne, p. 176.

25 E.28/58.

26 A. B. Emden, *A Biographical Register of the University of Oxford to A.D. 1500* (Oxford, 1957-9), Vol. I, pp. 15-16.

27 *Wars of the English in France during the Reign of Henry VI*, ed. J. Stevenson (Rolls Series, 1861-4), Vol. I, pp. 103-46; cited in Ramsay, *Lancaster and York* II, p. 67.

28. *An English Chronicle of the Reigns of Richard II, Henry IV, Henry V and Henry VI*, ed. J. S. Davies (Camden Society, Original Series, no. LXIV, 1856), p. 79.

Chapter II

1 *Political Poems and Songs*, ed. T. Wright (Rolls Series, 1859, 1861), Vol. II, p. 224.

2 *Rot. Parl*. V, pp. 176-83; *SD*., pp. 285-90.

3 R. Virgoe, "The Death of William de la Pole, Duke of Suffolk", *BJRL*. 47 (1965), pp. 489-502.

4 *Political Poems* II, p. 234.

5 Kingsford, *Prejudice and Promise*, pp. 154-71.

6 E.101/409, no. 11, fo. 38v.

7 KB.9/261, no. 47.

8 E.404/63, no. 13; *The Great Chronicle of London*, ed. A. D. Thomas and I. D. Thornley (1938), pp. 178-9. A second appeal is mentioned in E.404/65, no. 106.

9 KB.9/256, no. 13.

10 KB.9/72 is the file for her trial.

11 Baldwin, *King's Council*, pp. 188-93; *Correspondence of Thomas Bekynton*, ed. G. Williams (Rolls Series, 1872), Vol. I, pp. 155-9.

12 It was held at Eltham in the 26th year (1447-8). The same warrant covers expenses in the parliament of 1449, suggesting that there had been no intermediate assembly (E.404/65, no. 246).

13 *Political Poems* II, pp. 221-3.

14 KB.27/745, Rex 6d.

15 *Rot. Parl.* V, p. 226.

16 *ibid.* IV, pp. 433-8; examined by J. L. Kirby in "The Issues of the Lancastrian Exchequer and Lord Cromwell's Estimates of 1433", *BIHR.* XXIV (1951), pp. 121-48.

17 A. Steel, *The Receipt of the Exchequer 1377-1485* (Cambridge, 1954), pp. 203-284, and tables; cf. Ramsay, *Lancaster and York* II, pp. 250-67.

18 Exchequer L.T.R., Enrolled Accounts, no. 7, rot. 24-28.

19 *The Household of Edward IV*, ed. A. R. Myers (Manchester, 1959), pp. 6-7.

20 E.404/57, no. 130.

21 *Rot. Parl.* V, p. 183.

22 Historical Manuscripts Commission, *Third Report* (1872), Appendix, p. 280.

23 The more important are listed in *Cambridge Medieval History* VIII, p. 403, note.

24 C.1/19, no. 65 (Somerset's deposition); *CPR. 1436-41*, p. 418, and *1446-52*, p. 313.

25 Kirby, *loc. cit.*, p. 123; Exchequer Issue Rolls, no. 765.

26 E.404/65, no. 78, and 63, no. 158; *CPR. 1446-52*, p. 260.

27 *ibid.*, p. 307.

28 *ibid.*, p. 215; *Rot. Parl.* V, p. 150.

29 E.404/67, no. 37.

30 E.404/63, no. 65; 64, nos. 154-5; 65, no. 210.

31 *e.g.* E.404/57, no. 130; 62, no. 188. For this subject, see G. L. Harriss, "Preference at the Medieval Exchequer", *BIHR.* XXX (1957), pp. 17-40.

32 C.1/18, nos. 211-13.

33 *CPR. 1446-52*, pp. 201-2.

34 *Wars of the English* II, p. 766.

35 *PL.* I, nos. 56, 66, 132, 263.

36 *CCR. 1454-61*, p. 77.

37 *PL.* I, no. 124.

38 R. Somerville, *History of the Duchy of Lancaster*, Vol. I (1953), p. 420.

39 *CPR. 1441-6*, p. 403; *1446-52*, pp. 4, 208.

40 *PL.* I, nos. 144-5.

41 *PL.* I, no. 138.

42 *CPR. 1446-52*, pp. 388, 592, 595.

43 *PL.* I, no. 134.

44 KB.9/267, nos. 1-42. This is the commission's file.

45 Exchequer L.T.R., Pipe Rolls, no. 296, Norfolk & Suffolk, rot. 2d. This gives the total of Tuddenham's fines in the margin against the entry of £1,442 as the total of fines imposed by the commission. Sheriff's Accounts, bundle 20, no. 23, lists his fines: it is not complete.

46 *PL.* I, no. 60; KB.9/259, no. 70; *Collections for a History of Staffordshire*, New Series, Vol. III. (William Salt Archaeological Society, 1900), pp. 197-9.

47 E.28/78.

48 KB.9/266, no. 51; *CPR. 1446-52*, pp. 324, 329, 461.

49 E.404/69, no. 176.

50 *Rot. Parl.* V, p. 200.

Chapter III

1 KB.9/109, no. 25; E.404/66, no. 15.
2 KB.9/73; *Six Town Chronicles*, ed. R. Flenley (Oxford, 1911), p. 129.
3 *CCR. 1447-54*, pp. 194-5.
4 KB.9/263, no. 20, part 4.
5 *Original Letters Illustrative of English History*, ed. H. Ellis, Series II (1827), Vol. I, p. 114; J. Stow, *Annales, or a General Chronicle of England* (1631), p. 387.
6 *The Brut* II, p. 472; KB.9/230a, no. 24.
7 *CPR. 1441-6*, pp. 200, 422; E.28/81 (9 August).
8 H. M. Lyle, *The Rebellion of Jack Cade* (Historical Association Pamphlet G.16, 1950).
9 Historical Manuscripts Commission, *Eighth Report* (1881), Appendix I, Section 2, para. 267a.
10 Stow, *Annales*, pp. 388-9; *SD*. pp. 290-1.
11 Hist. MSS. Comm. VIII, *loc. cit.* The original – at Magdalen College, Oxford – may well be the articles which Sir John Fastolf's servant obtained in the rebel camp (*PL*. I, no. 99).
12 Jacob, *Fifteenth Century*, pp. 495-6.
13 KB.9/133 and 134; Kingsford, *Eng. Hist. Literature*, p. 348.
14 KB.9/109; *CPR. 1446-52*, pp. 420-1.
15 Gascoigne, *Loci*, pp. 42, 175; Kingsford, *op. cit.*, pp. 355-6.
16 *CPR. 1446-52*, p. 388.
17 "Some Ancient Indictments in King's Bench referring to Kent, 1450-1452", ed. R. Virgoe, *Documents Illustrative of Medieval Kentish Society* (Kent Archaeological Society, Record Publication XVIII, 1964), pp. 215-43.
18 *CPR. 1446-52*, pp. 460-1, 469, 472, 503; KB.9/133 (Wilts.).
19 KB.9/49.
20 E.404/67, no. 38; *CPR. 1446-52*, p. 435; KB.9/49.
21 *Rot. Parl.* V, p. 224.

Chapter IV

1 J. T. Rosenthal, "Fifteenth-Century Baronial Incomes and Richard, Duke of York", *BIHR*. XXXVII (1964), pp. 233-9.
2 E.404/57, no. 130; 59, nos. 161, 163.
3 *PPC*. V, p. 263; Exchequer Issue Rolls, no. 749 (10 July).
4 E.404/62, no. 188.
5 *PPC*. VI, pp. 52-3.
6 *Cambridge Medieval History* VIII, pp. 404-5.
7 *CPR. 1446-52*, p. 185; cf. *1436-41*, p. 140, and *1441-6*, pp. 45, 345.
8 *Registrum Johannis Whethamstede*, ed. H. T. Riley (Rolls Series, 1872-3), Vol. I, pp. 160-1.
9 Para. 1: KB.9/265, no. 121; *CPR. 1446-52*, pp. 443-5; KB.27/762, Rex 8 and 15.
Para. 2: *Rot. Parl.* V, p. 182; *CPR. 1441-6*, pp. 283, 436 and *1446-52*, pp. 1, 202.
10 E.404/62, no. 188; 67, nos. 37, 172.
11 *PPC*. VI, pp. 92-3.
12 *Rot. Parl.* V, p. 255.
13 *Six Town Chronicles*, p. 134; E.28/80 (15 August); C.81/1546, no. 54 (1 September).

14 R. Butler, *Some Notices of the Castle and the Ecclesiastical Buildings of Trim* (Trim, 1854), p. 79; cited in *Dict. National Biography*, *s.n.* Richard.

15 *PL*. Introduction, pp. xciii-vii; Vol. I, no. 114.

16 *Rot. Parl.* V, pp. 172-4; *SD*. pp. 284-5.

17 *PL*. I, nos. 132, 212.

18 *PL*. I, no. 113.

19 *Political Poems* II, p. 222.

20 *PL*. I, no. 173. Undated, but probably February 1451, when Norfolk was about to act as a commissioner of oyer and terminer (see *ibid.* 92).

21 KB.9/118, no. 22; *CCR. 1447-54*, p. 476.

22 *PL*. I, nos. 174-6, 179; KB.9/118.

23 KB.9/271, no. 117.

24 K. B. McFarlane, "Parliament and 'Bastard Feudalism'", *TRHS*. 4th series XXVI (1944), pp. 56-7.

25 *Six Town Chronicles*, pp. 106, 136-8, 157; *Wars of the English* II, pp. 769-70; Stow, *Annales*, p. 392.

26 B. P. Wolffe, "Acts of Resumption in the Lancastrian Parliaments", *EHR*. LXXIII (1958), p. 603.

27 *Rot. Parl.* V, p. 216; *SD*. pp. 292-4; *cf.* Kingsford, *Eng. Hist. Literature*, pp. 364-5.

28 *Wars of the English* II, p. 770; J. S. Roskell, "Sir William Oldhall", *Nottingham Medieval Studies* V (1961), pp. 111-12.

29 *PL*. III, no. 994.

30 *Incerti Scriptoris Chronicon Angliæ*, ed. J. A. Giles (1848), part IV, p. 45.

31 *CPR. 1446-52*, p. 455; *1452-61*, pp. 671-2.

32 C.53/190, m. 27.

33 *CCR. 1447-54*, p. 326.

34 Wolffe, *loc. cit.*, pp. 604-8.

Chapter V

1 A. R. Myers, "A Parliamentary Debate of the Mid-Fifteenth Century", *BJRL*. 22 (1938), p. 403.

2 Ancient Petitions, no. 7364; C.1/16, no. 484; and see p. 211 below.

3 *Calendarium Inquisitionum post mortem sive Escaetarum* (Record Commission, 1806-28), Vol. IV, pp. 66-7; Gray, *EHR*. (1934), p. 616.

4 I have to thank Dr Ralph Griffiths for suggesting this explanation.

5 E.404/40, no. 148.

6 *CPR. 1436-41*, pp. 133, 411.

7 E.28/64-5; *CCR. 1435-41*, p. 396.

8 *CPR. 1436-41*, p. 532; E.28/68.

9 *PPC*. V, pp. 158-61, 165, 173-5; Chancery Miscellanea, bundle 93, file 4.

10 *PPC*. V, p. 203.

11 *CCR. 1447-54*, pp. 45, 442; *CPR. 1446-52*, pp. 89, 138, 191, 298.

12 *Catalogue des Rolles Gascons, Normans et François*, ed. T. Carte (1743), Vol. I, pp. 223, 225, 233; E.404/59, no. 119; Exchequer L.T.R., Foreign Accounts, nos. 84, rot. C, and 91, rot. M; *CPR. 1441-6*, p. 424.

13 *PPC*. V, p. 240.

14 KB.27/767, Rex 3d.

15 *Six Town Chronicles*, p. 106.

16 E.404/68, no. 176.

17 E.101/410, nos. 6, ff. 32-4, and 9, ff. 11-12.

18 E.404/68, nos. 96-7, 99. In *Issues of the Exchequer, Henry III – Henry VI*, ed. F. Devon (Record Commission, 1847), p. 478, Buckingham is mistakenly said to have raised forces for the king in September 1450.

19 *Wars of the English* II, p. 770.

20 KB.9/267, no. 44.

21 *Six Town Chronicles*, p. 139.

22 J. Smyth, *Lives of the Berkeleys*, ed. J. Maclean (Gloucester, 1883), pp. 65-8; *CPR. 1446-52*, p. 511.

23 *ibid.*, p. 525.

Chapter VI

1 *PL.* I, nos. 148, 158-9, 172.

2 E.404/68, no. 176.

3 KB.9/85, no. 10.

4 KB.9/65a, no. 1.

5 Roskell, "Sir William Oldhall", p. 104, and see note 13 below.

6 Stow, *Annales*, p. 393.

7 *Original Letters illustrative of English History*, ed. H. Ellis, Series I (1825), Vol. I, pp. 11-13.

8 *Chronicon Angliæ*, ed. Giles, IV, p. 43; *Six Town Chronicles*, p. 139; E.404/68, no. 79.

9 *CPR. 1446-52*, p. 537.

10 *PPC.* VI, p. 116.

11 E.28/80, printed from a transcript in the British Museum in *PPC.* VI, pp. 90-2. Its editor there dates it to 1450, the original having only 17 February. Although York is not named, the letter can be more readily fitted into the chronology for 1452. Moreover, Sudbury undoubtedly did receive letters from York in 1452 which called on its citizens to attend him. The mayor and councillors fearfully asked the chancellor and keeper of the privy seal to send them royal letters forbidding all assemblies, and they were sent a letter under the privy seal, which may well have been that of 17 February (C.81/1458, no. 12).

12 *CPR. 1446-52*, p. 577.

13 Information about the risings and subsequent sessions comes from KB.9/7 (Cambs.), nos. 4, 10; 15 (Devon), nos. 20, 23-5, 33-4, 39; 26 (Essex), nos. 24, 28, 30; 34 (Hereford), no. 48; 40 (Herts.), nos. 5-6; 65a (Lincs.), nos. 19-21, 29, 33, 36, 39-41; 94 (Northants.), nos. 2-5, 12, 21; 103 (Salop), nos. 2, 16; 105 (Somerset), nos. 1d-e, 4b, 7b; 118 (Suffolk), no. 33. In some of the indictments, the year of the conspiracy is said to have been 1450, presumably in error.

Details of the king's progresses as shown on Map II come from E.101/410, no. 9, and C.81/766-7, 1371.

For York's estates, see those confiscated in 1459 as shown in *CPR. 1452-61*, pp. 530-74, *passim*: also *Ministers' Accounts*, Vol. I (Public Record Office Lists and Indexes, no. V), pp. 362-9.

14 E.101/410, no. 9, fo. 21.

15 *PL.* Introduction, pp. cxii-cxxiv; *The Brut* II, p. 520; Kingsford, *Eng. Hist. Literature*, pp. 367-8; *Great Chronicle*, pp. 185-6; *The Chronicles of London*, ed. C. L. Kingsford (Oxford, 1905), p. 163; *Reg. Whethamstede* I, pp. 161-3.

16 *CCR. 1447-54*, pp. 327, 334.

17 *Reg. Whethamstede* I, p. 85.

18 C.67/40.
19 KB.27/774, Rex 27; *Rot. Parl.* V, p. 248.
20 *ibid.*, p. 249. An indictment of Devon and Cobham for rising, with others, at Ilminster and Yeovil on 18 February 1452, was taken by commissioners in Somerset; it bears a note that it was sent to parliament in January 1454 (KB.9/105, no. 4b).

Devon was in fact imprisoned in Wallingford Castle (G. L. Harriss, "A Fifteenth-Century Chronicle at Trinity College, Dublin", *BIHR.* XXXVIII (1965), p. 216).
21 Roskell, *loc. cit.*, p. 105.
22 Ramsay, *Lancaster and York* II, p. 151; see also Jacob, *Fifteenth Century*, p. 504.
23 KB.9/103, no. 15; Kingsford, *op. cit.*, p. 368.
24 C.67/40, mm. 20-1; *Six Town Chronicles*, p. 107.
25 Ramsay, *op. cit.* II, p. 161; *Rot. Parl.* V, p. 230; Myers, *BJRL.* 22, p. 230; *CPR. 1452-61*, pp. 406-10.
26 *Rot. Parl.* V, pp. 265, 329.
27 E.404/68, no. 129.
28 *CPR. 1446-52*, p. 580; *1452-61*, p. 54.
29 *ibid.*, p. 102.

Chapter VII

Here *CW.* denotes *Transactions of the Cumberland and Westmorland Antiquarian and Archaeological Society*, New Series.

1 *Reg. Whethamstede* I, pp. 168-9, 391-2.
2 E.404/57, no. 279.
3 *Feudal Aids* (Public Record Office, 1899-1901), Vol. I, pp. 244-5.
4 Much of what follows is based on my "The Wardens of the Marches of England towards Scotland, 1377-1489", *EHR.* LXXII (1957), pp. 593-615.
5 Exchequer, Augmentations, Ancient Deeds, nos. 6258, 6466, 8541.
6 Gray, "Incomes in 1436", *EHR.* (1934), p. 615.
7 E.404/47, no. 194; 52, no. 211.
8 *PPC.* V, pp. 66-80; *CPR. 1436-41*, p. 289.
9 *Excerpta Historica*, pp. 2-3; *CCR. 1429-41, passim*, and *1441-7*, pp. 150-1, 195-8; *Reports of the Deputy Keepers of the Public Records*, no. 34 (1873), pp. 242-3.
10 T. Madox, *Formulare Anglicanum* (1702), pp. 146-7.
11 C.139/104, no. 11.
12 *CPR. 1441-6*, pp. 44, 93-4.
13 *ibid.*, pp. 191, 429; *CPR. 1452-61*, p. 544.
14 *English Chronicle*, p. 117.
15 *Deputy Keeper's Report* 34, pp. 178, 192, 209, 210; *CPR. 1441-6*, p. 458.
16 *Rot. Parl.* IV, p. 490; Justices Itinerant, Gaol Delivery Rolls, no. 208, mm. 39d, 41, 43-5.
17 C.139/25, no. 24; Augmentations Deeds, no. 6258.
18 E.404/52, nos. 212-14; *CPR. 1429-36*, p. 516.
19 *Rot. Parl.* V, p. 347.
20 R. L. Storey, "Disorders in Lancastrian Westmorland: some Early Chancery Proceedings", *CW.* LIII (1953), pp. 69-80.
21 Gaol Delivery Rolls, nos. 211, m. 44, and 213, m. 16.
22 *Rot. Parl.* IV, p. 163.

23 J. Nicolson and R. Burn, *History of Westmorland and Cumberland* (1777), Vol. I, p. 387.
24 F. W. Ragg, "Cliburn Hervy and Cliburn Tailbois; Part I", *CW*. XXVIII (1928), pp. 253-4; M. A. Rowling, "John Clybborne's Appeal to the Earl of Salisbury", *CW*. LXIII (1963), pp. 178-83.
25 *CPR. 1436-41*, pp. 124, 595, and *1441-7*, pp. 64, 191; Chancery Files, series C, file 180; C.139/92.
26 *Rot. Parl.* V, p. 168.
27 M. A. Rowling, "William de Parr, King's Knight to Henry IV", *CW*. LVI (1956), pp. 87-103.
28 Printed by F. W. Ragg in *CW*. X-XXVIII (1910-28), *passim*.
29 F. W. Ragg, "De Threlkeld", *CW*. XXIII (1923), pp. 198-9.
30 Storey, *CW*. (1953), p. 79.
31 F. W. Ragg, "An Indenture in English of 1431", *CW*. IX (1909), pp. 283-4.
32 Nicolson and Burn, Vol. I, pp. 96-8; *CPR. 1461-7*, p. 34.
33 Chancery Files, C.180.
34 *List of Sheriffs* (Public Record Office Lists and Indexes, no. IX), p. 27.

Chapter VIII

1 *PPC*. VI, p. 65.
2 Augmentations Deeds, no. 6435.
3 E.28/80 (3 April).
4 Bean, *Estates of the Percy Family*, pp. 84, *n.*, 93, *n.*
5 *CPR. 1446-52*, pp. 41-2.
6 *ibid.*, p. 307; E.28/79.
7 *PPC*. VI, p. 161.
8 *Catalogue of Ancient Deeds* (Public Record Office, 1890-1915), Vol. IV, no. A.8559; Historical Manuscripts Commission, *Twelfth Report* (1890), Appendix VI, p. 3.
9 Bean, *op. cit.*, pp. 89-96.
10 *CCR. 1447-54*, pp. 467-8.
11 *CPR. 1446-52*, pp. 269, 281.
12 *Calendar of Papal Letters* (Public Record Office, 1894-   ), Vol. X, pp. 109-10, 600, 608.
13 Chancery Files, C.180.
14 E.28/85 (11 July); *Rot. Parl.* VI, p. 63.
15 C.139/25, no. 22.
16 *The Itinerary of John Leland*, ed. L. T. Smith (1906-10), Vol. I, p. 69.
17 J. N. Bartlett, "The Expansion and Decline of York in the Later Middle Ages", *Economic History Review* XII (1959-60), pp. 28-9; E. Miller, in *Victoria County History of Yorkshire: York City* (1961), p. 82.
18 KB.9/149, no. 7/2.
19 *PPC*. VI, pp. 140-1; E.28/83.
20 KB.9/149, no. 8/5.
21 *PPC*. VI, pp. 141-2.
22 KB.9/149, no. 12/23.
23 *PPC*. VI, pp. 147-50; *CPR. 1452-61*, pp. 121-3.
24 E.28/83.
25 *CPR. 1452-61*, p. 64.
26 KB.27/778, m. 1d.
27 KB.9/148, nos. 3, 8, 16; 149, nos. 5/2, 6/7.

28 *Initium fuit maximorum dolorum in Anglia. Wars of the English*, Vol. II, p. 770.
29 KB.9/149, nos. 4/25, 8/5, 12/24.
30 YORK CITY LIBRARY: City Chamberlains' Accounts, 1453-4.
31 *PPC.* VI, pp. 159-63.
32 KB.9/149, no. 11/3. This is a memorandum in a "privy seal" hand.

Chapter IX

1 *Rot. Parl.* V, p. 236.
2 *CPR. 1446-52*, pp. 326, 401.
3 Storey, *EHR.* (1957), pp. 604-5.
4 *PPC.* V, pp. 268-75.
5 E.28/80 (22 March); C.53/190, mm. 19-28.
6 *CPR. 1446-52*, pp. 523, 580.
7 His income in 1436 was assessed at £205 (Gray, *EHR.* (1934), p. 618). In 1439, his wife received a third of her mother's lands, an addition of about £100 (Ross, *Estates of Richard Beauchamp*, p. 15). His pensions amounted to £1,330 a year (*CPR. 1441-6*, pp. 54, 277, 324; *1452-61*, p. 28). His offices included that of constable of Windsor Castle; he was paid £500 a year, nominally for its repair (*CPR. 1436-41*, pp. 188, 443).
8 Basin, quoted in *Complete Peerage*, Vol. XII, part I, p. 53, *n.* c.
9 E.28/83 (27 July).
10 *CPR. 1452-61*, p. 60.
11 *Chronicon Angliæ*, ed. Giles, IV, p. 44; *Reg. Whethamstede* I, p. 163; *Rot. Parl.* V, p. 241; for the date, see Ramsay, *Lancaster and York* II, p. 166.
12 KB.9/273, nos. 2 and 7.
13 D. Henderson and R. D. Gillespie, *A Text-Book of Psychiatry* (Oxford, 1956), pp. 328-9. Mr G. O. Douglas, lecturer in Clinical Psychology at Nottingham University, kindly discussed Henry's symptoms with me and suggested that they might have been due to schizophrenia.
14 *PPC.* VI, pp. 163-4.
15 *CPR. 1452-61*, pp. 143-4.
16 *PPC.* VI, p. 183.
17 *PL.* I, no. 195.
18 *CPR. 1452-61*, pp. 662, 664; *Rot. Parl. V*, p. 249.
19 C.81/1546, nos. 73-4 (6 and 9 February 1454); *PPC.* VI, pp. 218-19.
20 *PL.* I, no. 191.
21 *PL.* I, no. 195.
22 *PL.* I, no. 195.
23 *Rot. Parl.* V, pp. 238-43.
24 E.28/83-4.
25 E.404/70, part 3, no. 81, and 71, part 1, no. 52; Baldwin, *King's Council*, pp. 175, 198; *SD.* pp. 253-5.
26 *PPC.* VI, pp. 168-9.
27 *ibid.*, pp. 172-3; *CPR. 1452-61*, p. 202.
28 G. L. Harriss, "The Struggle for Calais: An Aspect of the Rivalry between Lancaster and York", *EHR.* LXXV (1960), pp. 34-8.
29 *PPC.* VI, pp. 206-7.

Chapter X

1 *CPR. 1452-61*, p. 143; *Rot. Parl.* V, p. 249.
2 KB.9/149, no. 8/4; 148, no. 7.

3 *PPC.* VI, pp. 178-9; KB.9/149, no. 11/12.

4 Bean, *Estates of the Percy Family*, p. 74.

5 *CCR. 1447-54*, p. 360; *Rot. Parl.* V, p. 264; see also Harriss, *BIHR.* (1965), p. 216.

6 *PL.* I, no. 195.

7 *PPC.* VI, pp. 130-1 (mistakenly attributed to 1453), 175-6, 180-1, 184-5.

8 KB.9/148, no. 15.

9 KB.9/149, no. 4/27. Other indictments concerning this assembly written in the usual law court hand are 148, no. 11, and 149, nos. 5/3, 9/8. The last two repeat the charges in 149, no. 4/27, and this would seem to rule out any argument that the king's council altered the record after it had been received by the commissioners of oyer and terminer.

10 *PPC.* VI, pp. 130-1.

11 KB.9/148, nos. 13, 15.

12 KB.9/149, nos. 8/2, 6/3, 9/7 (in a "privy seal" hand); *PPC.* VI, pp. 189-97.

13 Duchy of Lancaster, Patent Rolls, nos. 23, m. 4, and 24, m. 4d.

14 *ibid.*, 24, m. 4d.

15 *Chronicles of London*, p. 164; Chancery Files, C.181 (*corpus cum causa*).

16 Lancaster Pat. Rolls, no. 23, m. 3; *CCR. 1454-61*, p. 13.

17 According to one chronicle, Exeter was released before Salisbury resigned the great seal (on 7 March 1455). This chronicler, however, is extremely confused. He reports events in this order: Kemp's death (22 March 1454); skirmish at Stamford Bridge (31 October 1454); Devon's operations and arrest (23 October – late December 1455); Exeter's arrest (23 July 1454); Henry's recovery (late December 1454); release of Somerset (5 February 1455), Exeter and Devon; the battle of St. Albans (22 May 1455). Salisbury was said to have resigned because he objected to Exeter and Devon being released (*Chronicon Angliæ*, ed. Giles, IV, pp. 44-8).

In reporting Exeter's arrest, the chronicler says that York put him in the Tower and then sent him to Wallingford; there is no mention of Pontefract. Actually, Exeter was ordered to surrender himself to Wallingford Castle by a letter under the king's sign-manual dated 3 February only (E.28/86; printed *PPC.* VI, p. 234). Another warrant of 26 June 1455 refers to him as being in Wallingford (*ibid.*, pp. 245-6). Now on 3 February 1455, Exeter was in Pontefract Castle, and on 13 March following Sir Humphrey Stafford was ordered to bring him to the king (see note 16 above). It should be noted that this was six days *after* Salisbury's resignation, and there is no suggestion that Exeter was to be given his freedom.

What may have happened is this. Assuming that the letter of 3 February belongs to 1455, when Henry's recovery enabled the court party to regain control of the administration, Exeter was required to place himself under a custodian (the duchess of Suffolk) whom it considered acceptable. In reply, he complained about his detention by Salisbury, and the outcome was the order to Humphrey Stafford and another to Salisbury to put Exeter in Stafford's charge. After Exeter had been brought to the king, the original intention of lodging him at Wallingford was carried out, and thus he was still there on 26 June following. (Any explanation which puts the letter of 3 February in a year other than 1455 must take account of Henry's sign-manual. This rules out 1454, when Henry was incapable. The sign-manual does prove that Exeter was under suspicion at a time when the court party was in control.)

These records do not provide a complete coverage of Exeter's whereabouts in 1455, but it should be recalled that his fellow-conspirator Egremont was kept in detention after the end of York's first protectorate. That Exeter was tried before his peers in the parliamentary session of 14 January to 12 March 1456 is shown by a note that the indictment for his rebellion was to be produced there (KB.9/149, no. 5/3). He may have escaped judgment by producing the letters of general pardon granted to him on 18 August 1455 (C.67/41, m. 32).

The chronicler is clearly in error on the subject of Devon's release. He was not under arrest early in 1455, but he was a year later and was freed in February or March 1456 (see p. 173 above). The chronicler is correct only in stating that Exeter and Devon were released at the same time, but the year was 1456, and Salisbury's resignation in 1455 must obviously have been due to entirely different reasons.

18 CCR. 1454-61, pp. 318, 350.
19 E.28/85.
20 King's Bench, Controlment Rolls, no. 89.
21 C.67/41, mm. 33, 32, 30, 27, 22, 20, 3.
22 CPR. 1452-61, pp. 219-20.
23 *The Whitby Cartulary*, ed. J. C. Atkinson (Surtees Society, LXIX, LXXII, 1879, 1881), Vol. II, pp. 694-5; *Six Town Chronicles*, pp. 109, 143, 158; *Chronicon Angliæ*, IV, p. 45; *Reg. Whethamstede* II, p. 303; Bean, *Estates of the Percy Family*, p. 99 n.
24 *Chronicles of London*, p. 167; *Six Town Chronicles*, p. 110; *Three Fifteenth Century Chronicles*, ed. J. Gairdner (Camden Society, second series, XXVIII, 1880), p. 149.

Chapter XI

 1 *PPC.* VI, p. 273.
 2 *Rot. Parl.* V, p. 16.
 3 KB.9/11, mm. 14, 17.
 4 York described Blount as "my servant" in a letter of 1455-8 (*Original Letters*, ed. Ellis, Series II, Vol. I, pp. 125-6). See also p. 154 above.
 5 From information kindly provided by Mr. T. B. Pugh, who cites Longleat MS. 6411, mm. 1d, 2d.
 6 KB.9/12. This small file is the principal source for this chapter. Some of the incidents are also to be found in *Collections for a History of Staffordshire*, New Series, Vol. IV (William Salt Archaeological Society, 1901), pp. 123-6.
 7 *PPC.* VI, pp. 180, 192.
 8 *ibid.*, p. 192; E.28/84.
 9 E.28/83 (22 July).
10 Exchequer K.R., Bille, bundle 16, file 9.
11 C.67/41, mm. 19, 16, 7.
12 *PPC.* VI, p. 250.
13 F. Madan, *The Gresleys of Drakelowe* (Wm. Salt Society, 1899), pp. 57-8.
14 C.67/41, mm. 8, 4.
15 *Rot. Parl.* V, pp. 367-8.
16 Somerville, *Duchy of Lancaster*, pp. 367-8.
17 C.139/160; *CCR. 1461-8*, p. 320.
18 Ancient Petitions, nos. 4795-6, 6597-8; *Staffordshire Collections*, Original Series, Vol. III (1882), pp. 187, 192-4, 196-7; New Series, Vol. VII (1904), pp. 50-7.

19 KB.9/280, no. 27.
20 C.67/41, m. 20; 43, m. 40.
21 *CPR. 1461-7*, pp. 100, 304.
22 KB.9/13, no. 21; *CPR. 1467-77*, p. 504.
23 *CPR. 1477-85*, p. 524.
24 *Calendar of Inquisitions Post Mortem*, Second Series (Public Record Office, 1898-1956), Vol. II, no. 832.
25 KB.9/280, no. 67.
26 Dunham, *Lord Hastings' Indentured Retainers*, p. 23.

Chapter XII

1 *PL.* I, no. 226.
2 *CCR. 1454-61*, pp. 9, 44; *CPR. 1452-61*, p. 266; *Foedera*, ed. T. Rymer (1704-35), Vol. XI, pp. 361-2.
3 *English Chronicle*, p. 78.
4 Harriss, *EHR.* (1960), p. 39.
5 *CPR. 1452-61*, pp. 671-2.
6 See note 17 of Chapter X.
7 *CCR. 1454-61*, p. 71.
8 *Chronicon Angliæ*, part IV, p. 47.
9 *Rot. Parl.* V, p. 280.
10 *PPC.* VI, pp. 339-41; C. A. J. Armstrong, "Politics and the Battle of St. Albans 1455", *BIHR.* XXXIII (1960), pp. 11-14.
11 *Deputy Keepers' Report* 34, p. 175.
12 Armstrong, *loc. cit.*, pp. 22-50.
13 Ramsay, *Lancaster and York* II, p. 184.
14 Armstrong, *loc. cit.*, pp. 51-2; *PL.* I, no. 253.
15 *PL.* I, no. 243; E.28/86.
16 *Rot. Parl.* V, pp. 280-3; Armstrong, *loc. cit.*, pp. 58-62.
17 Harriss, *EHR.* (1960), pp. 40-6.
18 E.404/70, part 3, no. 73. The date of their new indenture was 9 August 1455, not 1454 as in my "Wardens", *EHR.* (1957), pp. 606, 614.
19 Somerville, *Duchy of Lancaster*, p. 420.
20 *CPR. 1452-61*, p. 243.
21 *PPC.* VI, pp. 265-7; *Cal. Papal Letters* XI, p. 30; Gascoigne, *Loci*, p. 16.
22 *Rot. Parl.* V, pp. 279-80.
23 Wolffe, *EHR.* (1958), pp. 610-12.

Chapter XIII

1 *CPR. 1446-52*, p. 526; *1452-61*, pp. 18, 91.
2 *PPC.* VI, pp. 166-73, 355-6.
3 KB.9/16, no. 76.
4 *PPC.* V, p. 408. The original draft (E.28/84) appears on the same membrane as the letters printed in *PPC.* VI, pp. 189-93.
5 *CCR. 1447-54*, p. 512.
6 Armstrong, *loc. cit.*, p. 65.
7 *Rot. Parl.* V, pp. 282-3.
8 C.67/41, m. 8; *Rot. Parl.* V, p. 332.
9 The following reports of disorders are found in KB.9/16. They are the subject of Mrs Radford's "The Fight at Clyst in 1455", *Transactions of the*

Devonshire Association XLIV (1912), pp. 252-65, and are more briefly listed by J. R. Lander in "Henry VI and the Duke of York's Second Protectorate, 1455 to 1456", *BJRL.* 43 (1960), pp. 60-4.

10 *CPR. 1436-41*, p. 125.
11 Ancient Petitions, no. 6864, partly printed, with some errors, by Mrs Radford in *Transactions of the Devonshire Association* XXXV (1903), pp. 251-78; KB.9/16, no. 50; *PL.* I, no. 257.
12. "The Fight at Clyst", pp. 259-61.
13 Lander, *loc. cit.*, pp. 50-8.
14 *Rot. Parl.* V, pp. 284-5.
15 *PPC.* VI, pp. 267-71; E.28/87.
16 *Six Town Chronicles*, pp. 109-10.
17 *PL.* I, no. 275.
18 *CPR. 1452-61*, p. 304.
19 E.404/71, part 2, no. 53.
20 *Rot. Parl.* V, p. 332.
21 *CPR. 1452-61*, pp. 308, 393, 398.
22 *English Chronicle*, p. 75.
23 *CPR. 1452-61*, pp. 562, 605, 607.

Chapter XIV

1 *The Brut* II, p. 525.
2 *Chronicle*, p. 251.
3 Chancery Files, C.191 (*corpus cum causa*).
4 *PL.* I, no. 275.
5 *Rot. Parl.* V, p. 321.
6 C.81/1464, nos. 1-6; *PL.* I, no. 285.
7 *CPR. 1452-61*, pp. 278, 291.
8 Ramsay, *Lancaster and York* II, pp. 194-5; *Wars of the English* I, pp. 323-6.
9 E.28/82 (15 July), 83 (25 May, 19 July), 86 (6 June). For Griffith's earlier career, see R. Griffiths, "Gruffydd ap Nicholas and the Rise of the House of Dinefwr", *The National Library of Wales Journal* XIII (1964), pp. 256-68.
10 Somerville, *Duchy of Lancaster*, pp. 640, 648-9; *CPR. 1452-61*, p. 245.
11 *Rot. Parl.* V, p. 279; Ancient Petitions, no. 5703.
12 *PL.* I, no. 285.
13 KB.9/35, no. 71.
14 C.81/772.
15 *PL.* I, nos. 281, 285.
16 KB.9/35, nos. 32, 60-6, 72, 115.
17 *CCR. 1454-61*, pp. 158, 190.
18 *Rot. Parl.* V, p. 347; *PL.* I, no. 298.
19 KB.9/35, no. 52; *CCR. 1454-61*, p. 158.
20 E.404/71, part 1, no. 60; part 3, no. 43.
21 *CPR. 1452-61*, p. 348; *PL.* I, no. 305; C.81/773.
22 *PL.* I, no. 305; *CPR. 1452-61*, pp. 340, 353, 360, 367.
23 KB.27/784, Rex 6, 7, 22; *CCR. 1454-61*, pp. 222-3.
24 H. T. Evans, *Wales and the Wars of the Roses* (Cambridge, 1915), pp. 97-109.
25 E.404/71, part 2, nos. 77-85.
26 *ibid.*, part 3, nos. 33, 38, 50.
27 *Chronicles of London*, p. 167; *PL.* I, no. 298; E.404/71, part 2, no. 12.
28 Storey, *EHR.* (1957), p. 614.

29 *CPR. 1452-61*, p. 335; Somerville, *op. cit.*, p. 538.
30 *Deputy Keepers' Report* 35 (1874), p. 88.
31 *PL.* I, no. 298.
32 *BIHR.* (1960), p. 69*n*.
33 *CCR. 1454-61*, p. 287.
34 *Chronicles of London*, pp. 276-9; *English Chronicle*, pp. 88, 96.
35 KB.9/287, no. 53.
36 C.53/190, mm. 8-12.
37 *CPR. 1452-61*, pp. 400-10, 413.
38 *Chronicles of London*, p. 168; *Six Town Chronicles*, pp. 111-12; *PL.* I, nos. 313, 315; *Reg. Whethamstede* I, pp. 295-308; *CPR. 1452-61*, p. 428.
39 Ramsay, *op. cit.*, II, pp. 210-11; *cf.* Jacob, *Fifteenth Century*, p. 515.
40 C.53/190, mm. 9-11; *Rot. Parl.* V, pp. 369-70.
41 R. M. Jeffs, "The Late Medieval Sheriff and the Royal Household, 1437-1547" (unpublished Oxford D.Phil. thesis, 1960-1), pp. 146-7; *cf.* Jacob, *op. cit.*, p. 514; E.404/71, part 1, no. 58, and part 4, no. 25.
42 *English Chronicle*, p. 78; *Six Town Chronicles*, p. 113; *Reg. Whethamstede* I, p. 340.
43 *PL.* I, no. 325.
44 E.404/71, part 3, no. 77; *Wars of the English* II, p. 511.
45 A. H. Burne, *More Battlefields of England* (1952), pp. 140-9.
46 *Rot. Parl.* V, pp. 346-50, 367; *SD.* pp. 311-12.
47 *PL.* I, nos. 355, 364.
48 *English Chronicle*, pp. 80-3; *Reg. Whethamstede* I, pp. 339-42.
49 *CPR. 1452-61*, pp. 533-54.
50 *Reg. Whethamstede* I, pp. 346-56; J. P. Gilson, "A Defence of the Proscription of the Yorkists in 1459", *EHR.* XXVI (1911), pp. 512-25.
51 J. R. Lander, "Attainder and Forfeiture, 1453 to 1509", *The Historical Journal* 4 (1961), pp. 145-6; and "Marriage and Politics in the Fifteenth Century: The Nevilles and the Wydevilles", *BIHR.* XXXVI (1963), pp. 125-6.
52 *English Chronicle*, pp. 86-98.
53 *PL.* I, no. 346.
54 *Chronicles of London*, p. 171.
55 Lander, *BIHR.* (1963), p. 127.
56 *Rot. Parl.* V, pp. 351-2.
57 *ibid.*, pp. 375-9; *SD.* pp. 313-18; T. F. T. Plucknett, *Taswell-Langmead's Constitutional History* (Eleventh Edition, 1960), pp. 496-8.

Conclusion

1 Listed by Lander, *BIHR.* (1963), pp. 151-2.
2 KB.27/804, m. 67; *cf. English Chronicle*, p. 107; C.1/31, no. 485.
3 Storey, *EHR.* (1957), p. 615.
4 *The Arrivall of Edward IV*, ed. J. Bruce (Camden Society, original series, I, 1838), p. 6; John Warkworth, *A Chronicle of Edward the Fourth*, ed. J. O. Halliwell (Camden Society, original series, X, 1839), pp. 13-14; C. L. Scofield, *The Life and Reign of Edward the Fourth* (1923), Vol. I, pp. 569-71.
5 KB.9/296-307.
6 J. R. Lander, "Council, Administration and Councillors, 1461 to 1485", *BIHR.* XXXII (1959), pp. 151-66.
7 KB.9/21, no. 28; 299, no. 25.

8 KB.9/106, no. 83.
9 *Calendar of Charter Rolls* (Public Record Office, 1903-27), Vol. VI, pp. 144-152, 155-67, 176-80.
10 KB.9/21, no. 28; 299, no. 25.
11 *Leviathan*, cap. xxi.

Appendix I

Unpublished Crown Copyright material in the Public Record Office is reproduced by permission of the Controller of H.M. Stationery Office.

1 KB.9/231, no. 33.
2 KB.27/715, Rex 19. KB.9/231, no. 3, is a mutilated copy of the coroners' transcript.

　　My intention to print this document was fortuitously anticipated by Mrs. Aston, who published it in "A Kent Approver of 1440", *BIHR*. XXXVI (1963), pp. 86-90.
3 *The Brut* II, p. 474; *CPR. 1436-41*, p. 266.
4 *The Brut* II, p. 472.
5 E. Hasted, *History of Kent* (Canterbury, 1797-1801), Vol. VII, pp. 32-3.
6 *The Brut* II, p. 476.

Appendix II

1 T. F. T. Plucknett, *A Concise History of the Common Law* (Fifth Edition, 1956), pp. 445-6.
2 *CPR. 1422-9*, pp. 106, 161, 273, 343, 381, 477, 531; *1429-36*, pp. 67, 102, 182, 246, 331, 334, 493, 502.
3 *CPR. 1422-9*, p. 341.
4 *CPR. 1441-6*, p. 322; *Rot. Parl.* V, p. 111; H. L. Gray, *The Influence of the Commons in Early Legislation* (1932), p. 323.
5 *CPR. 1436-41*, pp. 118, 124-6, 171.
6 Thus there are pardons mentioned in KB.27/705, Rex 24, and 740, Rex 4, which do not appear in *CPR*.
7 *CPR. 1441-6*, pp. 295-366, *passim*.
8 *Rot. Parl.* IV, pp. 504-5; C.67/38.
9 C.67/39.
10 C.67/40; *Reg. Whethamstede* I, pp. 86-91.
11 C.67/41; *Rot. Parl.* V, pp. 283-4.
12 C.67/42; *Reg. Whethamstede* I, pp. 291-5.
13 C.67/43.
14 *Reg. Whethamstede* I, pp. 86, 290.
15 E.404/57, no. 144.
16 KB.27/740-7, Rex sections.
17 C.1/19, no. 487, printed as *PL*. I, no. 180: C.67/40.
18 C.81/1371, nos. 37-8.
19 KB.27/705, Rex 31d.
20 KB.27/706, Rex 3d.
21 KB.27/744, Rex 1d.
22 KB.27/741, Rex 35d.
23 *CPR. 1436-41*, pp. 275-6.
24 Gilson, *EHR*. (1911), p. 516.

Appendix III

1 *CPR. 1446-52*, p. 432; and see pp. 56-7 above.
2 KB.9/267, no. 23; 272, nos. 1-5.
3 Many of the sources are printed or summarised in *The Records of the City of Norwich*, ed. W. Hudson and J. C. Tingey (Norwich and London, 1906), Vol. I. The Introduction gives an account of constitutional developments in the city, including these disturbances. References are given here mainly to sources not quoted in this volume.
4 KB.9/84.
5 F. Blomefield, *An Essay towards a Topographical History of the County of Norfolk* (1805-10), Vol. III, pp. 154-5.
6 W. I. Haward, "Economic Aspects of the Wars of the Roses in East Anglia", *EHR.* XLI (1926), pp. 175-6.
7 KB.9/241, no. 20.
8 *PPC.* V, pp. 15, 17; *CPR. 1436-41*, p. 86.
9 KB.9/229, no. 249.
10 *PPC.* V, pp. 33-4; *CCR. 1435-41*, p. 94; *Historical Collections of a Citizen of London*, ed. J. Gairdner (Camden Society, second series, XVII, 1876), p. 180.
11 *PPC.* V, pp. 76-7; *CPR. 1436-41*, pp. 76, 126, 587; *Calendar of Fine Rolls* (Public Record Office, 1911-   ), Vol. XVII, p. 12.
12 E.28/63 (12 December); *CPR. 1436-41*, p. 357.
13 Chancery Miscellanea, bundle 123, file 12.
14 *Chronicles of London*, p. 150; repeated by Hall, *Chronicle*, p. 208; KB.9/84, no. 4.
15 Chancery Misc. 70, file 2, no. 61.
16 *CPR. 1436-41*, pp. 552-3, 576.
17 KB.9/240, no. 25.
18 KB.9/267, no. 24.
19 Ancient Petitions, no. 6474.
20 E.404/59, no. 150.
21 E.28/72 (8 February), 71 (29 January).
22 KB.27/746, Rex 29.
23 E.28/71 (undated).
24 Gascoigne, *Loci*, pp. 42, 175.
25 KB.9/85, nos. 6 and 15.
26 Haward, *loc. cit.*, pp. 186-7.
27 *Cal. Charter Rolls* VI, pp. 144-8.

Appendix IV

1 E.404/63, no. 77; *Issues of the Exchequer*, p. 459.
2 K. H. Vickers, *Humphrey, Duke of Gloucester* (1907), p. 274.
3 *The Brut* II, p. 482.
4 *CCR. 1435-41*, p. 381.
5 *ibid.*, pp. 395, 420.
6 *PL.* I, no. 27.
7 The attack on Letheringham is reported in a commission of 1 September 1448 (*CPR. 1446-52*, p. 236) and in a petition from Wingfield heard by the council on 15 July 1452 (E.28/81). The latter shows, however, that the compensation was awarded by the arbitration of the bishop of Norwich, William, *then* earl of Suffolk, and John Fortescue, chief justice. (Suffolk was

created marquess on 14 September 1444 and Fortescue was appointed chief justice on 20 January 1442.) Their award of damages for the attack was presumably made at the same time as the assignment of revenues was arranged, *i.e.*, in May 1444, when Wingfield was also confirmed as Norfolk's steward (*CCR. 1441-7*, pp. 213, 215). Norfolk's bond (*ibid.*, p. 196) was probably made soon *after* the council learned of the assault, but not necessarily since bonds were not always respected.

8 KB.9/257, nos. 44, 53-9.
9 KB.27/747, Rex 7; *CPR. 1446-52*, p. 130.
10 *Letters of Queen Margaret of Anjou*, ed. C. Monro (Camden Society, original series, LXXXVI, 1863), p. 155.
11 *CPR. 1446-52*, p. 236.
12 *Six Town Chronicles*, p. 123.

Appendix V

1 KB.9/34.

Appendix VI

For general reference, see *The Complete Peerage* XII, part II, pp. 372-86; and C. D. Ross, *The Estates and Finances of Richard Beauchamp, Earl of Warwick* (Dugdale Society Occasional Papers, no. 12, Oxford, 1956).

1 "John Ross's Historical Account of the Earls of Warwick", ed. T. Hearne, with *Historia Vitae et Regni Ricardi II* (Oxford, 1729), p. 237.
2 *Cal. Fine Rolls* XVII, pp. 97-9.
3 *CPR. 1343-5*, pp. 251-2.
4 Plucknett, *Concise History of the Common Law*, pp. 720-1; J. Fortescue, *De Laudibus Legum Anglie*, ed. S. B. Chrimes (Cambridge, 1949), pp. 14-15; Lyttleton's *Tenures*, cap i.
5 *CPR. 1446-52*, pp. 262-3, 235-6.
6 C.139/135.
7 *CPR. 1446-52*, p. 324.
8 *ibid.*, p. 409.
9 E.404/67, no. 226.
10 *CPR. 1446-52*, p. 451.
11 Exchequer L.T.R. Escheators' Enrolled Accounts, nos. 44-5. A lease by the crown dated 8 May 1460 of certain lands forfeited by Warwick in 1459, as it is shown in *Cal. Fine Rolls* XIX, p. 268, can be read as indicating that he had been holding only a fourth part of numerous manors; in other words, it suggests that the Beauchamp lands had been partitioned among four claimants. Dr. Ross has made this assumption (p. 19, n. 2), presumably on the authority of this printed record and the licence of 1449. The entry in the *Calendar* is misleading. Its original indicates that only the first of the various properties shown was a quarter part, *viz.* "Concessimus . . . custodiam quarte partis manerii et dominii de Hanslape, manerii et dominii de Querndon, manerii et dominii" (etc.). (Chancery, Fine Rolls, no. 267, m. 6). There is no doubt that "quarte partis" is intended as a singular: the words are written in full. One would expect a plural had the term been intended to apply to the following manors.
12 E.404/70, part I, no. 47.
13 *CPR. 1461-7*, p. 119.

14 *Complete Peerage* I, p. 29, note a; *CPR. 1446-52*, pp. 264-5.
15 Ross, p. 6, n. 1.
16 Not in *CPR.* but see *Cal. Fine Rolls*, XVIII, p. 157.
17 *ibid.* XVIII, pp. 111, 157-8, 268; XIX, p. 34.
18 E.28/83 (27 July); and see p. 135 above.
19 Ross, p. 6, n. 1.
20 Dr Ross states that Warwick appeared to have gained possession of most of the Despenser lands (p. 19, n. 2). But Dr Ross does not take into account Warwick's position as the royally appointed custodian of George's lands.
21 *CPR. 1452-61*, p. 533.
22 *Cal. Fine Rolls*, XVII, p. 97.
23 Above, p. 135.
24 Above, p. 163.
25 Above, p. 134.

INDEX

This is primarily an index of persons and subjects. The names of many places are omitted but their counties are shown

A

B